# THE
# PROTEAN
# SELF

# THE
# PROTEAN SELF

### Human Resilience
### in an Age of Fragmentation

## ROBERT JAY LIFTON

BasicBooks
*A Division of HarperCollinsPublishers*

Grateful acknowledgment is made for permission to reprint from the following:

"Crucifixion" by Hayden Carruth, p. 55. Copyright © Hayden Carruth 1992. Reprinted by permission of the author.

*Designed by Ellen Levine*

93 94 95 96 ◆/HC 9 8 7 6 5 4 3 2 1

Library of Congress Cataloging-in-Publication Data

Lifton, Robert Jay. 1926–
    The protean self : human resilience in an age of fragmentation / Robert Jay Lifton.
        p. cm.
    Includes bibliographical references and index.
    ISBN 0–465–06420–5
    1. Self—Social aspects—History—20th century. 2. Civilization. Modern—20th century—Psychological aspects. 3. Pluralism—Psychological aspects. 4. Resilience (Personality trait)
I. Title
BF697.5.S65L53   1993
155.2—dc20                                            93–27068
                                                           CIP

*For Kenneth Jay Lifton,*
*brave and talented in his spirit of renewal*

*Everything is possible in history.*

—José Ortega y Gasset


*It's absolutely useless to look for [the self], you won't find it, but it's possible in some sense to make. I don't mean . . . making a mask . . . but you finally begin. . . to make and to choose the self you want.*

—Mary McCarthy


*Blessed be down-to-earth! Blessed be highs!*

—Seamus Heaney

# CONTENTS

# PREFACE

It has taken me decades to give the protean self its due. I began to think about it almost thirty years ago and published versions of a prelimary essay on it in the late 1960s and early 1970s. Although until now I have written little more on the subject, it has never left me.

Proteanism seemed to strike a nerve in people, as the essay has been reprinted in more collections than has anything else of mine. Readers have frequently told me that its focus on a many-sided self in constant motion reflects their own experience. But at least a few have been highly offended, even outraged, by the concept. Once, I recall, following a lecture of mine at the University of Sussex in England, a senior faculty member accused me of contributing to the downfall of Western civilization. My own view is that the protean self can help people renew their relationships to cultures, Western and non-Western, that are now under duress.

Throughout my explorations and meanderings, dialogues with friends and close colleagues have provided intellectual lifeblood. Erik H. Erikson conveyed to me, as no one else could, ways of thinking about psychological resilience and historical influence. Leslie Farber taught me much about what fiction and literary criticism can mean to psychological thought. David Reisman took me to the far reaches of human complexity and possibility. During early years, I was able to explore with Kenneth Keniston new ways of looking at openness and change, and with Eric Olson, root psychological perspectives in those areas. With Kai Erikson and John Mack, I have shared ideas and commitments of many kinds, as I have also with Nicholas Humphrey, Jerome Bruner, and Michael Basch. Many of these conversations took place in Wellfleet, Massachusetts, at the meetings on psychology and history my wife and I have hosted since the mid-1960s. Other participants have included Norman Birnbaum, Margaret Brenman-Gibson, Peter Brooks, Cathy Caruth, Harvey Cox, Ronnie Dugger, Daniel Ellsberg, Jean Bethke Elshtain, Richard Falk, Robert

Holt, Gerald Holton, Phyllis Palgi, Richard Sennett, Eugene Weiner, and
Howard Zinn.

In recent years, I have had the good fortune to work closely with
Charles B. Strozier and to carry on a continuous conversation with him
remarkable in its affection and sweep. At our Center on Violence and
Human Survival, Michael Perlman made many-layered contributions, as
did Michael Flynn, Ayla Kohn, and Laura Simich. I am especially grateful
for the generous participation of the men and women whose interviews
are discussed all through the book. Strozier, Perlman, and Kai Erikson
read the entire manuscript and responded in ways that improved both
the book and my own understanding of it.

One seldom talks about dialogue with spouses and children, but I
know it to exist, infused with love. Mine with Betty Jean Lifton has
reached every molecule of my being and thought. With my daughter,
Natasha Karen Lifton, I have experienced the excitement of emerging
psychological colleagueship; and with my son, Kenneth Jay Lifton, to
whom this book is dedicated, colleagueship in connection with preserving life on the planet.

Lucy Silva, my assistant, not only wore out computers with the endless
drafts she prepared, but managed to coordinate everything, myself
included. Phoebe Hoss demonstrated once more why she is one of the
great manuscript editors of our time. And Jo Ann Miller of Basic Books
has been a wise and sensitive editorial guide.

*Wellfleet, Massachusetts*
*July 1993*

# Chapter 1

# THE CHANGING PSYCHOLOGICAL LANDSCAPE

WE ARE BECOMING FLUID and many-sided. Without quite realizing it, we have been evolving a sense of self appropriate to the restlessness and flux of our time. This mode of being differs radically from that of the past, and enables us to engage in continuous exploration and personal experiment. I have named it the "protean self" after Proteus, the Greek sea god of many forms.

The protean self emerges from confusion, from the widespread feeling that we are losing our psychological moorings. We feel ourselves buffeted about by unmanageable historical forces and social uncertainties. Leaders appear suddenly, recede equally rapidly, and are difficult for us to believe in when they are around. We change ideas and partners frequently, and do the same with jobs and places of residence. Enduring moral convictions, clear principles of action and behavior: we believe these must exist, but where? Whether dealing with world problems or child rearing, our behavior tends to be ad hoc, more or less decided upon as we go along. We are beset by a contradiction: schooled in the virtues of constancy and stability—whether as individuals, groups, or nations—our world and our lives seem inconstant and utterly unpredictable. We readily come to view ourselves as unsteady, neurotic, or worse.

But rather than collapse under these threats and pulls, the self turns out to be surprisingly resilient. It makes use of bits and pieces here and there and somehow keeps going. What may seem to be mere tactical flexibility, or just bungling along, turns out to be much more than that. We find ourselves evolving a self of many possibilities, one that has risks

---

The sources for quotations and research findings can be found in the notes keyed to the individual text pages and beginning on page 233.

and pitfalls but at the same time holds out considerable promise for the human future.

I first encountered this pattern when interviewing Chinese in Hong Kong in the mid-1950s, in connection with the "thought reform" (or "brainwashing") they had been subjected to on the mainland. They described a series of identity shifts related to their monumental struggles with an ancient family system, their encounter with a wide variety of Western political and cultural ideas and ideologies, their embrace of communism followed by their conflicts with and break from it, and their subsequent exposure to a dizzying array of influences in the noncommunist world. I observed even more dramatic changes in Japanese university students I interviewed in Tokyo and Kyoto during the 1960s, as part of a study of individual psychology and historical change. A student still in his early twenties could describe a personal journey from childhood emperor worship during the Second World War, to embrace of democracy and all things American during the U.S. Occupation, and of Western principles of individualism (especially as conveyed by films), to a return to traditional Japanese cultural elements, to intense Marxism and romantic communist activism, to periods of hedonism with heavy drinking and random sex, to immersion as a young executive in a powerful corporation (an adjustment accompanied by dreams and fantasies of kicking over the traces and escaping from both company and country by means of endless travel and pleasure seeking).

I was to encounter similar explorations much closer to home when studying (with Eric Olson during the early 1970s) innovative young American professionals. This group of lawyers, writers, artists, and teachers had experiences that paralleled those of the Japanese students, except for the emperor worship and foreign occupation. At about the same time, I was also interviewing Vietnam veterans and participating in rap groups with them. They, too, underwent impressive personal transformation. Young men who had volunteered for the Vietnam War out of near-automatic patriotism, intense forms of male machismo, and attraction to violence could, within a brief period, condemn that form of patriotism and change not only their worldviews and political beliefs but their attitudes and behavior in their intimate relationships as well. They could develop a new freedom, as one put it, "to just move anywhere and feel anything."

The protean self did not suddenly appear in full bloom. It emerged from a certain social and historical context. What we call the self—one's inclusive sense (or symbolization) of one's own being—is enormously sensitive to the flow of history. In the case of the Chinese and Japanese I interviewed, that flow took extreme forms of war and upheaval. While America has undergone no such large-scale twentieth-century disaster, our history has included colonization and revolution, movement toward the western frontier, the carnage of our civil war, massive immigration, participation in at least five major wars outside of our territory during this century, and continuous technological development and social change—all of which have had a formidable influence on the contemporary self (see chapter 3). For these historical forces not only manipulate the self from the outside but shape it importantly from within.

Historical influences contributing to the protean self can be traced back to the Enlightenment and even the Renaissance in the West, and to at least the Meiji Restoration of the nineteenth century in Japan (see chapter 2). These influences include the dislocations of rapid historical change, the mass media revolution, and the threat of human extinction. All have undergone an extraordinary acceleration during the last half of the twentieth century, causing a radical breakdown of prior communities and sources of authority. At the same time, ways of reconstituting the self in the midst of radical uncertainty have also evolved. So much so that the protean self has become a modus vivendi, a "mode of living" in our time. This is especially true in our own country, and American proteanism is the primary subject of this book.

The malleability of the self can even be sustained under despotism, as evidenced by the worldwide movement, during the late 1980s, for freedom and broader human possibilities: the democracy movement in China, the overturning of Soviet-dominated communist states throughout Central and Eastern Europe (Poland, Czechoslovakia, Hungary, East Germany, Romania, Bulgaria, and Albania), and the struggle against apartheid in South Africa.

Individual and collective malleability were also evident both in the shift in Soviet-American relations during the late 1980s, when unrelenting antipathy and mutual nuclear threat turned to shared commitment to reduction of stockpiles and peaceful cooperation; and in the subsequent breakup of the Soviet Union and replacement by a confusing array of independent republics. These radical turnabouts reflected equally radical ones in the mindsets of not only Mikhail Gorbachev and Boris Yeltsin, of Ronald Reagan and George Bush, but of legions of decision makers and millions of ordinary people in the former Soviet Union and the United States. There followed in turn the stunning developments in the American presidential election of 1992, including the emergence of a bizarre but formidable third-party movement led by Ross Perot and, most dramatic of all, the victory of a previously unknown political figure, Bill Clinton.

The postcommunist chaos throughout Central and Eastern Europe— its most extreme expression the war and genocidal policies in the former Yugoslavia—reflects darker patterns that can result from large-scale change (see chapters 9 and 10). The same is true of the civil wars and widespread starvation occurring in various parts of Africa. There are also the persisting American national confusions and antagonisms, whether associated with economic duress and unemployment, race, crime and drugs, or major breakdowns in such areas as education and health care. Nor are these national and international antagonisms and breakdowns the last word; rather, they are part of a continuing pattern of upheaval and change.

Of the greatest importance here is the fact that virtually no one anticipated these developments. In Czechoslovakia, for instance, the successful "revolutionaries" were taken aback by the "surprising quickness of the collapse" of the Communist regime and had to "define and redefine the identity of the state." There are many reasons for that failure to anticipate either the liberating revolutions or the subsequent expressions of chaos, but one of them is surely our underestimation of the self's capacity for shifts and reversals. With that recognition, we now sense that human history has become increasingly open, dangerous, and unpredictable. It has also become more visible to people everywhere, as the mass media bombard us with its tragedies and achievements.

Consider some of the headlines in a single issue of the *New York Times* (of 25 January 1993): "Peacekeeper to Peacemaker: UN Confronting New Roles"; "Pentagon Chief Warns Clinton on Gay Policy" (the new President's advocacy of permitting homosexuals in the military); "Thurgood Marshall, Civil Rights Hero, Dies at 84"; "Yugoslav Leader Threatens Croats" and "Balkan Negotiators Urge an End to the Latest Fighting in Croatia"; "In Deception and Denial, an Epidemic Looms: AIDS in Latin America"; "East Europe Says Barriers to Trade Hurt Its Economies"; "Bentsen Suggests Broad Energy Tax Will Be Proposed" (by the new Clinton administration to help lower the budget deficit); "Now Hungary Adds Its Voice to the Ethnic Tumult"; "U.S. Watching Iraq for Air Defenses"; "As Civil War in Angola Intensifies, Pretoria Denies Aiding Rebels"; "3 Deaths in Somalia May Halt Port Visit by European Group" (in connection with the American military effort to bring food to the starving population); "Guatemala Indians in a Joyful Return from Exile"; "Israel Cool to Admitting a New Ethiopian Group" (of Christians descended from Jews); "Germany Plans to Make It Easier for Some to Obtain Citizenship" (foreigners who have lived in the country for many years); "California Inmates Win Better Prison AIDS Care"; and "'Ingles, No!' Puerto Ricans Shout as Language Bill Nears Approval." In just one day's headlines we encounter a dizzying array of twentieth-century fragmentations, deformations, and human struggles. No place on the globe is immune from them.

Over decades of observation, I have come to see that the older version of personal identity, at least insofar as it suggests inner stability and sameness, was derived from a vision of a traditional culture in which relationships to symbols and institutions are still relatively intact—hardly the case

in the last years of the twentieth century. If the self is a symbol of one's organism, the protean self-process is the continuous psychic re-creation of that symbol. Although the process is by no means without confusion and danger, it allows for an opening out of individual life, for a self of many possibilities. As the poet Galway Kinnell tells us, "Here I arrive there."

The mythology is itself many-sided. As Homer tells us in the *Odyssey*, Proteus first takes "on a whiskered lion's shape,/a serpent then; a leopard; a great boar;/then sousing water; then a tall green tree." No mere chameleon, Proteus is also capable of prophecy, but only if seized and chained, and held to his original shape. The shapeshifting can be equated with wisdom ("Who of those who listen to the poets could teach it, so variegated is it"). And in a different version of the myth, Proteus is not a sea god but an Egyptian king and "the most honorable of all men," a pillar of strength and a *preserver* of values. Thus, in a play of Euripides, Proteus is the protector of the beautiful Helen and enables her to "preserve my chastity inviolate" for her husband, Menelaus.

I do not invoke this mythology as an exact guideline of the contemporary self: it has no single "interpretation," and commentators have differed in their sense of its meaning. Rather, I view it as a metaphor for a contemporary phenomenon—a metaphor sufficiently rich to suggest the blending of radical fluidity, functional wisdom, and a quest for at least minimal form. Indeed, the mythological metaphor can suggest that free expressions of proteanism depend upon the existence of relatively established corners of the self. (I was confronted with that principle, soon after the publication of my first essay on the subject, by a graduate student who declared, somewhat whimsically but not without accusation: "I tried being a protean man [that is, undergoing continuous change], and it didn't work!")

Though variation is the essence of the protean self, that self has certain relatively consistent features. Central to its function is a capacity for bringing together disparate and seemingly incompatible elements of identity and involvement in what I call "odd combinations," and for continuous transformation of these elements (chapter 4). At the same time, the protean self must cope with, and sometimes even cultivate, feelings of fatherlessness and homelessness, associated with shifts in authority and mentorship (chapter 5). One may take on the psychology of a survivor and undergo symbolic forms of death and rebirth that contribute further to shapeshifting. At the same time, one always seeks a degree of form, grounding, and cohesion.

Mockery and self-mockery, irony, absurdity, and humor enable the protean self to "lubricate" its experiences and to express the absence of "fit" between the way the world presents itself and the way one actually feels about it (chapter 6). The emotions of the protean self tend to be free-floating, not clearly tied to cause or target. Not just individual emotions but communities as well may be free-floating—that is, removed geographically and embraced temporarily and selectively, with no promise of permanence. The protean self has an uneasy relationship to the holding of ideas—a condition of considerable significance for present and future politics, religion, and general intellectual life. Idea systems can be embraced, modified, let go, and re-embraced, all with a new ease that stands in sharp contrast to the inner struggle people in the past endured with such shifts. Work patterns may also be transformed—though affected, of course, by class and economic status; and a sizable number of the people interviewed for this book more or less created their own jobs. Social attitudes and styles of protest also undergo shifts, retreats, and unpredictable reassertions.

One seeks lasting human ties and sustained ethical commitments; while these, too, can be uncertain and susceptible to their own shifts, they can also be subject to various kinds of renewal (chapter 7). Indeed, a large question for the protean self, and one that cannot be answered simply, concerns its capacity to sustain and live out moral principles in the midst of psychological flux. For the entire life cycle, no longer governed by formal rites of passage, tends to be subject to considerable improvisation. The protean self tends also to be aware of historical process and of planetary connections, but is uncertain how to understand and act on that awareness. The overall quest involves a struggle for larger human connectedness, for ways of symbolizing immortality in the form of attachments that transcend one's limited life span. I will discuss first all of these traits in composite form, drawing mostly from interviews and from literature (chapters 4–7), and then three people in some detail in order to illustrate ways in which protean patterns operate over the course of individual lives (chapter 8).

I base this view of the protean self on a wide variety of observations in Asia, Europe, and the United States during the 1950s, 1960s, and 1970s. But I draw most heavily on recent (1987–1990) research (on nuclear threat and the American self) performed with my colleagues at the Center on Violence and Human Survival at John Jay College of the City University of New York. We interviewed four highly disparate groups—social activists, civic leaders, black poor, and Christian fundamentalists; and I make particular use of interviews I conducted.* From this research, as from a broad range of literary and artistic sources, I sought to tease out and describe specific protean characteristics. I make no claim of scientific or random sampling, but only of close study of evidence from many directions.

---

*I have used pseudonyms consisting of a first name and a last initial for people interviewed. In addition, I have altered certain identifying details that do not affect the substance of interviews.

In all of these groups, I found that while the protean self may have experienced much pain and trauma during and after childhood, it is able to transmute that trauma into various expressions of insight, compassion, and innovation. Young American lawyers I interviewed during the 1970s, for instance, brought such compassion to working with the poor and exploring new possibilities in their own intimate relationships, while honing their technical skills in teaching positions at mainstream law schools. Similarly, many in the groups more recently interviewed have drawn energy from their own pain in going about their experiments and improvisations. Indeed, that earlier pain, as a remembered part of individual history, can contribute to what I call "grounded imagination"—ideas and actions that transcend immediate arrangements while being rooted in personal and professional knowledge and experience.

There is also the matter of the proteanism of the researcher, of how an American Jewish psychiatrist in his late twenties found himself interviewing Chinese in Hong Kong and, a bit later, Japanese students in Tokyo and Kyoto; and subsequently many others in America and elsewhere who were far from being mental patients. That personal sequence (more replete with struggle and uncertainty than it may sound in retrospect) began with my being sent to Japan and Korea, after just two years of psychiatric residency training, by the United States Air Force, which had, by means of the doctor draft, claimed my far from enthusiastic services. Spending eighteen months in East Asia undermined, once and for all, my vague but previously uncontested life plan of a sensible mixture of private practice and teaching, which was to follow upon psychoanalytic training.

Upon completing my two years in the military, I arranged to be discharged in Japan so that my wife and I could spend a year traveling around the world. But we got only as far as our second stop, Hong Kong, where we were to stay for eighteen months. There I was able to meet and talk with Chinese and Westerners who had been subjected to thought-reform programs on the mainland, an experience that had come to interest me greatly since conducting interviews, as my last military assignment, with returning American prisoners of war who had been put through similar procedures. After some weeks, and with considerable trepidation, I made a crucial decision—to seek a foundation grant that would enable me to stay on in Hong Kong for the systematic research I wished to undertake. After returning to America, I was able, over the years, to combine further study with teaching, writing, and research in various part of the world, always involving psychology and history. My increasing inclination was to question received dogma. When completing my book on thought reform, I gently suggested parallels to that process in the psychoanalytic training I was then undergoing. I believe now that, in elaborating the protean concept, I have been both observing a widespread phenomenon of our time and reflecting my own experience of that phenomenon.

The protean self has at least three manifestations. It is sequential—a changing series of involvements with people, ideas, and activities, as was especially vivid during the late 1960s and early 1970s, but has continued to occur more quietly (and as a sustained pattern) in much of American culture. Proteanism can also be simultaneous, in the multiplicity of varied, even antithetical images and ideas held at any one time by the self, each of which it may be more or less ready to act upon—a condition sometimes referred to as "multimind." And it is social, so that in any given environment—office, school, or neighborhood—one may encounter highly varied forms of self-presentation: everything from a conventional, buttoned-down demeanor, to jeans and male beads and earrings, to the "blissed-out" states of members of religious cults, to any conceivable in-between.

Much that I say in this book about multiplicity is consistent with contemporary cultural and intellectual expressions now designated as "postmodern." I had used that adjective in connection with proteanism as early as the late 1960s. However convoluted the term has since become, it is meant to suggest a significant late-twentieth-century break, or at least a transition, from what is called the "project of modernity"— equally hard to define but seen as taking shape from the Enlightenment of the eighteenth century and including various forms of liberating knowledge and experience, along with confining expressions of rationalism, sweeping ideological claim, and technicism.* In fact, tendencies toward multiplicity to the point of fragmentation are rampant in both the modern and the postmodern, but the latter embraces these tendencies—"swims, even wallows, in the fragmentary and the chaotic currents of change." In that sense, proteanism is consistent with what is called the "contingency, multiplicity, and polyvocality" of postmodernism in the arts and with its "playful, self-ironizing" patterns. Because postmodernism has taken on a vast and many-sided theoretical structure of its own, I shall use the word sparingly and attempt to focus my observations and interpretations on how people behave, experience themselves psychologically, and express themselves imaginatively.

I must separate myself, however, from those observers, postmodern or otherwise, who equate multiplicity and fluidity with disappearance of the self, with a complete absence of coherence among its various ele-

---

*"Modernity" in this broader sense should be differentiated from "modernism," a nineteenth- and twentieth-century movement in art, though the terms are often used interchangeably, leading to considerable confusion between the two meanings.

ments. I would claim the opposite: proteanism involves a quest for authenticity and meaning, a form-seeking assertion of self. The recognition of complexity and ambiguity may well represent a certain maturation in our concept of self. The protean self seeks to be both fluid and grounded, however tenuous that combination. There is nothing automatic about the enterprise, no "greening of the self," but rather a continuous effort without clear termination. Proteanism, then, is a balancing act between responsive shapeshifting, on the one hand, and efforts to consolidate and cohere, on the other.

Although Proteus is male, there is virtually no manifestation of the protean self that either sex cannot express. Any differences are mainly in nuance. Men are given more opportunity by society, especially in connection with occupation, to experiment with forms and combinations. Women, on the other hand, perform (at least in American society) a special form of protean juggling in combining commitments to home, childbirth, and nurturing, with occupational and intellectual pursuits. At the same time, women in our study were more focused on grounding, more concerned with sustaining intimate relationships and relationships in general. That overall emphasis upon connection can discourage protean exploration in some women. But in others it contributes to that exploration either by providing elements of structure that free one for bold protean forays, or by suggesting an ideal model (of, say, significant work or an authentic relationship) for what one constantly seeks. (These tendencies are apparent, for instance, in the intensely protean patterns of Carol C., as I discuss in chapters 4 and 5.)

The fundamental similarities, along with the subtle differences, will be evident at various points in the book. But within individual life stories, it is difficult to ascribe with any certainty a particular tendency to gender as such. While I believe that there are significant psychobiological differences between men and women, they are orchestrated and recast by cultural forces. All these elements, in turn, open out and recombine within the protean process, so that differences become further obscured and emerge mainly in the form of relative emphasis. Also important here is the protean tendency to extend or reverse existing conventions concerning gender roles, "to go against the grain of one's sex," as Susan Sontag once put it. A few lines from W. S. Merwin sum up the complexity (not to mention the liquidity) of male and female proteanism: "deep/in the green sea/I saw two sides of the water/and swam between them."

The burgeoning of psychotherapists, psychotherapies, and spiritual disciplines, especially in America, is still another manifestation of the churnings of the protean self, of the struggle with the idea of change itself. These therapies are a recent, sometimes excessive, expression of our longstanding commitment to the self's freedom and right to realization. Therapists themselves are highly disparate in orientation, protean in their own divisions, whether within psychoanalysis, recent regressive therapies, or twelve-step programs for more varieties of addiction and trauma than were, until recently, known to exist. Whatever their elements of self-indulgence, our psychological and spiritual explorations both contribute to and reflect our proteanism.

Many public figures exemplify the protean self. Among Americans are such divergent representatives as Malcolm X, who declared, "My whole life has been a chronology of—*changes*"; and the broadcast network tycoon William Paley, described by his biographer as a man who virtually invented himself, and who "like many people who invent themselves . . . came to venerate the invention." But Václav Havel is perhaps the most dramatic exemplar of public proteanism. This absurdist playwright and disciple of Samuel Beckett underwent a sudden transition from being his country's leading dissident and political prisoner to becoming its leader and the first postcommunist president of Czechoslovakia; then, with the breakup of the country, its retired elder statesman at the age of fifty-six and, after that, the first president of the new Czech Republic. He has also been able to articulate his own ambiguous multiplicity:

> I get involved in many things, I'm an expert in none of them. . . . In general, . . . though I have a presence in many places, I don't really have a firm, predestined place anywhere, neither in terms of my employment nor my expertise, nor my education and upbringing, nor my qualities and skills. . . . I write mercilessly skeptical, even cruel plays—and yet in other matters behave almost like a Don Quixote and an eternal dreamer. . . . For many people I'm a constant source of hope, and yet I'm always succumbing to depressions, uncertainties, and doubts.

He goes on to ask: "How does it all fit together? Why don't these paradoxical qualities cancel each other out instead of coexisting and cooperating with each other? . . . How can I—this odd mix of the most curious opposites—get through life, and by all reports successfully?" This book is an attempt to answer such questions, and not for Havel alone.

The same historical forces can, however, produce an apparently opposite reaction: the closing off of the person and the constriction of self-process. It can take the form of widespread psychic numbing—diminished capacity or inclination to feel—and a general sense of stasis and meaninglessness. Or it can lead to an expression of totalism, of demand for absolute dogma and a monolithic self. A prominent form of totalism in our day is fundamentalism (see chapter 9). Broadly understood, fundamentalism includes a literalized doctrine, religious or political, enclosed upon itself by the immutable words of the holy books. The doctrine is rendered both sacred in the name of a past of perfect harmony that never was, and the center of a quest for collective revitalization. But the totalistic or fundamentalist response is a reaction to proteanism and to the fear of chaos. While proteanism is able to function in a world of uncertainty and ambiguity, fundamentalism wants to wipe out that world in favor of a claim to definitive truth and unalterable moral certainty. The "death sentence" imposed on the writer Salman Rushdie, an Indian-born Muslim, by Ayatollah Khomeini, the Iranian Muslim imam (or supreme guide), symbolizes painfully the contemporary struggle between proteanism and fundamentalism (see chapter 10). Khomeini was reacting to Rushdie's highly irreverent treatment of leading Muslim religious figures in his novel *The Satanic Verses,* depictions that were part of the author's wildly imaginative proteanism and of the novel's central question: "How does newness come into the world?"

In the waning years of the twentieth century, we have witnessed something close to a worldwide epidemic of fundamentalism: religious forms in Christianity, Judaism, Hinduism, and Islam; and political forms in various expressions of extreme nationalism (such as the Serbian attack on other groups and demand for "ethnic cleansing" in what was formerly Yugoslavia) and of neo-Nazi views in Germany and elsewhere. The issue of *control,* of stemming the protean tide, always looms large. Yet the polarization between proteanism and fundamentalism turns out to be less than absolute. In research interviews, fundamentalists revealed themselves to be frequently confused and ambivalent concerning their own principles, and susceptible to a proteanism of their own. Proteanism and fundamentalism represent, however, a basic historical dynamic that is crucial for this study and for the world in general.

For many years, I have been exploring the dark side of human behavior—Chinese thought reform (or "brainwashing"), the Vietnam War, Hiroshima, and, darkest of all, Nazi doctors. I have done so in the hope that, by probing the psychology of evil and destructiveness, we would be better able to combat this behavior and seek alternatives. In this book, transformation becomes itself the subject. The protean self represents an alternative to violence. Violence always has an absolute quality: behavior is reduced to a single, narrow focus; and in that sense, violence is a dead end. Proteanism, in contrast, provides a capacity to avoid dead ends.

Proteanism involves choice. My conviction is that certain manifestations of proteanism are not only desirable but necessary for the human future. For proteanism can provide a path to the species (chapter 11). That is, proteanism presses toward human commonality, as opposed to the fixed and absolute moral and psychological divisions favored by fundamentalism. In that sense, Khomeini's condemnation of Rushdie was a fundamentalist attack not only on proteanism but on species consciousness. For there is a trajectory, never automatic but always possible, from the protean self to the species self: to the formation of a sense of self based significantly upon one's connection to humankind. Here as elsewhere, proteanism provides no panacea for grave human problems. What it does offer is a potential for change and renewal, for tapping human resiliency. In any case, proteanism is integral to our historical situation, to our contemporary fate.

# Chapter 2

## HISTORY AND THE SELF

*The social process does not mold a new being merely to housebreak
him; it molds generations in order to be remolded, to be reinvigorated
by them.*

—Erik H. Erikson

MYTHS REVEAL PSYCHOLOGICAL and historical possibilities, as
bequeathed by human evolution. Myths do not dwell on what we now call
our inner life, but tell stories in which psychological traits are transfig-
ured into concrete actions of gods or mortals. We hear nothing about
Proteus's feelings about changing: we are simply told about the changes
he undergoes under certain pressures. Proteus suggests, in fact, a particular human evolutionary achievement, the capacity for flexible imagination and action. The appearance of this *"open-ended behavioral repertoire"* is
related to a perception of time. That perception includes a concept of
death, a concern about the future, and "a proclivity for looking both ways
when crossing the street (or ravine)."

All of these behaviors are associated with the development of the
frontal or symbolizing area of the brain ("Bigger brains were and are better brains") and provide a variety of adaptation—a potential for proteanism—not available to other animals. That enlargement of the brain
depends upon, and partly results from, the development of culture—that
is, of historically transmitted patterns of meaning. Culture is inseparable
from symbolization; and both had developed by the appearance of Neanderthal man one hundred thousand years ago, as we know from the existence of a variety of stone tools and other artifacts of burial rites and religious rituals.* The potential for proteanism is, then, inherent in certain

---

*It is now believed that even in much earlier hominoids, appearing one million years ago, there
was what could be called a precultural form of scavenging on the part of "Homo . . . [the] generalist . . . [who] roamed very widely and used all kinds of resources."

fundamental characteristics of the evolution of the human mind: the knowledge that we die, which is crucial to a sense of self; our emergence as the "cultural animal" for whom the resources of culture are "ingredient, not accessory, to human thought"; and our capacity to symbolize, to make endlessly imaginative use of the self's cultural and psychological resources.

Human beings are highly social animals. For most of our existence, we have been embedded in immediate relationships and functions, particularly those involving kinship, communal ritual, and cultural custom. For all but a tiny portion of the one hundred thousand years since the emergence of Neanderthal man (or the million years since the appearance of species *Homo*), one behaved in certain ways toward the people around one, according to status, role or occupation, and geographic place. One did so because one was required to (and would be shamed or punished if one did not) and because one wished to (had internalized these requirements and made them one's own). That has changed during the past two centuries or so in connection with three historical forces that have brought about the release of proteanism. These forces—historical dislocation, the mass media revolution, and the threat of extinction—are inseparable from the modern and postmodern state and are related to our surging technologies and our equally surging ideas and feelings of self.

## Historical Dislocation

Historical (or psychohistorical) dislocation consists of the breakdown of social and institutional arrangements that ordinarily anchor human lives. The dislocation can be brutal, as in wars, epidemics, and the many forms of murder and cruelty human beings have inflicted upon each other. But the dislocation is a product of historical change in general, whatever its relation to destructive or creative forces, when that change is too rapid and extreme to be readily absorbed; it then impairs symbol systems having to do with family, religion, social and political authority, sexuality, birth and death, and the overall ordering of the life cycle. The symbol systems have by no means disappeared, but they have become less effectively internalized, more a matter of external requirement. Hence, there is a loss of a sense of fit between what individuals *feel* themselves to be and what a society or culture, formally or informally, *expects* them to be.

While historical fragmentation of this kind can result in dangerous forms of fragmentation of the self (see chapters 9 and 10), it can also lead to impulses toward renewal. One's loss of a sense of place or location, of home—psychological, ethical, and sometimes geographical as well—can initiate searches for new "places" in which to exist and function. The protean pattern becomes a quest for "relocation," an effort to overcome spiritual homelessness. Elements of proteanism are likely to emerge at such times as the Renaissance and the Enlightenment in Western history, and the Meiji Restoration in Japan of the late nineteenth century. During these upheavals, symbols of longstanding authority are undermined, confronted, or shattered in ways that can produce powerful and painful collective experiences of death and rebirth. There is an outpouring of death imagery, publicly and privately, as well as feelings of separation, disintegration, and stasis (what I call "death equivalents") and a questioning of larger human connectedness or symbolic immortality. At such times, our psychological viability as the cultural animal, or what might be called the "immortalizing animal" (they are virtually the same), is under duress—until new combinations can reanimate our perceived place in the great chain of being. In the process, the individual sense of self can experiment and expand.

Recent scholars of the Renaissance stress its multiplicity: its contradictory profusion of rational humanism and "pagan" neoplatonism; its elaborate struggles within, against, and on behalf of religion; and its rush of new forms of artistic and political self-expression. Not only did secular culture gain ground from religion; but, more important from our standpoint, "the bond between the sacred and the secular . . . disintegrated." Principles compatible with proteanism were articulated: for instance, the late fifteenth century declaration by Giovanni Pico della Mirandola that God created man "as a creature of indeterminate nature," and told Adam that he need be "constrained by no limits, in accordance with thine own free will, in whose hand We have placed thee," so that he himself, the first man, "shall ordain for thyself the limits of thy nature" and, as "the maker and molder of thyself . . . mayest fashion thyself in whatever shape thou shalt prefer." But Pico was one of a small company of elite Renaissance innovators who stood apart from ordinary people and remained, moreover, subject to the very church authority they questioned. Pico still wrote from a God-centered medieval worldview, was forced to recant some of his propositions, and underwent a period of arrest following a clash with Pope Innocent VIII.

The Enlightenment of the eighteenth century further developed much of the Renaissance ethos. Seventeenth-century science and philosophy (Newton, Spinoza, Locke, and Bacon) could now be extended into a supreme faith in the rational and the scientific, constituting an intense "sacralization of the secular." The dark side of the Enlightenment has become all too clear in the twentieth century. Nazi biological visions, Communist social engineering, and draconian nuclear scenarios by the United States and the former Soviet Union—all these had roots in Enlightenment claims to pure rationality and in the subsequent emergence in the modern world of an "activist, engineering attitude toward nature and toward itself." But rather than assume an inevitable line from the Enlightenment to the death camps, we do better to see these as having drawn upon certain Enlightenment attitudes while violating many others, and incorporating a great deal of malignant ideation from very different historical and cultural sources. There was much more than an "engineering attitude" in the great Enlightenment motto "Dare to know!" Responses to that exhortation helped inspire what was most liberating in both the French and the American revolutions, including the still invaluable American influences of Thomas Paine, Thomas Jefferson, and Benjamin Franklin. Both in general, and particularly from the standpoint of this study, there remains significant truth in the historian Hans Blumenberg's view of the Renaissance-Enlightenment-modernist development as "self-emancipation."

Certain parallels can be found in the Meiji Restoration of 1868 and the subsequent Meiji era, as different as these were from Western developments. In a highly group-oriented non-Western culture, there could not be an Enlightenment stress on either individualism or universalism. Yet the Meiji Restoration did succeed in ending the formal structure of Japanese feudalism and establishing the beginnings of a modern Japanese nation-state. Strikingly, it achieved this in the name of a *restoration* of the emperor's religious and political centrality, reminiscent perhaps of the restoration of ancient Greek philosophical principles during the Renaissance, but the Japanese restoration was much more dramatic in its embrace of ancient imagery on behalf of an intense historical turn toward modernity. In a non-Western society embracing a wide array of Western influences, Meiji Japanese innovators could encompass staggeringly diverse cultural elements: highly traditional Japanese loyalties together with new Western forms; mixtures of emperor-centered state Shinto, everyday people's Shinto, Buddhism, and Christianity; elements of Confucianism along with Western philosophy and Western-inspired egalitarianism, individual rights, legalism, democracy, and Marxism. In that sense, the Meiji Restoration prefigured much of the confused proteanism I observed in Japanese youth following their country's later upheaval in its defeat in the Second World War.

As a generally shared experience, however, proteanism is essentially a twentieth-century phenomenon. Only in this—and presumably the next —century does the pattern of psychological multiplicity and change take hold in everyone. The Renaissance, the Enlightenment, and the Meiji Restoration involved relatively small, talented groups of innovators who helped open out their societies in ways that anticipated broader psychological fluidity. The process was importantly propelled by such staggering historical developments as the industrial revolution and the wars, genocides, tyrannies, famines, and economic deprivations of the past two hundred years or so. In our own century, we begin to encounter the "peculiar phenomenon of the integration-disintegration of modern society," in which there is "no longer . . . a system but only a lot of sub-systems." Our dislocations, then, stem from the combination of a general acceleration of historical change and the displacement of unprecedented numbers of human beings: émigrés and immigrants from anywhere to somewhere else, whether as refugees from war or political or economic duress, or as people caught up in the trials and possibilities of mass urbanization and flight from that urbanization. Whereas in past centuries people struggled from time to time against the authority of churches, kings, and feudal lords, contemporary men and women exist in a psychological landscape void of clear authority or viable community, so that the protean self must virtually reconstitute its own society.

## Mass Media Revolution

Any one of us can, at any moment, have access to any image or idea originating anywhere in the contemporary world or from any cultural moment of the entire human past. The mass media revolution responsible for this eerie "omni-access" has evolved mostly over the twentieth century and has so intensified during recent decades as to constitute a "revolution within the revolution." The process has been most extreme in advanced industrial societies, where the primary medium is television. But in societies of limited technology, other media can have their own extremity: the 1979 revolution in Iran followed upon a barrage of audiotapes of speeches by its exiled leader, the Ayatollah Khomeini, to herald his triumphant return.

Much has been said, quite justifiably, about the trivializing and distorting effects of the media. But that is far from the whole story. Media images may also open out the self and energize it. People all over the world, glued to television set and radio, could imaginatively experience the stunning international events of 1989–90. That was true for me and just about everyone around me—in New York where I live and in various cities I visited at that time in the United States, Germany, and Italy. We could be among the young Germans scaling and dismantling the notorious Berlin Wall; among the hundreds of thousands of Czechs and Slovacks listening to the elfin-playwright, Václav Havel, addressing them as their new president in the atmosphere of a great festival; with Nelson Mandela, as he proudly strode out of prison after twenty-seven years of incarceration; or with the millions of Chinese marching exuberantly for democracy through Tiananmen Square. In this vicarious participation, the observer's self can be *there,* newly expanded and sensitized, forever a little changed.

The same all-pervasive broadcast and print media—buttressed now by fax machines and radically expanded telephone communications— enabled the people most active in carrying out these events to relate them to all that was happening elsewhere, and in some cases to learn more about what was going on right around them. Chinese exchange students in Boston, for instance, played an important part in the Tienanmen Square uprising by faxing American and European news stories back to Beijing, thereby informing protest leaders about the international effects of their movement and also about repressive steps taken by Chinese officials. More than that, protest leaders in Czechoslovakia and Germany were influenced by the dramatic events in China just a few months before, as were the despotic leaders they eventually deposed, in realizing how much bloodshed would be required for the survival of their own regimes. Those events in Europe had, in turn, enormous impact on subsequent antiapartheid developments in South Africa.

Beyond doubt is the enormous contemporary impact of the media on the individual self, as well as our general psychological ignorance concerning the nature of this impact. Marshall McLuhan, the Canadian classicist turned media maven, was here a brilliant if flawed intellectual pioneer. Early in his work, McLuhan drew upon the social critic Lewis Mumford's idea that the printing press, with standardized and interchangeable parts, contributed greatly to the breakdown of the medieval balance between "the sensuous and the intellectual, . . . image and sound, [and] the concrete and the abstract." In 1962, McLuhan depicted the "galaxy" of effects brought about by Gutenberg's fifteenth-century invention of movable type, but went much further in claiming that each new technological medium has "created its own environment" and acted on "human sensibilities" in a "total and ruthless" manner. The printing press accentuated tendencies to "dissociate" meaning from the sound of letters and thereby to divorce the visual from other senses, resulting in a "visual homogenizing of experience in print culture." With the visionary bravado that characterized almost everything he did, McLuhan went on to attribute to this invention not only a traumatic "split between head and heart" but also such far-flung results as the emergence of modern nationalism and individualism and "the new world of the unconscious" (the latter a result of the flattening or "denuding" of conscious life and "the ever-mounting slag-heap of rejected awareness").

The Gutenberg galaxy was officially "dissolved," McLuhan thought, by Einstein's conception of "curved space" and then replaced by our new electronic media. These in turn created what he (drawing upon Mumford and the English writer and painter Wyndham Lewis) called a "global village," a world encompassed by a single communications network. Electronic media were revolutionary in creating "a total field of instant awareness," which McLuhan at first thought would create a marvelous new civilization making use of tribal "acoustic culture" and overcoming the imbalance of the senses and dissociated abstractions of "Gutenberg man." He was to reverse that judgment later in speaking of "discarnate man," divested of his body by electronic media, with a self that was little more than "an image or a pattern of information, inhabiting the world of other images and other patterns of information." The truth underneath McLuhan's polarizations had to do, I believe, with the influence of electronic media on such developments as our questioning of the linear logic of print, our attempts to engage senses other than the visual, and our tendency to substitute "information" for organic, physical involvement.

But this tendency could not in itself define the psychology of the contemporary self. Here McLuhan was probably misleading with his one-to-one equation between a particular medium and an all-encompassing psychological response. His famous slogan "The medium is the message" may, in fact, be quite wrong. What seems most important is not so much the specific character of an individual medium as the staggering array of images and ideas coming from all media—television, radio, and the press—and bombarding us from all sides. McLuhan may have come to recognize this when, with a characteristically serious put-on, he declared that he had changed his thinking, would no longer say that the medium is the message; he was now convinced instead that "the medium is the *massage*," meaning that "all media work us over completely, . . . leave no part of us untouched, unaffected, unaltered." McLuhan's position on the combined effects of the media was obscured by his pleasure in a certain gamesmanship, in misleading his audience to the point of intentional deception or hoax, and engaging publicly in what he called "probes" or explorations to which he did not want to be held.

Then, at a certain point during the 1960s, McLuhan himself went into a media-cultural orbit. He and his ideas, aphorisms, and slogans were suddenly everywhere. He was unique among 1960s gurus in being embraced not only by the media he was analyzing but also by both the counterculture (Abbie Hoffman was an early supporter) and much of mainstream business culture (he gave high-priced seminars to corporate leaders). Although McLuhan was frequently denounced as a charlatan or a madman, large numbers of people in many places were haunted by Tom Wolfe's famous question, "What if he is right?" The radical visions of the 1960s had converged with the extremity of McLuhan's concepts and personal style. But none of this would have happened had he not seized upon a truth that everybody sensed: the powerful human impact of the late twentieth century mass media revolution.

Perhaps the media revolution required for its prophet a person of McLuhan's odd and striking proteanism. His evolving self combined exquisite, innovative openness with vast rigidities and contradictions in a stunningly diverse series of influences and identity elements: the rustic from the western Canadian prairies whose mother constantly read poetry to him; the undergraduate student of literature (at the University of Manitoba) so traditionally oriented that he believed anything written after the mid-nineteenth century could be ignored; the Cambridge University disciple of I. A. Richards and F. R. Leavis, who could apply their then radical new criticism—their principles that language was infinitely flexible and elusive because "words won't stay put"—to his studies of communications and media; the academic radical who was always disdainful of conventional teaching methods and standard referencing or undue concern for content as opposed to "rhetoric"; the fierce convert to Catholicism who would wake up various of his six children at four in the morning to read the Bible to them; the hyperverbal con man whose nonstop monologues and avuncular puns, "jokes," and one-liners might lead anywhere (wildly unclear claims about "hot" and "cold" media, assertions that advertising was "the greatest art form in human history," and that governments could manage their economies "as easily as adjusting the thermostat in the living-room"); the authoritarian reactionary, sympathetic to fascist developments in Europe (admiring their "return to heroic enterprises"), who was distant from his children during their early years and sometimes beat them with a belt but later became tenderly involved in their lives; the believer in end-time theology (more characteristic of Protestant fundamentalism than of Catholicism), in a vision of the world soon coming to an end; and the peripatetic elusive guru for the rich and the powerful no less than the avant-garde, and, in important ways, for every subsequent student of the media.

The British novelist Penelope Lively writes eloquently, in *City of the Mind,* of the simultaneity of images as experienced, and handled more or less successfully, by her architect-protagonist:

> He is in London, on a May morning of the late twentieth century, but is also in many other places, and at other times. He twitches the knob of his radio: New York speaks to him, five hours ago, is superseded by Australia tomorrow and presently by India this evening. He learns of events that have not yet taken place, of deaths that have not yet occurred. He is . . . an English architect stuck in a traffic jam, a person of no great significance, and yet omniscient. For him, the world no longer turns; there is no day or night, everything and everywhere are instantaneous. . . . He is told so much, and from so many sources, that he has learned to disregard, to let information filter through the mind and vanish, leaving impressions—a phrase, a fact, an image. . . . He is an intelligent man, a man of compassion,

but he can hear of a massacre on the other side of the globe and wonder as he listens if he remembered to switch on his answering machine. He is aware of this, and is disturbed.

All this suggests that the phenomenon of worldwide media saturation is both new and crucial to the late-twentieth-century self. While that self invokes defenses of withdrawal and numbing, it remains continuously bombarded by ideas and images and is in some measure recast by them, made more fluid in response to the surrounding fluidity.

## "The World Is Ending"

The third historical development suggests not a noisy bombardment but a prospect of absolute silence. I have in mind a possibility I have been studying for decades: that of carrying out our late-twentieth-century technological capacity to annihilate ourselves as a species, and doing so with neither purpose nor redemption. That possibility initiates widespread imagery of extinction, of an end of humankind, imagery that casts doubt in each mind about the self's larger connectedness.

Contributing to such imagery are the genocides that have already occurred in the twentieth century. Most of all, the Nazi genocide of Jews, Gypsies, Slavs, and other groups demonstrated that it was possible for an advanced industrial society to apply its highest technology to the systematic killing of any group designated as undesirable. Nor is high technology required, as evidenced by earlier genocides carried out by the Turks and by the Stalinist Soviet Union and later ones in Cambodia, Africa, and the Indian subcontinent. And a genocidal project with middle-level technology has still more recently been mounted by Serbian forces in Bosnia among groups that constituted the former Yugoslavia. Also contributing to imagery of extinction are threats of apocalyptic proportions concerning the ecology of the earth itself and its human and animal inhabitants: vast and varied pollution, including radiation from nuclear accidents; the warming of the world, or greenhouse effect; the depletion of the ozone layer of the atmosphere; the destruction of rainforests; and devastating African famines resulting from combined natural and human causes. Increasingly, we have an amorphous but greatly troubling sense that something has gone wrong in our relationship to nature, something that may undermine its capacity to sustain life.

Contemporary awareness of the threat of extinction becomes a new version of the far-reaching human inclination to imagine the end of the world. So widespread are these images that "cultures without terminal visions of some kind in all probability never existed." Passionate concern for last things is expressed in the Old as well as the New Testament (though less in early Judaism than in later forms influenced by Persian Zoroastrianism); and Hindu tradition depicts four ages of world history, the last our own "age of darkness," which must end in catastrophe and dissolution. These religions drew upon still earlier primitive mythology, such as "the myth of universal conflagration, . . . of an end of the world by fire, from which the good will escape unharmed." Characteristically, the myth was "consoling" and regenerative because "fire renews the world"; and in that new world, "the dead shall rise [and] immortality shall come to the living." Also important in the mythology is a demonstration of human vulnerability to a greater power. That vulnerability combines with the regenerative principle in a mythological or religious narrative of world destruction and rebirth. Even in contemporary funda- mentalist Jewish and Christian end-time imagery, the ending is not final. History is abolished for the sake of bringing about something new and perfect: in Judaism, the arrival of the Messiah; and in Christianity, the Second Coming of Jesus and the glory of a new Jerusalem on earth.

This imagery of world destruction and purified restitution taps a universal potential of the individual self: under certain conditions, that is, the self equates its own demise and renewal with that of the world. Cultures have drawn upon this potential in elaborating their particular narratives for giving meaning to death as the harbinger of a better and purer individual and collective future. But there has been a jarring change in the cultural context for such narratives. Now we are in a situation where the world might actually be destroyed and we would be the ones to do it.

Well before the actual appearance of atomic and nuclear weapons, an abundant modern literature, beginning with the fiction of Mary Wollstonecraft Shelley, had been exploring our capacity to destroy the world with our own technology. Shelley makes clear in *Frankenstein: or the Modern Prometheus,* her most famous novel (published in 1818), that human responsibility for world destruction lies not only in creating the dangerous technology but in withholding from that technology the care it requires. Thus, the monster that the student-scientist Victor Frankenstein creates in his laboratory becomes destructive only when rejected, despite his poignant reminder to Frankenstein, "I am thy creature." A century later, H. G. Wells was to put forward a similar view of human responsibility when (in his 1914 novel, *The World Set Free*), more than thirty years before they were actually constructed, he wrote about "atomic bombs" that could destroy humankind. It would be accurate to term Wells the technological prophet not of extinction but of near-extinction, as his fiction tended to include last-minute expressions of human wisdom that could be applied to constructing a new world and eliminating war.

Despite the subsequent narrow "literary ghetto" of science fiction, its separation from the literary mainstream is often arbitrary and always incomplete. The better science-fiction writers (Karel Capek, J. G. Ballard, A. C. Clarke, Isaac Asimov, and Robert Heinlein, among others) join mainstream writers in an overall category of "speculative literature," which explores world destruction (and sometimes re-creation), by means of technology and science, that is imagined for the future or that already exists but is hidden from view. The British writer J. G. Ballard, a leading figure in science fiction whose work extends far beyond that genre, combines visions of the end of the world with specifically protean developments: descriptions of collective psychic transformation, in which "self and world are changing together, in answer to world-historical signals."

Three notable American mainstream writers have similarly incorporated science-fiction motifs in their bold explorations of the contemporary self: Kurt Vonnegut in his angry whimsy and gallows humor concerning imaginary planets, nuclear Armageddon, Nazi mentality, and the obscene mass dying resulting from the Allied "conventional" bombing of Dresden; Thomas Pynchon both in his plots and counterplots relating to technological threat and political repression and in his explorations of extreme psychic states of deadening as well as rebellion; and Don DeLillo, in the apocalyptic themes that haunt his novels and the specific depiction (in *White Noise*) of a vast, mysterious, deadly "toxic event." While these authors differ greatly in their treatment of science and technology, all connect them with some form of global catastrophe, with a vision of the end. All bring to bear zany expressions of imagination on the central question of meaning posed directly by the British novelist Martin Amis through a character in *London Fields:* "So in his own way [he] confronted the central question of his time, a question you saw being asked and answered everywhere you looked, in every headline and haircut: if, at any moment, nothing might matter, then who said that nothing didn't matter already?"

Also enormously influential in promulgating visions of extinction (but considerably less protean in imagination) are those novels and films that are more in the realm of popular culture and offer specific depictions of nuclear doomsday: notably Nevil Shute's *On the Beach,* Stanley Kubrick's *Dr. Strangelove* (the film adapted from Peter George's *Two Hours to Doom*), the television film *The Day After,* and the Soviet film *Letters from the Dead.*

Some contemporary critics view a great part of modern literature as a secularized version of ancient apocalyptic prophesy. That literature, moreover, transforms "the end" into "a predicament for the individual."

From that standpoint, much of the energy for the twentieth-century literary imagination stems from our increasing awareness of our capacity to extinguish ourselves. We may see an uneasy protean response to that capacity in the literature's combination of threat, absurdity, confusions, alienation, despair, and overall experimentation.

There are no precedents for the situation in which people find themselves today, at the end of the twentieth century. These historical currents interact with one another: the mass media revolution can further our sense of dislocation, which can make us more vulnerable to imagery of extinction, its impact in turn accentuated by media saturation. We have little knowledge of the overall consequences of this combination: indeed, we are just learning to ask a few pertinent questions. Those questions must take into account the capacity of the individual self, under such circumstances, for explorations and new combinations, for life-enhancing protean function.

## The Psychoanalytic Response

The Freudian revolution was called forth by these threatening historical forces. Although Freud has been described as the last great voice of the Enlightenment and a man of the nineteenth century, his probings of the human psyche were a response to turn-of-the-century pressures toward fragmentation. His work is a manifestation, rather than a cause, of that fragmentation. Together with his disciples, disciples-turned-heretics, and his later intellectual beneficiaries, he was to chart much of the breakdown of the twentieth-century self.

Yet, paradoxically, psychoanalytic concepts of self have tended to neglect, or even negate, principles of change and malleability. Freud himself is double-edged in this respect. His imaginative breakthrough is a stunning expression of late nineteenth- and early-twentieth-century proteanism. An intellectual hero who confronted late-Victorian sexual hypocrisy, he was a force for liberation and a spokesman for the complexity and many-sidedness of our mental life. For him the goal of psychoanalysis was "to strengthen the ego" and "to widen its field of perception and enlarge its organization"—that is, to further individual psychological exploration.

At the same time, Freud's discovery of the enduring influence of childhood experience led him to stress the relative fixity of what he called individual character. He made limited reference to a concept of self, preferring to emphasize the tripartite elements (id, ego, and superego) of the "psychic apparatus," and for the most part using the term *ego* when referring to that part of the psyche concerned with the ordering of inner experience and external encounters.* The ego was, moreover, always under duress from the disruptive instinctual energies of the id, being (in Freud's famous metaphor) "a rider . . . [on] his horse," often obliged to guide the powerful animal "along the path by which it itself wants to go." The ego is, in Freud's words, "hemmed in on three sides" by its "three tyrannical masters . . . the external world, the super-ego [or conscience] and the id." That side of Freud came close to saying that we are rendered helpless, even static, by our powerful instincts, and that our claims to an autonomous self are illusory.

Significantly, early disciples who broke with Freud—Adler, Rank, and Jung—all came to question that emphasis and to attribute greater autonomy to the self. Alfred Adler spoke both of the perils of "systematic self-restriction" and of the need to compensate for perceived weakness in order to give "ballast" to the self and approach the "self-ideal." Carl Jung wrote at length about the idea of self, recognizing that it could contain many subselves, and seeing in it a "transcendent function" that enabled it to bring together elements at variance with one another in "conjoined opposites." Otto Rank focused still more specifically on issues of autonomy through his concept of "will," which he defined as "a positive guiding organization and integration of self" and, in Freud's metaphor, permitted the rider to control the horse ("utilizes creatively, as well as inhibits and controls the instinctual drives"). Rank was also aware of many dimensions of the self (the social self, the sexual self, the immortal self, and so on), and spoke of broadly human "cultural development through a will to change." He denounced approaches that rendered therapy a "repetition . . . of the past—instead of . . . a new experience in the present," and thereby amounted to "a denial of all personal autonomy in favor of the strictest possible determinism, that is to say, to a negation of life itself."

Commentators on the heresies of Adler, Jung, and Rank have tended to neglect their common concerns with autonomy and mutability. Each might be said to have struggled to reassert something of the early spirit of the Freudian breakthrough while coming into conflict with its increasingly systematized content, as well as with Freud's need to maintain intellectual and creative control of the overall enterprise. Certain subsequent psychoanalytic developments—for instance, the American focus on "ego psychology" and the British school of "object relations"—have cautiously advocated greater mutability while holding to, and limited by, traditional Freudian structures. A number of neo-Freudians (such as Eric Fromm, Karen Horney, and Harry Stack Sullivan) were to free themselves sub-

---

*Freud did, however, employ such general terms as *consciousness of self, self-analysis, self-reproach,* and *self-observation.*

stantially from those structures: in Sullivan's case, with a concept of a "self-system," which, whatever early conflict it may contain, enables the organism to move in a "basic direction [that] is forward."

Erik H. Erikson, while still considering himself a Freudian, took a gigantic step toward psychoanalytic openness in evolving his concept of identity (in early work he called it "ego identity," then sometimes "inner identity," and it eventually entered an area others have called "self-identity"). In his hands, the concept of identity provided a newly liberating flexibility in self-definition (though Erikson spoke relatively little of the self as such) and equivalent responsiveness to changing social currents. All the while he was managing the difficult psychological task of placing both the patient and the ordinary person (and, for that matter, the researcher) into the flow of the larger historical process. Over decades of dialogue with him, I found Erikson to be a man with history in his bones. More than anyone else, he brought to psychoanalytic thought a sense of our vulnerability to the larger human environment. Yet his loyalty to psychoanalytic tradition, his keen awareness of his intellectual formation in the Freudian circle, caused him to walk a tightrope between orthodoxy and innovation, which perhaps precluded a forceful overall theory of self. Moreover, the requirements of identity theory, notably those of "inner sameness," can be at odds with the radical flux and fluidity of much contemporary experience.

I had briefer personal encounters with three other men who did much to open out our concept of self—R. D. Laing, Jacques Lacan, and Heinz Kohut. Laing's description of the "divided self" (the term came from William James) in schizophrenia was part of his brilliant rendering of our more general many-sidedness. During a number of intense exchanges with him, I was struck by his willingness to take chances with his own self-process. But I felt that both his theorizing and his personal function were damaged by his susceptibility to guruhood, a state that always takes its toll.

Jacques Lacan viewed the self as both multiple and profoundly elusive: Freud's project of replacing instinct with reason ("Where id was, there ego shall be") becomes "an extinction that is still glowing and a birth that is retarded," so that "I," as Lacan puts it, "can come into being and disappear from what I say." For Lacan, "I" and self are essentially forms of illusion. One observer characterized that approach as a "withdrawal of the self into the no-self." But in all this, Lacan gave great emphasis to a symbolizing principle.* Hence, even when engaged in purifying the

---

*This led me to suggest to him, during our one active exchange, that the logic of such an emphasis should lead to his working from the broader model of death and the continuity of life as a more inclusive symbolizing paradigm than the Freudian model of instinct and defense. His way of agreeing enthusiastically, while adding a bit of mockery and self-mockery, was to declare dramatically, "*Je suis Liftonian!*"—to which he added that only his roots in the Freudian tradition stopped him from following that logic.

Freudian message, a project that could have been static in many hands, Lacan managed to convey much about human fluidity.

Heinz Kohut painstakingly reversed the classical psychoanalytic emphasis by subsuming instincts and drives to a predominant concept of self. That provided a certain mutability, particularly since Kohut acknowledged "many selves" within the inclusive one. I came to his work late, but found much in common with him during several extended conversations. He did not like my saying publicly that he and Erikson had much in common (Erikson would not have been pleased by the remark either), but I believe they both extracted from psychoanalysis a wholistic concept of the person in which self and identity constitute more than their component parts. Kohut, like Erikson, quickly understood patterns of "doubling" (development of a functional second self) in Nazi doctors for their adaptation to evil. He could also acknowledge that a widespread fear of falling apart was at issue where he and others used the term *narcissism*, which suggested a further movement on his part from a classical to a more flexible position. Laing, Lacan, and Kohut experienced an irony in common: each took on a powerful charisma for an immediate group of followers, a process that inevitably "stops time," imparts a form of magic to intellectual exchange, and thereby undermines the original exploratory impulse.

But beyond the work of these leading figures, the idea of multiplicity of the self has recently been much in the air. James Hillman, from a Jungian tradition, has advocated a "polytheistic psychology" that recognizes "the inherent dissociability of the psyche and the location of consciousness in multiple figures and centers." And others have written books and papers describing such phenomena as "human plasticity," "the saturated self," "the empty self," "possible selves," "the dialogical self," "the decentralized identity," "many dimensional man," "the quantum self," as well as "multimind" and "the society of mind." All these highly varied concepts, among others, strongly suggest that the self, or at least its contemporary version, is far from the bastion of order it is often assumed to be.

Yet expressions of proteanism among theorists themselves may depend upon the existence of relatively established elements of the self. Lewis Mumford, in a review of Carl Jung's posthumous autobiography, *Dreams, Memories, Reflections* (1963), compared Jung's bold flights of imagination when communing with the spirits in his famous tower outside of Zurich with the early Freud's when spinning out startling thoughts about the human psyche during his late-night hours of solitude in his Vienna study. But, Mumford reminded his readers, these same two men met their patients punctually the next day. That is, they required discipline and stability in fundamental areas of psychological existence in order to be able to embark on their extraordinary imaginative forays. While inner and outer worlds have changed greatly since the time of Freud and Jung, the principle still holds.

A different scholarly tradition provides intellectual grounding for the kind of psychological radicalism now called for. I have in mind the twentieth-century principle of "symbolic forms" and "symbolic transformations," as put forward by the philosophers Ernst Cassirer and Susanne K. Langer. Their work emphasizes that human mentation consists of continuous creation and re-creation of images and forms. We perceive nothing, so to speak, nakedly; our only means of taking in the world of objects and people around us is through this unending process of reconstituting them. Thus, Cassirer tells us that all our knowledge of the world "is no mere receiving, no repetition of a given structure of reality, but comprises a free activity of the spirit," becomes a matter of "spiritual [that is, mental] formation."

Langer draws upon Cassirer, and also upon Alfred North Whitehead, in extending this position and emphasizing a principle of flux. She speaks of the "*transformational* nature of human understanding," of "the stream of symbols . . . [that] constitutes a human mind." The activity of that mind is "a constructive, not a passive thing," and its "symbol-making function is one of man's primary activities, like eating, looking, or moving about . . . the essential act of mind." This overriding principle of "symbolic transformation of experiences" is, then, the great human evolutionary achievement. So much so that, in her final magisterial three-volume study, she speaks of the "tremendous complexity" of our dynamic pattern of feeling as a "vital activity [that] goes on at all levels continuously . . . [and] make[s] mental phenomena the most protean subject matter in the world." In that characterization, so close to my own, she was echoing an earlier poetic statement: "The great dreams of mankind, like the dreams of every individual man, are protean, vague, inconsistent, and so embarrassed with the riches of symbolic conception that every fantasy is apt to have a hundred versions."

Langer is telling us that the human mind is capable of symbolizing virtually anything. We have become painfully aware that this genius can be destructive in the extreme: as in the Nazi vision of revitalizing the Nordic race, and humankind, by extirpating its lethal "infection," the Jews; or the nuclearistic vision of increasing weapons stockpiles, with readiness to destroy most life on the planet, as a means of maintaining the peace and keeping the world going. Yet that same symbolizing capacity is responsible for Mozart sonatas and the theory of relativity—and the basis for proteanism, for a sense of self that can be fluid and multiple.

The self becomes an engine of symbolization as it continuously receives, re-creates, and extends all that it encounters. Rather than the classical psychoanalytic concept of symbol making as a primitive, unconcious mechanism involving one thing standing for another (sticks or umbrellas equal penis, doors and gates equal female genital orifice, and so on), symbolization in this broader view becomes the all-encompassing mode of self function. And every manifestation of this formative process involves the entire self and all of its previous experience.

These principles of self are *biologically* grounded in the symbolizing (or "representational") function of the human brain, particularly the fore-brain, rather than in any principle of instinct. The symbolizing self is *developmentally* sensitive to influences from early childhood but never entirely "determined" in outcome by any of them. The evolving self, in constantly re-creating all such influences, traumatic or otherwise, becomes itself *causative* and always prospective or forward moving.*

The principle of the symbolizing self helps resolve several false dichotomies: symbolizations are *both* "rational" and "irrational," relate *both* to "inner" and "outer" worlds, are *both* individual and communal. Similarly, that principle enables us to engage the self's simultaneous involvement with proximate (or immediate nitty-gritty) experience having to do with people and events on an everyday level, on the one hand; and with an ultimate level of larger human connectedness (or symbolization of immortality), on the other.

I understand the self to function within a model or paradigm of life continuity, of the symbolization of life and death. In that model, at the immediate level occur struggles with connection and separation, with movement and stasis, and with integrity and disintegration. The ultimate level includes an inner sense, in the face of one's finite life span, of living on in one's children or group (the biological mode of symbolic immortality); in one's work or influence on other human beings (the creative mode); in one's spiritual principles (the religious mode); in what virtually all cultures symbolize as eternal nature (the natural mode); or, on a somewhat different level, through a psychic state of experiential transcendence, a form of intense or quiet ecstasy within which time and death disappear. The symbolizing self is, in my view, always involved on both proximate and ultimate levels of function, however we may choose to separate them for purposes of analysis. One seeks a sense of vitality generally associated with the proximate level (with connection, movement, and integrity), and a sense of larger human continuity or symbolic immortality associated with the ultimate one. But neither sense is significantly available in the absence of the other.

In functioning as an open system, the self is always capable of revising its own meaning structures, of what Langer calls "the constant reformulation of ... conceptual frames." The meanings are always in some sense ethical, whether or not perceived as such. As the philosopher Charles

---

*As the neuropsychologist Roger Sperry puts it in rigorous scientific terms, "The whole [in this case, the self] besides being 'different from and greater than the sum of the parts,' also causally determines the fate of the parts ... [so that] the qualitative, holistic properties at all different levels become causally real in their own form."

Taylor puts it, the self operates "in moral space," from a "frame or horizon within which I can try to determine from case to case what is good, or valuable, or what ought to be done, or what I endorse or oppose. . . . We are not selves in the way that we are organisms. . . . But we are only selves insofar as we move in a certain space of questions, as we seek and find an orientation to the good." That is, our innate need to symbolize eliminates our biological neutrality. That "orientation to the good" can become hauntingly elusive, but remains integral to the protean enterprise. The moral component is bound up with our capacity for self-observation, for symbolizing further our own symbolizations as a way of evaluating them. This ever-present capacity to divide oneself into observer and observed can all too readily lapse into forms of dissociation, but can also contribute to creative self-guidance. With constant symbolization, that guiding function can resemble a gyroscope or balance wheel; though keeping the enterprise on track, it is never able to control it absolutely.

Awareness of death becomes, we now see, central to human evolution because that knowledge could not be erased, only symbolized, and symbolizations stemming from it are powerful and ever present. Symbolization is, then, Cassirer tells us, our quintessentially human trait, our "specific difference . . . the way to civilization," to "progressive self-liberation." It is also the source of our "multiplicity and disparateness . . . [and] contraries [that] are not mutually exclusive, but interdependent." But since, in evolutionary terms, all this is quite recent, Langer can add: "That newest of natural phenomena—Mind—still faces the mystery of all things young, the secret of vital potentiality." That "vital potentiality" is, as I argue in this study, the proteanism of today.

These principles of self and symbolism are consistent with postmodern rejection of "grand narratives," or what are called "metanarratives." Rather, we may speak, as one observer does with truth and humor, of our "postindustrialized, postmodernized, postsemioticized, post-toastied, fairy-tale West." Things are tenuous, but we are open to a great deal, for it is "[a]mazing what the mind makes/out of its little pictures/the squiggles and dots,/not to mention the words."

But the symbolizing self centers on its own narrative, on a life story that is itself created and constantly re-created. To be sure, the self can fall from narrative and undergo perceived breaks and radical discontinuities in life story. It can also divide itself into many subnarratives sufficiently developed to form their own self-structures or subselves. The self never stands still: "A so-called steady state . . . is really not a changeless state but a slowly advancing act." And an astute if somewhat lyrical commentator described my protean perspective as one of "rolling configurations," which retain "serial equipoise" in the constancy of change.

The narrative sought is as much historical as it is psychological; hence, the inseparable connection between these two realms of experience. Susanne Langer thus tells us that it is "even conceivable . . . [that] the study of mental and social phenomena will never be 'natural science' in the familiar sense at all, but will always be more akin to history, which is a highly developed discipline, but not an abstractly codified one." Langer's argument is not that we should exclude from science our study of mind but that we should cease imposing on that study what she calls the "idols of the laboratory" and the "dream of mathematization." We do better to explore the interweaving of every level of historical encounter with every aspect of the self—and to do so in a particular geographical and psychological place, such as America.

Chapter 3

## AMERICA, THE PROTEAN NATION

*The American is always on the way to someplace else.*

*The outcome was always plural. Not one story but many stories.*

—Lewis H. Lapham

WERE PROTEUS to change his dwelling place from the seas that fed the Greek imagination, he would undoubtedly retire to those that embrace America. Indeed, the shapeshifter has become nothing short of a fixture here. Dislocated from our beginnings, we are the home of traditional flux. Our great cultural themes of the ever-beckoning frontier and of continuous influx of immigrants converged to create "an endless inpouring of strangers, who in the general movement become endlessly re-estranged." Whatever the costs, and they are considerable (see chapters 9 and 10), we see ourselves as people of metamorphosis.

That characteristic, according to the historian Daniel Boorstin, can be seen to define us: "No prudent man dared to be too certain of exactly who he was or what he was about; everybody had to be prepared to become someone else. To be ready for such perilous transmigrations was to become an American." And an American kept moving: "Men and women start out in one place and end up in another, never quite knowing how they got there, perpetually expecting the unexpected, drifting across the ocean or the plains until they lodge against a marriage, a land deal, a public office, or a jail."

The outpouring of experiments with the self during the 1960s and 1970s were, in that sense, very much in the American grain. Similarly, we invest recent history with a spirit of metamorphosis in our tendency to identify particular decades with specific sets of attitudes ("roaring 20s," "radical 30s," "swinging 60s," "me decade of the 70s," and so on). Over time, the process accelerates, so that "the 90's, which began in the 80's, feel nearly over. And it's only 1992." Even in 1992, an American newspaper columnist could declare with some truth: "We are a nomad people, always have been, leaving almost everything behind when we move on— place, family, job, religion, friends."

American self-invention and shapeshifting are prominent in our biography and fiction, as will be evident throughout this book: from Benjamin Franklin in the eighteenth century and Herman Melville in the nineteenth to such contemporaries as Frederick Barthelme, Ann Beattie, Saul Bellow, Don DeLillo, Ralph Ellison, Janette Turner Hospital, Jack Kerouac, Alison Lurie, Toni Morrison, Bharati Mukherjee, Grace Paley, Thomas Pynchon, and Kurt Vonnegut. And in American painting since only 1970 or so, the "profusion of individual discourses" has included "minimalism, conceptualism, neo-expressionism, neo-geo, graffiti, abstract illusionism, photorealism, 'bad' painting, pattern and decoration, and so on."

During the last years of the twentieth century, there has been a deepening of American confusion. With the end of the cold war, Americans lost a world-clarifying enemy. Over the previous decades, whatever our deficiencies or decline, whatever wrongs we perpetrated abroad or at home, we could still view ourselves, in contrast with Soviet evil, as steady in our virtue. Denied that contrast, we find it hard to see ourselves as steady in anything. This post–cold war psychological state taps earlier doubts and psychological dislocations and places new burdens on our political process and our sense of social cohesion. The novelist Ralph Ellison has written of Proteus as standing for both America's "rich diversity and its almost magical fluidity and freedom," on the one hand; and, on the other, for our distorted realities and "illusion which must be challenged, as Menelaus did in seizing Proteus," until America "surrenders its insight, its truth [which] lies in its diversity and swiftness of change."

## Rebirth on the Frontier

*Political principles, laws, and human institutions seem malleable,
capable of being shaped and combined at will. . . . A course almost
without limits, a field without horizon, is revealed: the human spirit
rushes forward and traverses them in every direction.*
                                            —Alexis de Tocqueville

The "great historic movement" of the American frontier did not begin
with the nineteenth-century treks to the American West. Rather, as the
American historian Frederick Jackson Turner points out, the "first . . .
frontier was the Atlantic coast . . . [which] was the frontier of Europe in
a very real sense." Thus, the original colonists from England were immigrants no less than were the subsequent waves of English, French, German, Irish, Scandinavian, Italian, Central and Eastern European, Jewish,
Chinese, West Indian, and Hispanic peoples over the last three centuries.
Early settlers carried European models of "civilization," which they "imi-
tated, burlesqued, adapted, and jury-rigged" in ways that "introduced
more fluidity" and provided "surprising possibilities for the individual to
move about." The great exemplar of what might be called founding proteanism was Benjamin Franklin, described by Herman Melville as "a
tanned Machiavelli in tents" who "having carefully weighed the world, . . .
could act any part in it, . . . printer, postmaster, almanac maker, essayist,
chemist, orator, tinker, statesman, humorist, philosopher, parlor-man,
political economist, professor of housewifery, ambassador, projector,
maxim-monger, herb-doctor, wit:—Jack of all trades, master of each and
mastered by none—the type and genius of his land." Franklin's classic
*Autobiography* records how he "tries out a series of identities and adapts
himself to the situation and the audience," always with "exhilaration in
performance." An eighteenth-century figure who thrived on Enlightenment principles of reason and experiment, Franklin was America's quintessential "self-made man" (though that term was not coined until 1832
by Henry Clay).

   From the late eighteenth century through the beginning of the twentieth, millions of people moved westward across the American continent.
Individual desire for land, economic betterment, and adventure all
played a part. Evolving national policies of expansion could come
together with individual yearning for a new start. It was a continuous
process, in which "the bonds of custom [were] broken," there was "a gate
of escape from the bondage of the past," and "new activities, new lines of
growth, new institutions and new ideals [were] brought into existence."
Moreover, the process would repeat itself, so that one frontier or border

settlement would give way to another, "West after West," and in ways that had enormous impact on the psyche of the entire American nation. The mythology of both the frontier and immigration centered on leaving behind the "old world" for a "new life" in a "new country," and thereby tapped the most fundamental of all mythic images, that of death and rebirth.

Early frontier proteanism was tinged with blood. The Puritans of seventeenth-century New England associated the native American population with sin and temptation, and their attacks upon them were often associated with their own struggles against religious backsliding in succeeding generations. They had initiated the pattern of "regeneration through violence" that was to characterize much of the frontier experience. Continuous warfare against the Indians culminated in the national policy of "Indian Removal," in which throughout the nineteenth century the latter were harassed, pressured, and attacked, and killed in large numbers, at best forced to move westward, a process in which "the language of paternalism preceded the burning of villages."

Indeed, the historian Richard Slotkin speaks of the true American founding fathers as

> the rogues, adventurers, and land-boomers; the Indian fighters, traders, missionaries, explorers, and hunters who killed and were killed until they had mastered the wilderness; the settlers who came after, suffering hardship and Indian warfare for the sake of a sacred mission or simple desire for land; and the Indians themselves, both as they were and as they appeared to the settlers, for whom they were the special demonic personification of the American wilderness.

Slotkin also points to a deep fear of acculturation, of becoming like the dark figures one was fighting. There was, then, considerable anxiety concerning this early proteanism, along with compensatory impulses toward purification by means of draconian policies of extermination. Yet all that fear and accompanying sense of exile was associated with a concept of the "errand into the wilderness," with a powerful vision of "life's renewal, of rebirth, of reason and a higher reality."

Daniel Boone, the great hero figure of the frontier, who was to help settle the Kentucky region and eventually move on to Missouri, had originally come from a Quaker family who had moved from Pennsylvania to North Carolina. Known primarily as an Indianlike hunter, he was also soldier, Indian fighter, and Indian captive, as well as a frontier landholder and official under American and then Spanish authority. Finally, Boone became, in the vast literature about him, a psychological repository of American virtues of courage, martial spirit, fierce individual autonomy, defiance of authority, and near-mystical combinations of continuous movement, pervasive entitlement, and dynamic achievement. Significantly, his legend varied according to region, so that Western writers stressed his "powers as [a] man" and as a "solitary, antisocial hunter"; Eastern writers saw in him "racial degeneracy—a white Indian"—or else "cleaned [him] up" and provided him with "specious social graces"; while in the South, he appeared in historical romances "either as a disguised aristocrat . . . or as a humble subordinate to some more aristocratic hero representative of southern virtues." Boone could be seen, then, as "a new man, the author and artificer of his own fortunes," as a strikingly protean figure of the American grassroots. So much so that, according to Turner, "[t]his perennial rebirth, this fluidity of American life, this expansion westward with its new opportunities, its continuous touch with the simplicity of primitive society . . . [provided] the forces dominating American character."

## Immigrants Forever

Just as the journey to the frontier was itself an outgrowth of immigration, so each wave of immigrants came seeking its own frontier. And many immigrants from many places experienced at least something of the myth shared with the frontier: they had a sense of resurrecting themselves, or their families over generations, from deadly oppression or victimization and achieving a "new life."

But for a considerable number, the new life brought the suffering, poverty, and victimization they thought they had left in the Old World. For example, a contemporary account of several shiploads of Irish fleeing the potato famine and arriving in America in 1847 via the St. Lawrence waterway, described "not one free from the taint of malignant typhus, the offspring of famine and of the foul ship-hold, . . . [and] the wails of children, the ravings of the delirious, the cries and groans of those in mortal agony." Those who survived could be subjected to fierce discrimination and anti-Irish and anti-Catholic sentiment. Many Eastern European Jews had comparable experiences, and anti-Semitic accusations could attribute to them "wiles that have hitherto been unknown and unthought of by civilized humanity." The suffering could be even worse for Asians: "No variety of anti-European sentiment has ever approached the violent extremes to which anti-Chinese agitation went in the 1870's and 1880's. Lynchings, boycotts, and mass expulsions still harassed the Chinese after the federal government yielded to the clamor for their exclusion in 1882." These vituperative expressions of nativism, along with racist visions of "swarms of hybrids," reflected widespread anxieties concerning the prospect of rendering the American landscape more protean.

Yet the immigrant's breakdown, loss, and humiliation could become part of family mythology as the theme of a new self reverberated down through the generations. The situation was a seedbed for protean exploration on the part of the young, as they balanced (or failed to balance) obligatory emotions in respect to weakening family and ethnic custom with the dazzling, frightening, always tempting offerings of American cultural experience. Indeed, a cardinal principle of the immigration process, spoken or unspoken, was that the next generation, and the one after that, could move to geographic, spiritual, and economic places denied their parents. There was always a cost. Thus, the last two lines of a poem written by an immigrant pants presser: "A stranger am I to my child; /And stranger my child to me." Although the poet attributes the estrangement to his extremely long work hours ("Ere dawn my labor drives me forth; /Tis night when I am free"), the conflicts in that generational journey could well have been as important an influence.

Some of that generational sequence, along with the staggering immigrant amalgams and the urban struggles of all immigrant groups are conveyed by Saul Bellow's depiction of a scene in a Chicago city college:

> And the students were children of immigrants from all parts, coming up from Hell's Kitchen, Little Sicily, the Black Belt, the mass of Polonia, the Jewish streets of Humboldt Park, put through the coarse sifters of curriculum, and also bringing wisdom of their own. They filled the factory-length corridors and giant classrooms with every human character and germ, to undergo consolidation and become, the idea was, American. In the mixture there was beauty—a good proportion—and pimple-insolence, and parricide faces, gum-chew innocence, labor fodder and secretarial forces, Danish stability, Dago inspiration, catarrh-hampered mathematical genius; there were waxed-eared shovelers' children, sex-promising businessmen's daughters—an immense sampling of a tremendous host, the multitudes of holy writ, begotten by West-moving, factory-shoved parents. Or me, the by-blow of a traveling man.

But Bellow's protagonist, Augie March, is energized by the struggle: "I am an American, Chicago born ... and go at things as I have taught myself, free-style, and will make the record in my own way."

Our protean perspective helps resolve some of the contradictions concerning the "melting pot" image. The idea of peoples of all nations being "melted into a new race of men" (as a naturalized New Yorker put it in 1782) is "as old as the Republic." Over a century later, a character in a New York play exulted: "America is God's Crucible, the great Melting Pot where all the races of Europe are melting and reforming! ... German and Frenchmen, Irishmen and Englishmen, Jews and Russians—into the

Crucible with you all! God is making the American."* Nathan Glazer and Daniel P. Moynihan created something of a sociological sensation with their conclusion that such an image was inaccurate for America, that we are instead characterized by a "pattern of subnationalities," and that "the tendency is fixed deep in American life." On the other hand, Glazer and Moynihan recognized that, if immigrants do not "melt" into American society they are "transformed by [its] influences, stripped of their original attributes, [and] . . . re-created as something new"—a clear statement of protean outcome. That "something new" takes the form of "still identifiable groups," so that "even after distinctive language, customs, and culture are lost, as they largely were in the second generation, and even more fully in the third generation," the ethnic groups are reconstituted as such. Variations in this regrouping occur, as influenced by specific events in subsequent generations. And the process is endless: "Religion and race define the next stage in the evolution of the American peoples. But the American nationality is still forming: its processes are mysterious, and its final form, if there is ever to be a final form, is as yet unknown."

Many of us—the overwhelming majority of Americans, in fact—have direct personal knowledge of this immigrant sequence. In my own case, a great-grandfather after whom I am named was known to me only as a mythological figure, said to be the designated wise man, the equivalent of a rabbi in an Orthodox Jewish village or *shtetl* near Minsk too small to support one. My grandparents fled persecution when immigrating as young adults during the last decade of the nineteenth century, but remained highly orthodox in religious practice and little acculturated to America. I have boyhood memories of walking hand in hand with my maternal grandfather, whom I loved, and becoming aware that we had no common language: he spoke extremely little English, and I even less Yiddish. For my parents, born in this country, had plunged energetically into American life, reserving their Yiddish for comments to one another they did not want the children to understand. My father defied his parents by resisting his Hebrew lessons and becoming an atheist; he went on to read Freud and Marx while a student at the City College of New York and became a modestly successful businessman, a Roosevelt liberal, and a passionate advocate of free higher education in New York City.

My parents strongly conveyed to me the expectation that I would go further and do more than they did. In the four generations I have known, including my adult children, there has been a sequence from religious to secular Jewish identity with each generation in turn combining its Jewish attachments with more extensive affiliations with non-

---

*But Israel Zangwill, the playwright, turned out to be a Zionist, thereby involved in an "anti-melting" crusade at least for Jews; he was later to retreat further from the play's stated position.

Jewish—that is, general and mixed—occupational, political, and social groups. A sense of Jewish identity, increasingly secular, has been strong in all the generations, though each in turn might be said to wear it a little more lightly. But in each there have been powerful personal forays back into various dimensions of felt Jewishness (as for me during my study of Nazi doctors). The result is never a literal return to an imagined past identity but a new combination in which earlier ethnic images are more strongly reconstituted within an evolving self.

## African Americans: "Double Meanings"

African Americans have been immigrants unlike all others. Portuguese and Spanish slavery began in the Americas early in the sixteenth century, was introduced into the colony of Virginia a century later, and quickly developed into "a regular institution . . . the normal labor relation of blacks to whites in the New World." Black immigration, then, was pure victimization. Where other immigrants underwent terrible ordeals in transport, only blacks were, through brutal commerce, imprisoned, chained, branded, and subject to cruelties that made the slave deck "resemble . . . a slaughterhouse"; where other immigrants underwent vicious discrimination and ethnic prejudice, only blacks remained under the total control of masters and were made into what I term "designated victims," people off whom the dominant population came to live not only economically but psychologically. They were victims, that is, of a particularly malignant white racism.

While there has been much debate on the psychological effects of slavery, it undoubtedly produced in blacks a combination of psychic damage and ingenious adaptation. The latter was exemplified by the escaped slave and great abolitionist leader Frederick Douglass. When, at the age of eight, a kind mistress began to teach him to read and write, he was struck by her husband's enraged declaration that "[i]f you give a nigger an inch he will take an ell [English linear measure equal to 45 inches]," and that "it would forever unfit him to be a slave." From that outburst, Douglass realized that denying literacy was the source of "the white man's power to enslave the black man." He approached white street urchins and exchanged bread for reading lessons, which he now understood as the pathway from slavery to freedom, his mistress having "given me the *inch*, . . . no precaution could prevent me from taking the *ell*." Slaves evolved survival mechanisms, drawing partly upon their African heritage, that could be convoluted and deceptive. To deal with their pain and seek some control over the situation that brutally controlled them, they (as one former slave put it) "cut capers in chains" to sustain themselves; and created stories and folk songs replete with irony and ridicule, social criticism and protest, and "double meanings." In one important series of slave tales, Brer Rabbit became "now trickster, ladies' man, and braggart, now wit, joker, and glutton, possessed the resourcefulness, despite his size and lack of strength, to outsmart stronger, larger animals." While there were notable slave rebellions, the more sustained resistance occurred as efforts to undermine psychologically white authority and become a "virtuoso of the system." In this spirit, Ralph Ellison has a former slave give deathbed advice to his son: "I want you to overcome 'em with yeses, undermine 'em with grins, agree 'em to death and destruction, let 'em swaller you till they vomit or bust wide open." For blacks, that is, the very struggle for existence led to continuous protean experiments.

The end of slavery, however welcome, further dislocated African Americans, as did the sequence of struggles during the reconstruction era, the establishment of the cruelly destructive sharecropping system, and the "great migration" to the North, which took place mostly during the first two-thirds of the twentieth century. Much of the family breakdown among blacks, many historians now believe, occurred under the duress of sharecropping rather than during slavery. Over these decades and beyond into our own time, with the emergence of a sizable black middle class and the continuing ghettoization of the poor and deprived, blacks refined and extended their techniques of dissimulation. In Ellison's *Invisible Man,* the president of a black college in the deep South stops before a mirror to prepare himself to meet an influential white: "He composed his angry face like a sculptor, making it a bland mask, leaving only the sparkle of his eyes to betray the emotion that I had seen only a moment before." He then berates a student guide for acceding to the white man's requests and showing him a seamy aspect of nearby black life: "Damn what *he* wants. . . . We take these white folks where we want them to go, we show them what we want them to see. . . . My God, boy! You're black and living in the South—did you forget how to lie?"

Ellison captures the characteristic pattern of "jive," deception, and dissimulation—along with an easy and radical personal flow—that characterize certain expressions of black proteanism. He plays off his first-person "invisible" narrator against a kind of doppelgänger named Rinehart, who is even more of a phantom as he never actually appears. The personal identities of each are stretched and diluted, and yet they remain powerful figures—the narrator as a brilliant rabblerouser and Rinehart as mythical con man–sexual hero–clergyman. The two share a "world . . . without boundaries. A vast seething, hot world of fluidity." Ultimately, the narrator recognizes, "You could actually make yourself anew" and "travel . . . up *and* down, in retreat as well as in advance, crabways and crossways and around in a circle, meeting your old selves coming and going and perhaps all at the same time."

The black philosopher and theologian Cornel West has more recently spoken of "the murky waters of despair and dread" and "the nihilistic threat to [the] very existence" of black America. He stresses the "breakdown of black culture," of "structures of meaning and feeling that [in the past] created and sustained communities [and] . . . embodied values of service and sacrifice, love and care, discipline and excellence." West sees the causes of this cultural breakdown in some of the history I have briefly recounted, but also implicates the exploitation of the "corporate market institutions" of our society, particularly in their use of "culture industries—television, radio, video, music—in which gestures of foreplay and orgiastic pleasure flood the marketplace."

Both Ellison and West, however, still envision protean glimmers of possibility. Ellison chastises certain blacks and whites for their "confusion, impatience, and refusal to recognize the beautiful absurdity of their American identity and mind." West advocates, along with his radical economic and political approach, a "politics of conversion": "Like alcoholism and drug addiction, nihilism is a disease of the soul. Any disease of the soul must be conquered by a turning of one's soul."

## Con Men and "Too Much of Anything Goes"

*You are of the opinion, Judge Temple, that a man is to be qualified by nature and education to do only one thing well, whereas I know that genius will supply the place of learning, and that a certain sort of man can do any thing and every thing.*
—James Fenimore Cooper

America's proteanism, and especially its con-man edge, is inseparable from the nation's status as a land of promise. Our deep-seated visionary tradition ("linking land boomers and poets, prophets and profiteers") renders Americans susceptible to the confidence man's false promise of better things. So much so that, following the arrest of a real confidence man in the mid-nineteenth century, a literary commentator declared: "It is not the worst thing that can be said of a country that it gives birth to a confidence man. . . . It is a good thing, and speaks well for human nature, that . . . men *can be swindled*." It is a good thing, that is, because it reflects Americans' faith in a good future and in those who offer it. But perhaps only an American could make that statement.

There is, in fact, a vast American literary tradition of fast-talking shapeshifters. An early manifestation was James Fenimore Cooper's Richard

Jones, in the 1823 novel *The Pioneers*. He is convinced that "a certain sort of man can do any thing and every thing," and his amoral frontier manipulations suggest how "Adam in the wilderness gives way to the con man in the clearing." The classic of this genre is Herman Melville's *The Confidence Man: His Masquerade,* published in 1857. Melville's otherwise nameless protagonist is a slippery shapeshifter of infinite trades or poses—merchant, philanthropist, speculator, healer, philosopher, and possibly slavetrader—who plays a "shell game of identity," involving his own and everyone else's. In this and other novels, Melville was posing radical questions about the capacity of people, especially in nineteenth-century America, to make the self over and live with more or less perpetual discontinuity and multiplicity. Thus, *Moby Dick*'s narrator, Ishmael, declares, "I try all things; I achieve what I can," and later asks, "Where lies the final harbor, whence we unmoor no more?" Melville was exploring the "'New World' as social concept," a "culture without authority," within which "Americans have had to confront each other as mere claimants, who can at best try to persuade each other who they in fact are."

Other nineteenth-century American writers contributed to this tradition without being, or creating, what we think of as con men. Walt Whitman was "as ready as Franklin to enter a series of roles—cultural bard, American Adam, common laborer, nurse, prophet, lover, scapegoat, booster." In proclaiming his own divinity, he declared himself to incorporate "Kronos, Zeus, Hercules, Osiris, Isis, Brahma, Buddha," as well as "Manito [the Native American spirit] loose, Allah on a leaf, the Crucifix engraved." Ralph Waldo Emerson gave a mid-nineteenth-century American blessing to "keeping the soul liquid . . . [and] resisting the tendency to too rapid petrifaction." For Emerson, "metamorphosis is the law of the universe"; "there are no fixtures in nature"; and "the quality of the imagination is to flow, and not to freeze." Henry David Thoreau, his disciple, added, "I have as many trades as fingers"; and "I left the woods for as good a reason as I went there. Perhaps it seemed to me that I had several more lives to live, and could not spare any more time for that one."

By the middle of the twentieth century, Ernest Hemingway was struggling against what he called the "shapelessness" of the world by imposing on it his version of precision and truth. Subsequent American writers, such as those of the Beat generation of the 1950s, took that shapelessness for granted. Their sense of perpetual motion was perhaps best personified by Neal Cassady—a model for Dean Moriarty in Kerouac's *On the Road,* an important character in Allen Ginsberg's *Howl,* and the "manic driver" of the Day-Glo bus carrying Ken Kesey and the Merry Pranksters and rendered mythic by the early Tom Wolfe. Others described Cassady in terms of "feverish activity," called him "the fastest man alive," and told how he would "burst in and out of ideas, coming to them, throwing them in the air, dropping them behind him and hurrying on to the next one."

Similarly, William Burroughs, an early associate of the Beats, explored drug reveries "in a spirit of raw kaleidoscopic self-intoxication," with "rapid shifts and indiscriminate couplings of scenes," creating "a world forever being reshuffled in the mind."

In the wake of the extraordinary upheavals of the civil rights movement, the powerful emergence of feminism, anti–Vietnam War protests, and the sexual revolution and other experiments of the 1960s and 1970s, Norman Mailer seized upon our culture's "fury of transformation," taking on the characteristic protean task of confronting "different orders of reality to be *willed* together." Women writers have provided fiction no less protean: Erica Jong, the female sexual picaresque; Joan Didion, choosing California as her venue for "com[ing] to terms with disorder"; and Joyce Carol Oates, describing ordinary people acting in extreme ways because of lacking "a fixed point within . . . [their] thinking" and being "unable to find a language for what is happening to them." Oates bears some resemblance to Russell Banks, the chronicler of violent white working-class men for whom proteanism—"the dream of starting over"—is a trap. The protagonist of Banks's novel *Continental Drift,* tells us, "The more a man trades off his known life, the one in front of him that came to him by birth and the accidents and happenstance of youth, the more of that he trades for dreams of a new life, the less power he has." A perceived formlessness goads many contemporary writers into intensified protean experimentation. Thus, John Barth, Donald Barthelme, Don DeLillo, and Jay McInerney can see the flux and fluidity through a glass darkly— as does Frederick Barthelme when referring to the "smell of too much freedom, too much anything goes, too much anything can happen, of everything else is too far away." But that flux and fluidity is a given, the very matrix of their work, and never quite without possibility.

Significantly, the con man reappears vividly in twentieth-century novels by F. Scott Fitzgerald, Saul Bellow, and Ralph Ellison. Fitzgerald's Jay Gatsby is "a crook as well as a dreamer," in whom "there is finally no distance between façade and self." Likewise, Bellow's Augie March says of himself, "I touched all sides, and nobody knew where I belonged. I had no good idea of that myself." An ever-hopeful "rogue-survivor," Augie believes that "there may be Gods turn up anywhere," and "at any time life can come together again and man be regenerated." Bellow prepares us here for Herzog, the protagonist of his next novel, a quintessential Jewish-protean seeker and "a representative modern intelligence, swamped with ideas, metaphysics, and values, and surrounded by messy facts . . . [who] labors to cope with them all." Ellison's *Invisible Man,* published in 1953, just one year before *Augie March,* calls his Rinehart "the personification of chaos; . . . intended to represent America and change," a "confidence man . . . in a country with no solid past or stable class lines," and "therefore . . . able to move easily from one to the other." More generally, Ellison is suggesting that black proteanism can epitomize much of the over-all American—indeed, universal—probing of deep disorder in order to uncover hypocricy and oppression and to suggest potential forms of order beyond them. Ellison, indeed, describes himself as aspiring to "a prose which is ... flexible, and swift as American change is swift, confronting the inequalities and brutalities of our society forthrightly, but yet thrusting forth its images of hope, human fraternity and individual self-realization."

## Grazing the Channels: American Media

*Sound bites, shortcuts, clips, trailers, minimalist fragmented "dialogue," . . . the speeded-up, almost decimated attention span of the bored, overstimulated viewer who must be caught, bought, on the wing as he or she is clicking past, "grazing" the channels, wanting to be stopped, but only momentarily.*

—Jorie Graham

Media bombardment has a special American intensity—and a special fascination for Americans. "Grazing the channels" is made easy and routine by the widespread availability of remote control equipment. But the channels one changes include those on one's own symbolizing brain, the channels of one's individual protean screen. That constant "grazing" becomes an increasingly important part of everyone's psychological existence, and in ways that can be far from trivial.

The novelist Don DeLillo powerfully evokes the bizarreness and absurdity of our relationship to the media through the words of three farcical authorities on "American environments": The first authority tells us, "For most people there are only two places in the world. Where they live and their TV set." The second refers to "the incessant bombardment of information"—"Words, pictures, numbers, facts, graphics, statistics, specs, waves, particles, motes"—causing everyone to suffer from "brain fade": "Only a catastrophe gets our attention." And the third authority, DeLillo's favorite, associates television with mystical forces (in ways that connect with McLuhan's stress on its relationship to the unconscious):

I've come to understand that the medium is a primal force in the American home. Sealed-off, timeless, self-contained, self-referring. It's like a myth being born right there in our living room, like something we know in a dreamlike and preconscious way. . . . Ancient memories of world birth, it welcomes us into the grid, the network of little buzzing dots that make up the picture pattern. . . . Look at the wealth of data concealed in the grid, in the bright packaging, the jingles, the slice-of-life commercials, the products hurtling out of darkness, the coded messages and endless repetitions, like chants, like mantras. "Coke is it, Coke is it, Coke is it." The medium practically overflows with sacred formulas if we can remember how to respond innocently and get past our irritation, weariness and disgust.

Media pundits, no less than media content, become objects of DeLillo's edgy laughter; though the pundit is being mocked, his message of the arcane all-controlling myth is not to be dismissed.

But DeLillo's ultimate comment on planetwide simultaneity came in his next novel, *Mao II:* "A person sits in a room and thinks a thought and it bleeds out into the world. Every thought is permitted. And there's no longer a moral or spatial distinction between thinking and acting." He goes on to say that we are so inundated that the terrorist alone can transcend the suffocating barrage:

There's too much everything, more things and messages and meanings than we can use in 10,000 lifetimes. Inertia-hysteria. Is history possible? Is anyone serious? Who do we take seriously? Only the lethal believer, the person who kills and dies for faith. Everything else is absorbed. The artist is absorbed, the madman in the street is absorbed and processed and incorporated. Give him a dollar. Put him in a TV commercial. Only the terrorist stands outside. The culture hasn't figured out how to assimilate him.

The self of the viewer is, DeLillo tells us, constantly being dissolved by the all-pervasive media images, to the point where it can be reached only by forms of violence and ways of life the media are unable to take in and reconstruct as their own.

Certain images of the media can transcend the endless trivia, with profound life-changing consequences. I discovered this in a very personal way in connection with the Vietnam War. One morning in November 1969, while on an airplane traveling from New York to Toronto, I picked up my copy of the *New York Times* to find a detailed front-page story about the massacre, carried out by American troops at My Lai a year earlier, of between four hundred and five hundred Vietnamese villagers, mostly old people, women, and children. I remember well, can still readily evoke, the shame and rage I felt at the time. After expressing these feelings at the beginning of the lecture I gave later that day at Toronto University, I returned home to rearrange my life and devote my main professional and personal energies to exposing painful human truths about the Vietnam War. Although one inevitably brings one's own prior experience to any such encounter (I had long opposed the war and was going to Toronto to speak on psychohistory and do a radio broadcast on nuclear-weapons issues), certain media narratives can powerfully connect with, awaken, call into question, prod, or expand narratives already within the self.

During the Vietnam War, the media influenced the function of the self in differing, even antithetical ways. On the one hand, violent images—of bombings, burnings, and deaths—could become so routine as to resemble a John Wayne film or a police-and-criminals television series, thus further numbing people toward the events of the actual war. On the other hand, once significant doubts about America's involvement in Vietnam set in, these same television images could be a constant source of discomfort, of guilt and shame, anger, and deepening opposition. So much so that it was generally believed, certainly by American military and political leaders, that journalistic coverage of the war, both print and electronic, played a major part in the eventual disenchantment of the American public in general. It was not so much a matter of journalists turning critical of the war—only a few did and usually belatedly—as of their gradually increasing capacity to gain access to, and record, what was actually taking place.

In any case, American military officials took as their lesson for future wars the importance of preventing any such on-the-spot reporting of extensive death and suffering. They applied this principle during the Gulf War of 1990 in the form of extraordinary new regulations regarding censorship and restrictions on coverage. The policy was greatly enhanced by the high-tech nature of the war, which imposed its own separation between the operation of the weapons and their human effects. The result was that newspaper, radio, and television coverage of the war, at least for Americans, was dominated by displays of the technological brilliance of weapons, by discussions of demanding tactical and organizational arrangements, and by continuous geopolitical and military commentary by "experts" (often retired generals and admirals). Yet at the same time there took place a quantum jump in media function, as epitomized by American Cable News Network's (CNN) twenty-four-hour coverage of the war, disseminated throughout the world. Viewers could feel themselves to be in the war zone as they witnessed its sights and sounds at any moment, night or day. But with death and destruction mostly filtered out of available images, the war seemed to have little unpleasantness.

Yet here, too, some truth made its way into these media images. For instance, a four-year-old child I knew expressed the fear that a missile was going to come out of his television set and get him. That fear bespoke two forms of recognition: first, that the war was dangerous and people were getting killed; and second, that the television set, around which American families spent long hours, was a central actor in all these events. Adults were not immune from these more troubled perceptions, which television images, however sanitized, could bring forth. Once more, people experienced the media in very different ways: a viewer's self could be numbed, or opened to fear and questioning.

## "Just Dust": American Endings

*Years before the world's nuclear arsenals made such a holocaust
likely or even possible, the prospect of global annihilation already
filled the national consciousness.*

—Paul Boyer

During the weeks and months following the atomic bombings of
Hiroshima and Nagasaki in August 1945, end-of-the-world imagery pervaded American culture. The day after Hiroshima, a *New York Times* editorial referred to "an explosion in men's minds as shattering as the oblit-
eration of Hiroshima." And a short time afterward, the same newspaper
referred to our capacity to "blow ourselves and perhaps the planet itself
to drifting dust." Indeed, during the years between 1945 and 1950, "the
Bomb" pervaded American intellectual life and popular culture, making
the "prospect of global annihilation" seem all too likely even before
existing weapons made it feasible. Though we were to embrace the very
object of our terror in order to diminish that terror, and develop a
mind-set I have called nuclearism, the imagery of extinction accompanying the bomb's entry into the world could never be eliminated.

In our research interviews at the Center on Violence and Human Survival, the nuclear threat readily blended in people's minds, consciously
and unconsciously, with the threat of environmental destruction.
Nuclear fear has not disappeared with the American-Soviet détente and
the collapse of the Soviet Union—partly because the weapons still exist
and pose great dangers (whether from the difficulties of destroying
them or from nuclear proliferation). There was, with the end of the cold
war, a shift in emphasis: fears associated with the environment became
greater and more actively expressed, while nuclear fear became more of
a background shadow. But imagery of extinction remains important for
the contemporary self. We are aware of our continuing capacity for literally bringing about that extinction; and that awareness makes contact, as
I have noted, with the larger human inclination to imagine the end of
the world.

Responses to imagery of extinction can vary greatly, as suggested by
the vignettes that follow. One may bring to it various forms of protean
malleability and capacity for transformation. Indeed, precisely those tendencies may be called forth by the threat itself.

Arthur M., an accomplished seventy-year-old lawyer, who views himself
to be much more inwardly chaotic than his dignified appearance suggests, imagines a post-bomb scene in which he and other people are
"running about wildly, flames, terror, a kind of general madness, hunger,

a general picture of devastation." In contrast, his wife, a strong and nurturing person, would be acting more purposefully, looking for her children and her husband so that she can "gather them all up and organize
them." He further imagines "a sense of a forlorn, waste universe, which is
dead and cold, empty and meaningless. . . . [a] sense of nothingness
[that] is mournful to me." Yet he holds to the belief that "somehow the
entire destruction of the civilized world would not happen. . . . If one survived, . . . there would be places to repair to and start all over again, . . .
primitive, ugly, exiguous and terribly unpleasant circumstances, but kind
of resuming [life] . . . again." He bases that expectation on the remarkable good fortune he has experienced in his own life in having survived
and transcended severe personal abuse and deprivation (see chapter 8).
In general, he struggles against his "mournful" imagery of extinction and
clings to a vision of collective renewal associated with his lifelong personal project of self-renewal.

Jessica C., a twenty-year-old black woman aspiring to become a popular
vocalist, is unable to imagine anything in her life more than five years
ahead because of her feeling that "there's not going to be a world at all."
She imagines the world "like burnt, like everything's . . . broken down . . .
and . . . there's . . . no people." She derives most of her images from TV
and films, particularly the television film about nuclear war, *The Day After,*
shown during the 1980s ("Everyone . . . died, . . . but the roaches were
still living. . . . They had to . . . burn the people because there were so
many dead bodies, . . . just truckloads of bodies"), but also from a film
about Hiroshima and from such additional films as *The Terminator* and
*The Seventh Sign.* She is not hopeful that any life will continue: "Let's just
say the world ends." For her this nuclear annihilation would be just an
extension of other destructive forces: "I mean, if it's not the water it's . . .
the ozone layer or AIDS. . . . If they do find a cure for AIDS, two years
from now there's going to be something even worse. . . . You can't
breathe anymore because the air is so contaminated, . . . and then the
rainforests. . . . They're just killing everything." She adds that, were she to
learn what would happen an hour or two before the bombs fell, "I would
. . . say bye to everyone, and I'll go get laid or something. . . . I'm serious.
That's what I'd want to do." She is, compared with the elderly lawyer,
much more oppressed by the likelihood of world destruction and less
hopeful of any form of human survival. But in her description of last-
minute sexual assertion, she is positing a general intensification of life
energies against the threat of extinction.

Carol C., a forty-year-old sculptor and social activist, describes a post-
bomb landscape as devoid of vegetation with "very little sense of human
remains, . . . just . . . dust, . . . no atmosphere—just a void." All death
would be "stripped of human dignity." And she says she experiences
"rage" when thinking about it. She associates such a scene with a number

of films on Hiroshima she has viewed, but also with what she has read about the Nazis and their concentration camps. Deeply involved with the natural world, her imagery also draws upon the nuclear accident at Chernobyl and her fear of another nuclear accident at a plant in her area or in relation to the Galileo space probe making use of plutonium fuel. All this to her is part of the "ongoing destruction" of the global environment. Her preference for "complete termination of humankind" rather than the existence of a survivor remnant both reflects that bitterness and her awareness of the horrors that would result for those who lived ("I don't want to be around the next day!"). She alternates between an image of total destruction, leaving only dust, and one of "something . . . that would regenerate from a seed, . . . one pine tree, . . . the chance to start over again." With it all, she is convinced that the "spirit . . . lives on," that "just because . . . there might be an atomic bomb, it doesn't wipe out my spiritual journey!"—and declares defiantly, "I'm not ready to die yet!" Like those of many people, her images are contradictory; her intense awareness of a possible planetary end renders everything precarious for her while at the same time vivifying and intensifying her protean quest.

Despite the end of the cold war, Americans approach the twenty-first century haunted by a sense of futurelessness—by the fear of being radically severed from larger human connectedness or the symbolization of immortality. But at the same time—as Carol C., Jessica C., and Arthur M. testify—another side of us lives "normally," makes plans, struggles with nitty-gritty life issues, and seeks to block out the occasionally conscious image that all may suddenly end. In pursuing this double life, we oscillate between protective numbing with a partial shutting down of the self, and sufficient openness to troubling feelings of meaninglessness and disintegration for these to serve as stimuli to self-exploration and change.

Proteus's sojourn in American waters, then, remains active, influences all that we do, and continues to define us as a people and a nation. For such is our history that we have never been other than protean. That essential proteanism imbues us with sometimes dangerous social and psychological vulnerabilities. But it also provides a sense that we need never stand still, and that transformation may be just around the corner.

# Chapter 4

## ODD COMBINATIONS

*All my life I've felt like I was just making things up, improvising as
I went along. I don't mean telling lies, I mean inventing a life.*
                                                              —Ann Beattie

*Mutually irreconcilable realities are wedded to each other.*
                                                              —Max Ernst

THE ESSENCE of the protean self lies in its odd combinations. There is
a linking—often loose but functional—of identity elements and subselves
not ordinarily associated with one another to the point of even seeming
(in Max Ernst's words) "mutually irreconcilable." The new combinations
may take one in unexpected directions and provide one with equally
unexpected capacities, as was the case with people in Prague at the time
of their revolution (discussed later in this chapter). These combinations
undergo shifts and transformations, subject as they are to the self's per-
meability to inner and outer influence (never fully distinguishable from
one another). But the rearrangements nonetheless permit a certain continuity amidst individual disruptions and explorations. The process is laid
bare in James Joyce's rendition of *Ulysses,* surely the great protean literary
journey of the twentieth century. Joyce's "Proteus" episode (his titles and
structure follow Homer's) portrays "a world dominated by metamorphoses which continuously produce new centers of relations."

As in the case of Joyce's protagonist, Stephen Dedalus, the protean self
is always confronted with the danger that these odd combinations will
not cohere. But it continually combines its fragments in order to avoid
fragmentation. One could say the same for much of modern and contemporary art, especially the cubist-collage tradition, as I shall also suggest. These attributes of the protean self result in a form of life (as conveyed by the fiction of Vladimir Nabokov) that is not "one-way motion"

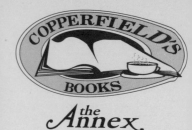

but "something much freer, with surprising jolts and changes of direction that nevertheless in retrospect fall into a unique pattern that character-ize[s] one person's individual fate."

The self's symbolizing function, its continuous restructuring of images and forms, feeds and maintains its evolving combinations. With symbol-ization, no relationship, idea, impulse, or blend of any of these is immune from modification or recombination. As a result, the self's belief and value orientations can become "like particles in modernity's acceler-ator." Precisely this transformative pattern provides the protean self with the everpresent capacity for emerging from "stuckness," from apparent thralldom to a particular stance. It can also create in one a sense of tem-poral freedom, the feeling that "time . . . is up for grabs"; and an inclina-tion to "tak[e] . . . the time to drift and think, afresh as in all beginnings."

## "How Many More Shapes . . . How Many More Selves?": Individual Narratives

Less lyrically perhaps, but with considerable effect, these patterns of com-bination and transformation can be observed in the following vignettes.

### "THESE MIRACULOUS RECESSES OF OUR MIND": MICHAEL W.

Michael W. was seventy-three years old when I interviewed him in Washington, D.C., and in semiretirement from a long and distinguished career in government and foundation work. He spoke of his early family experience in Tennessee as "culturally deprived" and in every way impov-erished. His parents constantly fought until their divorce, his mother working at menial jobs to keep things going amid such Depression poverty that they lived on leftover sandwiches sold at a drugstore for a penny each. He added, however, "It sounds probably worse than I felt it to be," as he had no basis for comparison; and when he turned out to be a good student, sympathetic teachers would "take me by the ear" and encourage further study, including college. He eventually won an inter-national scholarship, distinguished himself as a combat naval officer in the Second World War, did important work in assessing atomic bomb damage in Japan, became an administrator for the Marshall Plan in Europe, then served in government and in several foundations at high levels in work that took him to various parts of Europe, Asia, and Africa, always advocating projects that would benefit large numbers of people.

In discussing these experiences, he spoke of observing his own mental processes and noting that certain important images remain "in these . . . miraculous recesses of our mind . . . [and] genuinely affect all kinds of reactions." He gave as an example his childhood "romantic idea about China," which led to a lifelong preoccupation with that country. The "romantic idea" might also have contributed to the seeming coincidence of his actual travel to China on a naval vessel during the war. The adventurous character of the visit was to be amplified by an encounter, when providing food supplies to a Jewish ghetto in Shanghai, with an adolescent boy who was later to become a member of an American presidential cabinet. The desire to return to China was a major reason for Michael W.'s entering the State Department after the war, and he did consulting work with a large corporation for the same purpose. On his visits to China, he became deeply interested in Chinese art, both ancient and contemporary. He was especially struck by the capacity of contemporary Chinese artists to rebound from the "terrors" and rigidities of the Cultural Revolution of the late 1960s and other waves of persecution, by "how quickly the human spirit revived."

Michael W. still sees himself as "thrust by circumstances, fortuitous circumstances, into a whole series of situations and contexts": "I got scattered around but [not] by design and not by anything I can compliment myself on. . . . I happened to develop a little bit of sophistication in the social sciences and in international affairs, and I was, I guess, rather strongly interested in political matters. . . . Now I've become very much interested in the whole nonprofit sector of the American pluralistic system, . . . questions about philanthropy and donors." He wonders exactly what he has become: "I'm not quite anything. I mean I'm not really a qualified social scientist and . . . not really . . . a qualified specialist in international affairs, . . . it's been more eclectic random things. . . . Whatever the hell it adds up to, I'm not all that sure." But when looking back "at the kid I was in high school," he is "really kind of amazed [at] how the hell . . . I ever [got] into the things I got into."

He can recognize, however, that whatever the fortuitous circumstances, "I had the ability to kind of react to them, grasp them, and function in them." Just as he and his family scavenged for food when he was young, Michael W. was able to become a skillful psychological scavenger. His sustained vision of China came to represent a transcendence of his impoverished background, a sense of adventurous possibility, both geographically and in terms of his always evolving self.

"A VESSEL ON THE WATER": CAROL C.

Carol C., a woman of forty, combines her work as a sculptor in a small California seaside town with a continuous commitment to political activism on behalf of the environment, peace, and the homeless. During her early thirties she made a series of bold decisions: to give up a successful career as a therapist for children with learning disorders in order to pursue her art, to leave a home and a city in which she had thrived, and to "come out" as a lesbian. She told of a childhood experience that fed her protean capacities. When she was eight or nine years old, she would lie down on the ground in a secluded place, pleasurably "smell the grass," and then "astrologically project . . . myself" out into the "atmosphere" and "try to imagine life beyond the planet and let . . . my mind wander off to think about the endless space that is out there." Her relationship with her parents was often troubled, and she was aware of a "need to leave" and in some sense to live "out there," a feeling that could become "very scary": "There was a sense of losing touch with reality here," a reality that "required me to come back." She was describing a form of dissociation, a willed "out-of-body experience," but one that served her imaginative purposes. It was part of a practice she had developed still earlier of lying on the ground, "connecting with the earth," and calling forth a Christian image of "ashes to ashes." Under duress, including early death anxiety, she was making use of a form of controlled dissociation to expand the self into infinite realms and render it free to experiment on its own terms. In that sense, she was constructing a beginning model for her proteanism.

That experimentation included moral questioning. She was troubled by the question of black children having to believe in a "white Jesus," which "didn't seem fair to me"; and was upset when, following the disappearance from school of a black child she had befriended, she was told that the other girl "lived on the other side of the tracks and . . . wasn't anybody to worry about." As a teenager, Carol C. began to read books about Jewish experience, was particularly moved by the story of Anne Frank, and found herself "somehow identifying with that female child." She left home during her last two high school years to attend a Marxist school; joined demonstrations at her small western college protesting the firing of faculty members accused of being communists; and took part in what she called the "Chicago burning," the mass student, anti-Vietnam War protests during the Democratic convention of 1968. She found the latter experience "scary and creepy" because her government seemed capable of shutting down an entire city. At the time, she was influenced by SDS (Students for a Democratic Society), the Black Panthers, and the Communist party, but could follow none of them completely because of her early and consistent commitment to nonviolence. In subsequent political involvement, she has continued this pattern of working with various organizations while thinking through and acting upon her individual convictions.

Her work sequence also expressed her capacity for innovative combinations. After training in speech therapy for children with learning disorders, she excelled in that work to the point of becoming the head of a small department within a larger clinic. Also interested in the arts from childhood, she simultaneously studied and worked at sculpture. During her early thirties, she began to realize, "My art work had really reached a plateau, and I either had to accept that plateau . . . or commit myself to [the artwork]." She decided to "make that leap" (leave her safe job, move to another city, and immerse herself in her art), knowing that she could always fall back on her skill as a speech therapist, which she has since done on occasion when in need of money. She experienced the shift as both fundamental and combinatory, one of (here applying an architectural idiom to the self) "restructuring the whole groundwork—building an addition . . . [but] having to start at the foundation again."

Contributing to the shift that enabled her to "see . . . myself as a sculptor" was her immersion in feminist consciousness-raising groups: she learned of women who had shown great courage in pursuing creative or humanitarian goals, such as Gertrude Stein, Charlotte Dickins Gilman, Emma Goldman, Angela Davis, and members of the Maryknoll Sisters in El Salvador who had recently been tortured and killed. She associated the decision to acknowledge herself as a lesbian with an evolving bond with generations of women, with the feeling that "it just didn't end with me," and that "my sexuality is also part of my spirituality." Similarly, in making her career shift, she saw herself as rejecting the traditional female role of "caregiver . . . [who] tends to other people's needs," and as "trying to find some of my own passion." She understood the whole process—her career change, confirmation of sexuality, and evolving feminism—as in the service of authenticity and coherence: "I was beginning to listen to some inner voice"; and "there [were] a whole lot of dominoes kind of toppling from me at the same time." The "dominoes" were elements of self, or combinations of elements, which she now experienced as impediments to authentic self-process.

While undergoing these changes, she had dreams of journeys, of sea voyages. After one such dream of being on a ship that encountered a violent storm, she made a large clay sculpture in which she herself was the base of the boat, its sides coming out of her own body, with her arms the gunwales and her feet the bow; her head, which was the stern, "became the head of a bird." She wished, via the sculpture, "to allow myself to bend with the storm and still stay strong, to feel the pressure and the impact of it." She was struggling to strengthen a sense of self that was always vulnerable and always in passage. She came to recognize a death-related aspect to such "voyages"; and in that sense, her dream imagery contributed to a death-and-renewal process she was undergoing.

Carol C.'s most dramatic transformation emerged from her exposure to endless renditions of the Crucifixion as part of the oppressive, near-fundamentalist Lutheranism of her childhood. She rebelliously rejected all of its dogma and was critical of the Crucifixion imagery, which she found "bizarre" and grotesque: "It didn't seem human . . . that somebody would hurt somebody else like that." All the more so as she learned that "lots of people were killed for that Crucifixion, and the value of human life was . . . little." But as she took on her adult concerns about abuse of human rights and human beings, she came to feel that the Crucifixion "doesn't seem so far off any more." Her present associations to the Crucifixion suggest both her transformation of the image and the power of that transformation: "Pierced hands, pierced feet, dehydration, hot sun, semiconscious, delirious, flesh sagging, weight of a body," and finally, what has become a key word for her, "Torture!" She added, "A lot of people are tortured that way. They may not be on a cross, but they're tortured in some very similar ways, and it makes me angry and . . . really sad. . . . Emotionally it hurts." In that sense, the Crucifixion provides searing motivation for her social activism: "It's what propels me to do the work that I do now . . . in terms of justice." The Crucifixion for her has been transformed into a contemporary set of images organized around the principle of torture, that principle extending to any form of suffering caused by other human beings (or neglected by them), including not only physical infliction of pain but homelessness, AIDS, starvation, and poverty. Carol's view of the Crucifixion as a source of energy and illumination is reminiscent of lines in a poem by Hayden Carruth: "I saw another cross with another man nailed to it,/twisting and nodding, and then another and another,/ranks and divisions of crosses straggling like exhausted . . . legions upward among the misty trees, each cross/with a silvery, writhing, twisting, nodding, naked/figure nailed to it, and some of them were women."

Finally, in these combinations, she further transmutes early religious influence into a kind of natural mysticism. She spoke of "an existence that goes on beyond me, . . . that I call my spirit," with "this planet being one of many planets," and when "looking at every particle of sand on the beach . . . human life is relatively insignificant." She connects her work with clay to her love of natural elements, to "feeling the earth in my bloodstream" and "being . . . a vessel on the water." The questions she raises concerning her art apply to every facet of her life: "What is my process? How do I evolve?"

## "SO MANY DIFFERENT FACETS": ROSALYN K.

Rosalyn K., a thirty-year-old social activist and teacher from the Midwest, had difficulty delineating herself from her activist parents. During her last year of high school and her college years when "away on my own," she began to question family-instilled truths, to reject simplistic ideas about Us (activists) and Them (reactionaries), and to realize painfully that "the solutions weren't that easy." She also saw herself part of "the nothing generation, the Me generation" of the mid-1970s (while at the same time mocking media representations of it), an attitude that led to a sense of "non-identity" and escape into television watching ("I knew every commercial by heart"). These personal and social conflicts became associated with an ineffectual proteanism: "I couldn't move forward because I was moving sideways, just sort of taking in all the different possibilities and all the different sides of the story. . . . I really felt unable to act in this world." Yet in her confusion about political action, she found herself turning "inward" (though also outward) in mobilizing her intellectual energies to pursue her university studies in art and literature, philosophy, history, and questions of war and peace.

While she remembered no special moment of resolution, at some point soon after her college graduation she "decided to become an adult." For her that meant a combination of working for a living and resuming social activism at a more independent and responsible level. She was able to obtain a position in the Philadelphia city bureaucracy dealing with educational problems in young people, which she calls "my straight job" or "what I count on every day." Of great importance to this process of fluid self-delineation was her discovery of the writings of the American Pop artist Andy Warhol, which expressed her doubts and deep sense of absurdity. When others to whom she recommended them would complain that they were "boring" or "dumb," she would reply: "But that's what his art is about, it's about boring, . . . about just this nihilistic monotone. . . . I identified with . . . every word. . . . He spends . . . a whole chapter talking about which side of the pillow to sleep on. . . . He understood. That's exactly what life was for me." Warhol's writings connected her to a contemporary sensibility she could combine with her intellectual and political exploration in forming an adult self she could feel to be her own.

Her activism came to be varied: several years of grass-roots work with young people, old people, and community groups; more recent participation on steering committees of a number of leading peace organizations in East Coast cities where she works on issues of policy "less exciting, less romantic [than grass-roots work], . . . [but] I just sort of felt an obligation." She has been able to clarify her political convictions and (in keeping with her subculture) see herself as favoring "a decentralized participatory form of self-government, so that people really are making decisions about their own lives and not imposing them on others." She also fell in love with an older activist, with whom she lived for some years in a relationship she found "very exciting," an experience of valuable political discipleship, and an introduction to becoming "definitely a family" (including his children). She experienced considerable pain when they broke up, but retains feelings of affection for her friend and a sense of having learned and grown much in the relationship.

Important to Rosalyn K. are several additional interests—opera and ballet, her own painting, and baseball. The painting affords great satisfaction in "mak[ing] something," and the baseball provides an excruciating immersion in a sports fan's pleasure and pain. "You get all caught up in something you know . . . really won't affect your life. . . . You can win the World Series, but your work's going to be the same the next day." She looks back with pride and amusement at the impact made at a Washington pro-choice demonstration by a small group of women she helped bring together, who were carrying big signs, "Philadelphia Phillies fans for legal abortion." Concerning all these interests, she explains: "I'm not . . . somebody who's ever been an expert on anything. . . . I just reach a plateau with everything. . . . So my life has always had so many different facets to it." While sometimes yearning to be "a master of something," she also sees value in being able to "spread yourself out that way and cover many different things." She applies that principle of innovative combination to her continuing activism. She was involved in a protest against bringing nuclear weapons into New York Harbor: "We stood outside . . . that rush-hour traffic going on to the ferry, with all the cars backed up, . . . and said, 'Can you imagine evacuating New York City if there was a nuclear accident?'" And she helped plan a "wonderful action" called "Free Brunch at the Plaza," in which her group set up a soup kitchen at Trump Plaza and fed twelve hundred homeless people, and to which Donald and Ivana Trump were invited.

Rosalyn K. still has moments of deep uncertainty and what she calls "underlying despair." She overcomes these feelings by acting: "I feel more like a human being taking action, and maybe making a mistake, than I do sitting back and saying, 'Well, . . . it's not going to do anything anyway, you're just wasting your time.'" She experiences a never-ending struggle against two fears: that of becoming stuck or "paralyzed," on the one hand; and on the other, of being so fluid that she loses "continuity in my life" by engaging in an exaggerated proteanism: "This idea that we can do anything, we can have anything, we can be anybody—changing careers, . . . changing mates, changing locations—maybe we're going [to] too much extreme [in] that." She aspires to be like certain people she admires who remain activists, who "take care of their family and are still involved with their community at every level," yet "approach situations with an open mind and . . . don't have a pat answer, and somehow go through this world with a sense of optimism and hope, which is hard to do while working in the muck of everything." For Rosalyn, however, continuing uncertainty is a given: "If we knew what the problem was, and you could encapsulate it in that way, life would be a little easier." That uncertainty, along with the temporary state of things, is part of her sense of the world: "The value of things is not their length . . . like cities and civilization. . . . We spend all of our time just trying to keep something alive [here she was referring specifically to activist organizations]. Well, why should it last? Maybe this is not the best vehicle to move forward our ideas." So she varies her activities to work "with different political causes," to follow a life pattern that is "exciting but . . . also scary."

## SOURCES OF INNOVATION

These innovative combinations result from openness to self-process and sensitivity to the outside world; from a sequence of varied, often painful personal exposures that could be transcended or transformed; and from a wide array of historical and cultural influences. Whatever the apparent prominence of any one of these (Michael W.'s connections with larger history, Carol C.'s striking sequence of personal involvement, Rosalyn K.'s openness to new experience), all three interact in anyone with protean tendencies. For instance, Michael W. had to be considerably open in his self-process to be responsive to the great historical events of his time; and his resulting life experiences were as varied as either of the two women's. Similarly, Carol C.'s questing openness helped create her divergent life experiences; as did the larger historical forces acting upon her (the Vietnam War in the 1960s rebellion of the young, patterns of American feminism during the 1970s, and general developments in the divergent fields of speech therapy and American art). Rosalyn K.'s openness would not have resulted in the combinations she formed without her life experiences (leaving home while in high school, intellectual studies at college, work in education, and participation in activism) and without the historical developments encompassing those experiences (the Vietnam War, Watergate, and even the vicissitudes of the Philadelphia Phillies baseball team). In general, openness leads to varied life experiences and to ways of responding to them; and the ever-present and powerful historical and cultural events of our era, having been made psychologically available in varying depth by the media, prod everyone into at least a susceptibility to varied life experiences.

## "I PRESUME THERE IS NOTHING I CAN'T DO": GEORGE R.

For example, George R., an executive and management consultant long associated with a large Hartford accounting firm, has outwardly followed a conventional life pattern. The child of Catholic, working-class parents, George R. grew up in Chicago and was always "expected [to] pitch in, participate, work hard, perform." His father, authoritarian and caring, had immigrated from Poland to become a successful cabinet-maker and connected closely with his son in relation to two sustained activities: work together, over years, on building a summer house ("We cleared the land and put down seed and picked up rocks 'til my back was broken"); and an intense, closely shared immersion in sports. When George showed outstanding talent as a baseball player, his father exerted strong pressure on him to embark on a professional career that might take him to the major leagues. The young man's rejection of that plan, with the surreptitious help of his mother, for a career in business was a considerable defiance, especially since his father looked down on office work.

Upon entering the firm where he is still employed, George not only worked hard but showed enormous ingenuity in evolving policies for handling accounts of tax-free institutions. In this way, he developed what he calls "some very special programs," which have become broadly influential in his field. He brought to these accomplishments an ethical commitment toward "trying to create awareness that . . . we have a stake in what's happening in society, with nonprofit organizations being an important part of society." At the same time, his work frequently "gets stale, and that bothers the hell out of me." Constant innovation becomes for him a means of "keeping my sanity." As he explained, "I try . . . to push [things] . . . off the edge of the map . . . as far as I can without falling over the edge myself." George R. brings to other areas of his life this uneasy balance between stable outward conformity and edgy imaginative fluidity. He chooses to travel extensively, finding that he is professionally most creative that way, though aware that this threatens his family life. He is concerned about being "an absentee father": "You cheat that way and then try to make it up . . . in other ways," so "I work very hard trying to balance my act." In his religious practice, he is skeptical of almost all dogma, particularly that of an afterlife, though he believes that "we're gonna go *some* place." At the same time, he describes himself as "a regular churchgoer": "For me it's a very important private time . . . to sort of step back and think about who I am."

He finds himself always looking to the future, "scanning the environment" for change and escape, searching for "megatrends." He is serious about the possibility, during the next few years, of making a major change in his professional life; but he is aware of being confused about "whether or not I really want to stay here doing what I'm doing, or whether . . . I want to go into . . . a second career, or whether I want to do both." He is aware that, generally speaking, "severe change [in either his family life or his work] would . . . scare me for a while." But then he added, as though thinking out loud, "You know, I'm forty-seven years old.

How long are you gonna continue to work here?" He was speaking of "that sort of fear about where I want to end up with my life," because "I enjoy doing other things." Then, reverting to powerful early influences: "I like building houses." He sees what he is doing as "just a stop" on a journey, so that one day he might "spring . . . off into something else." In the meantime, "I always keep three balls in the air . . . I think that's the only way you can survive in the kind of crazy world we live in."

Although George tended to muzzle much of his proteanism, he seemed capable of taking the more radical plunge he constantly envisions. A product of the immigrant sequence discussed in chapter 3, he manifests a cautiously open self-process in responding to some of the powerful currents of recent American social and economic history. His balancing act between grounding and fluidity is no less demanding than that of the others I have discussed. But his proteanism has an element of unusual confidence: "I think you can set your own destiny and accomplish . . . pretty much what you care to in this world if you really want to. . . . I presume there is nothing I can't do." His larger problem is knowing just what it is that he "really wants" to do. Hence, his "three balls in the air" for what he calls survival but which includes high accomplishment and an ever-available escape hatch.


## "IT'S JUST A PROCESS OF NEW GROWTH": FRANCINE C.

In contrast to George, Francine C. (in her late fifties when interviewed) met discrimination as a woman, but managed to evolve a sense of self that took on its own idiosyncratic combinations. Discouraged in her early intellectual aspirations by her Baltimore middle-class parents, she was, like Michael, greatly helped by sensitive support from teachers and also from a female dean. But despite her outstanding record in graduate work in international relations, the government agency she joined would not appoint her to an overseas position because of a policy excluding women from such assignments (the assumption was that "it wasn't suitable [because] women needed to be protected"). She then proceeded to "construct a career in international affairs without . . . even going overseas." She states that she managed this "by sheer flukes," but actually brought considerable ingenuity to evolving a broad program ("You had to know a little bit about a great number of countries") of educational and cultural exchange. Her effectiveness in the work had to do, she thought, with her ability to empathize with people of highly varied backgrounds, a capacity "possibly" related to being a woman. But she was never able to fulfill her ambition of overseas service and realized that her division "had virtually no input in policy."

She was always aware of balancing her professional activities with her family life. She would invite people she met to her home if she thought them "of particular interest to my husband." And having always "wanted a child more than anything else," she focused strongly on her daughter's upbringing and saw herself as "a working mother." So much so that when, on one occasion, she mustered the courage to take an assignment that required her to leave her family for a month and travel all over the United States, she considered it "a revolution in my life."

Having to retire early from her job because of a partially incapacitating chronic illness, Francine began to teach at a local women's center and to immerse herself in what she calls "new disciplines." In her teaching, she combined material from feminist studies (which she interested herself in for the first time) with her own life experience. She has been drawn once more to the diversity of women she encounters, and is particularly excited about extending her extensive knowledge of various ethnic groups by probing the black female experience, "a new exposure for me." She speaks proudly of "black welfare mothers, by God, who are getting themselves college educations," and of "the strength that a lot of women are developing from one another."

Francine is not without resentments concerning the discrimination she encountered and regrets not having done better in raising her child. By implication, she partly blames herself for her adult daughter's reluctance to have children (because of "so many kinds of potential doom"). That attitude "distresses" Francine because she "would like to see the world continue" and wants very much for her husband to have a grandson: "He's so cute with little boys and . . . didn't have a son." But something radiating from Francine led the interviewer, a sensitive young female anthropologist, to comment to her that she seemed "very calm and happy," to which Francine answered, "Yes, in a strange way." Her "strange way" included creative forms of career assertion in the face of parental resistance and discrimination against women, a delicate balance of professional and domestic commitments, and the transformation of a severe illness into an opportunity for acquiring forms of knowledge that added coherence to her own life and enabled her to empower many others. She went on to explain that she has "learned a lot" from many directions, including much from her daughter, and that, more generally, "It's just a process of new growth."

## THE BORDERS OF FRAGMENTATION: EDWARD G.

Edward G. is, at the age of sixty, a respected social activist and a leading figure in a prominent Washington, D.C., peace organization. His

commitment to nonviolent protest and his personal struggle against fragmentation have involved an impressive and highly irregular combination
of religious, political, and experiential components. He associates his
movement toward pacifism with his rebellion against his North Carolina
father and grandfather, both of whom had distinguished military careers
and were conservative Republicans. But in the process he has struggled
with his own violence, recalling two painful incidents: one in which, as a
boy, he chased and caught another youngster who had bullied his
brother, and " was in the process of strangling [the other youngster] to
death" until a teacher intervened; and another, as an adult, when,
angered by a young woman who had kicked his cat, he "carried her out
the . . . door and dropped her." He understands violence as "unleashing
of something in the unconscious, . . . very frightening to see, . . . something all of us can do," but rejects it as "not something I would want to
have done to me and . . . not something I would want to do to anyone
else." He can accept his own violent dreams, including one in which,
brandishing a Chinese saber, he was "hacking people and destroying people" ("I was engaged in a struggle for my survival"); the violent content of
the dream seemed to him an expression of life power that could be transformed into nonviolent, but equally fierce, defense of other beings and
larger principles.

His evolving fluidity and his sense of self were greatly enhanced by living, during his twenties and thirties, "the life of a bohemian." That
involved, rather than alcohol or drugs, relaxed social and sexual mores
("Nobody's going to be surprised if the friend [one brings to a party] is
black, or . . . male, or . . . transvestite"); poetry and music; and, more
than anything else, continuous talk ("inconceivable to a Protestant family"). He further described it as "the middle class running toward [that]
kind of freedom," with people able to find "enough money loose in the
society that if we were willing to be poor we could be free and still [sur-
vive]." Though not without pain, those years were profoundly formative:
"We were young and confused, and it was a great time to be alive even
though you were depressed a large part of the time or your life was
chaotic as it always is. It was a wonderful, shaping experience." Many of
the "bright, sharp people" around him then are still his friends, and he
sees himself as having undergone a "permanent shift of values."

When asked whether he was religious, Edward G. answered, "I am, but
I'm an atheist"—which reflected the combinations encountered in several other activists. While still under the original influence of his family's
authoritarian Baptist religion, he joined the Prohibition party and also
became a pacifist (by that combination managing both to hold onto and
to reverse family influences). He found himself horrified by "that . . . figure of a genocidal God" depicted in the Old Testament, "a book which
made me want to have the courage to be an atheist." But for him that

God "somehow changed" in the New Testament, so that, despite his declared atheism, he found himself returning to the Gospels, which "remain very profound psychological documents," and then connecting them with readings in Eastern religions. He combined these attitudes in his view of death, which at first seems to be simply one of atheism: "That will be the end of it, . . . no heaven, . . . no immortality, . . . no afterlife." But he added, "I expect to dissolve like a sugar cube in water, . . . becoming part of something broader." And he went further: "No, I don't think there is a death in that [ordinary] sense"; he expressed in Tolstoyan fashion a form of symbolic immortality that is as Christian as it can be in the absence of a dogmatic structure.

He added a complicated original principle (though he believes it consistent with the Gospels) of "sending over": "The one who has been able to get rid of most of his money when he dies, lives; whatever you have left, you lose. Whatever you gave away you get to take across. You're not going anywhere, and nothing goes across that will be of help except . . . an image. But whatever you've held on to you've lost. Whatever you've gotten rid of you've saved." Following a drug experience as a young adult, during which he felt himself close to death, Edward realized that he was completely unprepared to die: "I haven't sent anything over," which also meant, "I haven't left anything behind," so that his life or death "didn't make a difference to anybody." He thus holds to both his atheism and his spirituality in a way that enables him to form a self in touch with death and death-related experiences; a way that, in turn, contributes to his capacity for empathy and to his ethical and political energies. Those energies have been applied in connection with a series of organizations on behalf of pacifism, nonviolent protest against war and militarism, and anticommunist socialism.

What is surprising about Edward G., given his abilities and high standing in his activist subculture, is his lifelong tendency toward psychological disintegration. He has for some time been on medication for depression and describes himself as "a little bit manic-depressive." And although he has long given up drinking, "I'm an alcoholic, and that involves a great deal of . . . self-inflicted pain." Another source of considerable pain has been the antagonism he has experienced in the past to his homosexuality (he told our young interviewer, "You can't tell from your age what it was like at that time when no one in the country, not anyone, . . . would admit they're homosexual"). Also, he is a man with significant fears—of physical violence on the part of someone else ("I'm a coward"), and of heights and closed spaces.

About all this, he disdains self-pity, and speaks of these troubling tendencies as "a very interesting pattern." He seeks hope from adversity in pointing out the frequent relationship between suffering and creativity (referring concretely to such groups as American blacks and artists of various kinds). One way he copes with the danger of individual collapse is to take a stand against the collapse of the world, as suggested by his reactions to a dream he had while still in high school. The dream evoked an end-of-the-world scene in which "buildings were being disintegrated because the molecular level was dropping"—"a very powerful dream, very haunting, things coming apart." Rather than put the dream aside, he reflected its message, by stressing the dangers of nuclear war, in a graduation speech he had been scheduled to make. The dream stayed with him, and over the years he has come to see it as "an example of . . . the bomb entering the unconscious . . . of the people at that time." Confronting this vast collective threat in sustained and serious ways has contributed greatly to his own psychological survival. His personal vulnerability remains an important part of his ingenious combinations.

## PROTEUS IN PRAGUE

I went to Prague in September 1990, ten months after the overthrow of the Czechoslovakian Communist government, to explore the experiences of people involved in that odd and moving sequence of historical events.

Jana P., an elegant woman writer in her fifties who had become a special assistant to the president of the new democracy, gave vivid testimony to the kinds of transformation and expansion of the self that took place. She told me how, as a successful journalist, she had been devastated by the official decision to shut down the magazine to which she had regularly contributed articles on various social issues. Then she discovered that, in addition, she had been blacklisted by the government so that nothing she wrote could legally appear anywhere: "It looked like the end of life. . . . I didn't exist anymore." While living with her infant daughter in a small village, she began to work with chronic psychiatric patients, mostly schizophrenics, in a facility where they had been hospitalized for decades. She found many of the patients to be "sources of pure poetry" and "much more free than the people . . . outside": "They could say whatever they wanted"; moreover, many had entered the hospital prior to Communist rule and had never really been exposed to its influence. Jana P. began to write sketches about these patients and to reflect on what was normal or abnormal: "In this mental hospital, I realized that these people are more reasonable than those people outside who are having [a] completely mad life . . . because it was all based on lying." She found, "These people helped me much more than I helped them."

Then, for the first time in her professional life, she turned to writing fiction. She found this extremely difficult because its imaginative process seemed to have "nothing to do with journalism"; and, as one who was professionally "accustomed to write with facts, . . . I was afraid to abandon this island." But she did just that, and "it saved my life." Through contacts with other dissidents, she was able to find outlets in underground publications circulated throughout the country and sometimes in books or periodicals published abroad.

Now she did not require "the world of these mad people," because she had discovered "the world of my [own] complete fantasy." She evolved ways to express that fantasy fully ("everything which [came] to my mind") and crossed boundaries between "what is dream and what is reality." As she began to write obsessively in this way, she felt herself "like being mad" and was thereby continuing her reversals concerning normality. For in this way she was separating herself from a regime at a "particularly horrible time"; and, like her dissident colleagues, she came to believe, "If you just express yourself [genuinely]," you engage in a political act of resistance and "you become . . . free." Her self-expansion was enhanced by yoga training she undertook with a guru who had spent years in India, which included meditation and breathing exercises and "went together with this . . . opening [of the] mind." Yet in her writing and in ideas and images she came to share with other dissidents, she saw an important connection with earlier traditions of Central Europe, notably the literature of Franz Kafka and Robert Musil.

She faced profound new difficulties when, with the success of the revolution, she was asked to become a special adviser to Václav Havel, the president of the new republic. Addressing immediate human problems meant "tension all the time" from widespread pain over "inherited . . . old structures" from the Communist regime which "don't work," and from people who, having been made dependent on a ruling regime, now demanded instant results. She found, moreover, that she was working virtually every minute ("sometimes . . . fifty-four hours a day!") and "always giving energy" that "just disappears" into anonymity, very unlike the situation of a writer producing an article or a book. Yet Jana P. greatly valued her new work. She found in it "something interesting because it's experience," because "in fact, life [itself] is so dramatic," and because "it's much better to be [in government] than to sit home and to write about some love affair."

She developed a new ability (which those who knew her found "astonishing") to make endless "fast decisions" every day, basing these on her improving "intuition" that helped her avoid making "serious mistakes" (knocking on wood as she said that). At the same time, as she told me then, she looked forward to completing her government service and "becoming a writer again"—which was just about to happen when I talked to her again during a second visit to Prague nineteen months later, when the country was breaking up and Havel was about to resign. She spoke with sadness about these developments and about Havel's personal ordeal, but then took me to the window of her office overlooking the city and said that, whenever she felt troubled, she looked out at that beautiful vista. She then spoke of all that she and her colleagues had accomplished in bringing about a nonviolent transition to democracy, and recognized that the historical moment of her group of dissidents seemed to be ending. She was also expressing, though indirectly, her recognition of the transformations, expansions, and strikingly innovative combinations of self she and others at the time had so effectively achieved.

Tomas M., a long-haired, irreverent journalist I also interviewed in 1990, had gained enormous respect among dissidents for his extraordinary achievements in editing one of the most important underground journals. Playful and self-mocking, he told me that, as a psychiatrist, I was the right person to speak to him because he had "acted crazy" to avoid military service and been confined for a period of time to a psychiatric hospital. Always rebellious and eccentric, he had written rock lyrics when younger, and was aware that "there is something in me that must do something different." He had been strongly influenced by the rock group Plastic People of the Universe, which played a prominent role in the revolution; he remembers being "really happy" during those years of opposition ("It was romantic—there was some danger"), while at the same time he had "the feeling I'm doing the right thing." A man always given to spontaneity and unbridled self-expression, he found himself, in joining the opposition, preoccupied with the seemingly antithetical principle of controlled dependability: "The first important thing . . . is that you have your own responsibility. If you will do this, it will exist. If you will not do this, nobody will do it." In taking over the dissident journal, he showed not only considerable courage but a steadfastness that impressed and somewhat surprised those who knew him. Now he continues to express his sense of responsibility by raising questions about the new regime and the behavior of its officials, even though some of them are his friends. He has also been writing articles about the racism manifested toward Vietnamese who had been working in Czechoslovakia.

As with many people I interviewed in Prague, Tomas M. could realize aspects of self that had before been only potential, and, in the process, carve out new combinations of content and capacity. Under certain kinds of duress, that is, the self can expand and thrive. I spoke to a professor of philosophy who, as a non-Marxist, was banned from university work and obtained jobs as a night watchman or a coal stoker. He did not greatly mind these jobs because they gave him considerable time during the day for philosophical work free of the ideological compromises forced upon people still working in universities. A journalism student I interviewed, widely admired for having started an opposition paper at his university, told me he did so "because that's what I knew how to do." Finally, Ivan

Klima, a novelist who, during the Communist regime, managed to publish several books abroad, wrote: "We live because there are a number of encounters ahead of us for the sake of which living is worthwhile."

# Literature and the Arts:
## "These . . . Many Dimensions"

Over the twentieth century, literature and the arts have lived on virtually nothing but odd combinations. Words and images pertain less to clarity and truth than to the complexity of component parts and, above all, to the search. Recently these patterns have become particularly striking—whether in literature, painting and sculpture, the performing arts, or architecture—as can be seen from even briefly stated examples from these areas.

### "ENTHRALLMENTS AND FUTILITIES": LITERARY COMBINATIONS

American novelists participate actively in the exploration of multiplicity and uncertainty that has been characteristic of modern literature. In this literature, the idea of "a stable, impervious, monolithic human identity" has given way to expressions of "volatility, versatility, variety, variance, vagary, vertigo," all following a pattern of "duality" and "dynamic inconsistency." But writers of fiction must imagine *some* combination within the self if they are to tell their story. In Saul Bellow's "post-quixotic, post-Copernican U.S.A. where a mind freely poised in space might discover relationships utterly unsuspected by a seventeenth-century man sealed in his smaller universe," his protagonist, Herzog, is so burdened by this diversity that he must "disencumber . . . himself of a succession of false ideas of self"—or, more likely, of a succession of false selves. A writer/protagonist of Don DeLillo's catches "the back-and-forthness. The way things fit almost anywhere and nothing gets completely forgotten." In speaking of "the spray of talent, the spray of ideas. One thing unlike another, one voice unlike the next. Ambiguities, contradictions, whispers, hints," DeLillo is referring to the odd juxtapositions of the novelist's own self as well as those of his characters. For "[w]hen there is enough out-of-placeness in the world, nothing is out of place."

Bharati Mukherjee, the Indian-born American writer, tells how these combinations are enhanced by emigration. Here one was "out of God's sight," and earlier destinies were "cancelled" in favor of "new fates": "We could say or be anything we wanted." These American transformations—of both landscape and person—are blinding in their speed and yet profoundly compelling: "I feel at times like a stone hurtling through diaphanous mist, unable to grab hold, unable to slow myself, yet unwilling to abandon the ride I'm on." There are parallels in the work of Vladimir Nabokov, a very different kind of writer from a very different (Russian) culture, but also an émigré. *Lolita,* his novel celebrating the "nymphet" as love object, is an evocation of "the American highway, the American motel, motor court, tourist home . . . all this floating, farcical easiness of America"; and the nymphet herself becomes "another discreet phenomenon of life on the endlessly shifting scale of being."

The principle of the combining self at risk has been starkly exemplified by Günter Grass, the German novelist and visual artist, both in his life and in his work. *The Tin Drum,* his magnum opus (which I will discuss in chapter 5, in relation to the literature of survival), is as much a dazzling foray into mid- and late-twentieth-century proteanism as it is an evocation of the experience of Nazi evil. In his pursuit of "a career in which novels and politics are twinned," Grass has been a fierce moral presence in his society and elsewhere: "Martin Luther with a sense of humor." The American critic John Leonard further sums up the components of the Grass self as "a good liberal, a practical radical, a ferocious democrat, a self-made orphan, a citizen without portfolio and a prophet without honor; a Bad Boy and a skeptic; a holy fool instead of a court jester; incapable of simplifying [himself] in the gridwork of profit-taking and self-congratulation; ashamed of [his] very own white male perks"—and concludes that all this is "very hard cheese. And certainly not advisable if you want a Nobel Prize."

Robert Frost once described a similar principle of risk for poetry in terms of the "ideals of form," within which "all our ingenuity is lavished on getting into danger legitimately so that we may be genuinely rescued." But poets no longer have access to a clear direction of "rescue." With the breakdown of fixed poetic criteria, they experiment with forms previously considered nonpoetic—including those of conversation, confession, dream, and just about every other kind of discourse. Poetic multiplicity and flow can also be associated with place, as in Amy Clampitt's evocation of New York City: "from Manhattan, a glittering shambles/of enthrallments and futilities." Significantly, smaller places can serve similar purposes, as Anne Carson makes clear in her poem sequence with prose, "The Life of Towns." Carson tells us, "Towns are the illusion that things hang together somehow," and goes on to play with the idea first in prose ("Matter which has painted itself within lines constitutes a town. Viewed in this way the world is, as we say, an open book"), and then in a series of short poems that, within an ironic frame, manage to evoke a stunning variety of narrative moods and cultural landscapes, as some of the titles suggest: "Apostle Town," "Desert Town," "Town of the Death of Sin," "Love Town," "Town on the Way through God's Woods," "Death

Town," "Luck Town," "Memory Town," "September Town," "Wolf Town," "Town Going to Sleep," "Town of the Wrong Questions," "Freud Town," "Bride Town," and "Judas Town."

## "A WILLFUL ECLECTICISM": ARTISTIC FORAYS

Paul Klee, in a 1924 talk entitled "On Modern Art," spoke of "a conception of a whole which is constructed from parts belonging to different dimensions." As we sensitize ourselves to this art, he went on, we can "with any given picture . . . experience easily and quickly the phenomenon of simultaneous contact with these many dimensions." That principle of multiplicity has since been radicalized, so that during recent decades, art has created "meanings [that] are explosive, ricocheting and fragmenting throughout its audience." A work of art "becomes a situation, full of suggestive potentialities, rather than a self-contained whole, determined and final."

By the early 1960s, the art critic Harold Rosenberg was speaking of the "replacement of tradition by historical consciousness" that opens art to immediate experience while releasing it from the "one-way push" of the past; but at the same time, artists and their audiences undergo a lasting uneasiness having to do with this new-found freedom and its "anguish of possibility." Rosenberg also announced that the radical innovation of the powerful post–Second World War abstract expressionist movement was "to dispense with the *representation* of the [artist's psychic] state in favor of *enacting* it in a physical movement," and therefore introduced the term "action painting." Robert Motherwell, who died in 1991 and was a survivor of the school, spoke of its search for a certain attitude toward reality and concluded, "The process of painting *is* the search."

Yet, rather quickly, there were movements away from and against abstract expressionism in a dazzling—some would say, blinding—sequence, to kinetic art, to Pop art, to every variety of collage and assemblage, to conceptual art, to destructive art, to large wrappings of coastlines with cloth or canvas, to periodic disappearances and reappearances of the human figure, to various forms of minimalism; to the recent developments in painting mentioned in chapter 3 (neo-expressionism, neo-geo, graffiti, abstract illusionism, photorealism, "bad" painting, and pattern and decoration); and to the "great plethora of possibilities" beyond painting itself, including "video, performance, body art, . . . hyper-realism in sculpture, story art, monumental abstract sculpture (earthworks)," all characterized by "a willful eclecticism." In these expressions, art can make contact with every dimension of American popular culture, including graffiti, the most vernacular of all forms and also perhaps the most fluid and multiple. Meaning something like "small scratches," graffiti could be made up of virtually anything—letters of names, abstract designs, political slogans, representations of urban life—to the point of becoming "a cross between Grandma Moses—the authenticity of the 'folk' tradition—and street-smart, Third World exoticism."

But the protean breakthrough in twentieth-century art had begun long before in such movements as cubism and the related phenomenon of collage. Cubism originated in Paris in 1907 and was later described by Naum Gabo, the Russian sculptor and theorist, as "a revolution . . . in which . . . the formal unity of the external world . . . was suddenly laid down on . . . canvases, torn in pieces and dissected as if it were a mere anatomical specimen," reflecting "the inner world of [the artist's] perceptions with all its component parts." In the historical "moment of Cubism" between 1907 and 1914, Picasso and Braque conducted an extraordinary artistic dialogue that contributed much to the overthrow of prior artistic conventions. New knowledge, technologies, and modes of feeling changed the meaning of both time and space and led both to "a liberation from the immediate" and to an expanded sense of self in which, as the "Cubist poet" André Salmon put it, "Everything is realizable everywhere with everything." Cubism provided a new model of the human relationship with nature that permitted "multiplicity of viewpoints" and expressions of what was continuous within the "discontinuity of space." The focus was now on elaborate interactions and on a "configuration of events," consistent with the emphasis of twentieth-century science on the interplay of multiple forces and shifting viewpoints. Significantly, cubism, unlike subsequent movements influenced by it (Dadaism, surrealism, and abstract expressionism), preceded twentieth-century horrors, beginning "not in despair, but in affirmation."

The principle of collage was an extension of the cubist impulse to combine disparate elements, reveal component parts, and open closed surfaces. In 1912, Pablo Picasso inserted a piece of oilcloth into his cubist still-life painting; then he and Braque experimented with pasting in various paper objects in other works, Picasso in particular introducing visiting cards, labels, matchbox covers, cigarette or tobacco packages, cloth, and printed matter. But only in the hands of Max Ernst, the Dada and surrealist artist, was the collage itself—the "assembling . . . [of] pictorial components into unforeseen and unexpected combinations"—to become the work of art. Hence, Ernst's famous declaration: "It is not the paste that makes the collage."* From 1919 on, Ernst produced a brilliant

---

*Ernst recalls, as the source of his work on collage, a vision he had in 1919, after perusing an illustrated catalogue whose advertisements included objects so varied and unrelated that "its sheer absurdity provoked in me a sudden intensification of my faculties of vision—a hallucinatory succession of contradictory images, double, triple, multiple, piling up with the persistence and rapidity characteristic of erotic memories and visions of half-sleep." Such images, he felt, "demanded to be united on new planes, in a new unknown [the plane of contradiction and disagreement]."

sequence of collages characterized by "mutually irreconcilable realities . . . wedded to each other"—also an apt chacterization of the self's broader embrace of odd combinations. Subsequent developments in collage and related assemblages ultimately broke down all barriers between high art and low culture, so that artworks could include combinations of "beat Zen and hot rods, mescalin experiences and faded flowers, photographic bumps and grinds, . . . jukeboxes, and hydrogen explosions."

Contemporary performance art is a further movement away from the art object and toward art as experience and presentation. One version can be found in photographs by William Wegman (also a conceptual artist) of his Weimaraner dog named Man Ray (after the leading American Dada painter and photographer); the absurd and affecting poses result in a "transformation of . . . dog into artist," and in a theater of the self with ongoing transformation. Judy Chicago, very differently, suggests a feminist sequence from being a minimalist artist named Judy Gerowitz (her new name chosen to divest herself of all that had been imposed upon her through male social dominance), to feminist artist (in one visual series, "Pasadena Lifesavers," she used the circular format to express her "central core," her vagina), to creator and teacher of feminist performance art programs. One of her students, Faith Wilding, developed a performance litany of all that a woman waits for in our culture (wearing a bra, being asked to dance, the perfect man, an orgasm, and so forth), such performances, as Chicago explained, providing men with opportunities to "feel themselves 'other' and thereby force them to identify with us on a psychic level." And Laurie Anderson, a celebrated multimedia performance artist, cultivates "chance collisions with whatever occurs at [the] margins." She says, "I'm interested in fact, images, and theories which resonate against each other, not in offering solutions"—but in the process, "she submits her own identity to perpetual nomadism."

## COMBINING THE COMBINATIONS

Finally, there are particularly striking articulations of cultural layering—combinations of combinations. One such example is that of contemporary architecture, where much of the cultural dialogue on postmodernism has taken place. Here the stress is on a pluralism that includes in a single building an eclectic array of influences from varied historical periods without being committed to a single historical style—the most consistent element perhaps the self-conscious irony and playfulness with which the enterprise is carried out. Critics of this theoretical approach have pointed to exaggerations in the claimed break with modernism (and neglect of the considerable variation of that tradition) and to superficiality in the buildings themselves. "We look at architecture now almost the way we look at television—demanding new images, new pictures, new scenes, all the time . . . [so that] image *is* reality in our culture, a reality that comes faster and faster, in ever more facile form." But advocates of the approach stress its openness to the past as well as to the "locus of meanings" we struggle with in the present. At its best, this approach renders divergent architectural concepts in ways that mirror the contemporary self and blend multiplicity with genuine renewal.*

Among writers notable for such cultural layering I would include Don DeLillo, James Joyce, and Salman Rushdie. DeLillo names his novel *Mao II* after a pencil drawing of the Chinese leader by Andy Warhol, the American pop artist who conducted a "vast and uninterrupted dialogue" with mass culture. On the one hand, DeLillo recognizes that the artist (through his series of Mao drawings as well as Mao wallpaper over which silk screens were hung) has converted a revolutionary hero into a Warhol "superstar," and notes "how it is possible to fuse images . . . and to steal auras." On the other hand, DeLillo also invokes Mao as an inspiration for terrorists and (like Sun Myung Moon) an activator of a fierce contemporary end-time surge. Such forces are able to break through the endless "messages and meanings" of contemporary culture and be heard, while novelists, in contrast, are increasingly unable to do so. DeLillo believes that Warhol, in his tame rendering of Mao, has grasped that point and at the same time depicted our culture's omniverous capacity for exploitation. DeLillo thus orchestrates a merging of novelistic and visual insights to suggest the elaborate cultural layerings of the contemporary American self.

James Joyce achieved his poetic rendering of metamorphosis by probing in "criss-cross" fashion all aspects of the modern cultural universe. *Ulysses* has been seen (by both Umberto Eco and Carl Jung) as a "cubist" enterprise in which Joyce decomposed the mind into various component parts and exposed himself to "the terror of Chaos" in order to emerge with a "music of ideas." He so immersed himself in cultural layerings that the story of a single day became "the history of the world and of civilization." Above all, Joyce charted an endless cultural chain of encounters, oppositions, contradictions, and visions to constitute "the world with which contemporary man must deal." He provided a treatise on metaphysics as well as a handbook of anthropology and psychology in the service of imagining new and believable forms. He was a prophetic voice depicting our twentieth-century cubist-protean fate.

---

*Charles Jencks points to Kisho Kurokawa's Museum of Modern Art in Hiroshima as an example of architectural multiplicity in its "ambiguity between several languages." These include the glistening metallic surfaces of the modern or neo-modern; roofs proportioned like traditional sixteenth-century Edo storehouses; "controlled ambiguity" in references to the atomic bomb; and a circular form that suggests, in addition, community and religiosity, so that the entire building becomes "coherently multivalent."

If *Ulysses* reflected the fragmentation and imaginative breakthrough of the early twentieth century, Salman Rushdie's *Satanic Verses* carries us one step further toward the twenty-first—this work considerably less formal than its great predecessor, its protagonists more antiheroic, and its self-combinations still more radical. When, at the beginning of *Satanic Verses,* an airplane blows up, Rushdie refers to the physical remnants of the plane and then tells us that "equally fragmented, equally absurd, there floated the debris of the soul, broken memories, sloughed-off selves, severed mother-tongues, violated privacies, untranslatable jokes, extinguished futures, lost loves, the forgotten meaning of hollow, booming words, *land, belonging, home.*"

But those very fragments, those "sloughed-off selves," can give rise to something new:

> *How does newness come into the world? How is it born?*
> *Of what fusions, translations, conjoinings is it made?*
> *How does it survive, extreme and dangerous as it is?*

Rushdie flies the protean banner in declaring that *Satanic Verses* "celebrates hybridity, impurity, intermingling, the transformation that comes of new and unexpected combinations of human beings, cultures, ideas, politics, movies, songs. It rejoices in the mongrelisation and fears the absolutism of the Pure." Pointing out that the word *translation* comes from the Latin for "bearing across," he describes people like himself as "translated men." But in rejecting the usual supposition "that something always gets lost in translation," he "cling[s], obstinately, to the notion that something can also be gained." What is gained by this "postmodern prophet of the confluence of cultures" is the imaginative power—and the importance for all of us—of the new combinations achieved.

Chapter 5

# SOURCES OF FLUX
# AND FORM

*What I am is an editor of my own past. I collect versions of my pre-history, arrange them, rearrange them, and then tell them to you.*
*—Janette Turner Hospital*

GREATLY CONTRIBUTING to the odd combinations and transformations of the protean self are certain vicissitudes having to do with loss or absence, as well as with perceived threat. The first category includes feelings of fatherlessness, homelessness, and the absence of clear mentorship—feelings that can be painful but are at the same time necessary to the protean self. That sense of being personally adrift renders one, in turn, vulnerable to perceptions of threat to personal and collective existence, which cause the protean self to take on much of the psychology of the survivor. These vicissitudes can lead to confusion, and certainly to restlessness and flux. Yet they also provide strong motivation, and a certain content, for the self's quest for form. That quest can never quite be completed, but it can result in the achievement of what I call integrative expressions of proteanism.

## Varieties of Fatherlessness

*Let the dead bury the dead.*

*—James Joyce*

Early in my explorations of proteanism, I was struck by Jean-Paul Sartre's comments on his father's death before he was born. Rather than bemoan the loss, Sartre celebrated it in his mock-grandiose style, with an attack on the father–son relationship in general: "There is no good father, that's the rule. Don't lay the blame on men but on the bond of paternity, which is rotten." He was, as he further explained, liberated in advance: "Had my father lived, he would have lain on me full length, and would have crushed me." Rather than carry the burden of an Aeneas, the mythical Trojan hero who wandered along the Mediterranean carrying his father on his shoulders, Sartre was free to "move from shore to shore, alone, and hating those invisible begetters who bestraddle their sons all their life long." More than that, he could imaginatively reverse roles: "I left behind me a young man who did not have time to be my father and who could now be my son." And still in the spirit of liberation, Sartre completed the brief passage with a playfully ambiguous self-judgment: "Was it a good thing or bad? I don't know. But I readily subscribed to the verdict of an eminent psychoanalyst: I have no superego."

His father's absence, Sartre is telling us, left him free of the heavy authority of the past, free to create himself. In most cultures, the father is identified with social and moral authority, while the mother (very much present for Sartre) represents more intimate and organic personal connection. In celebrating release from not only paternal authority but the more general burden of social origin, Sartre resembles Joyce's young Stephen Dedalus: "Soul free and fancy free. Let the dead bury the dead. Ay. And let the dead marry the dead." And in arrogating to himself the fatherhood of his father, Sartre subsumes paternal authority within his own evolving self and lays claim to a reversal in mentorship frequently associated with proteanism. Similarly, the young Stephen Dedalus says of himself as he observes his father and two cronies drinking and reminiscing: "His mind seemed older than theirs: it shone coldly on their strifes and happiness and regrets like a moon upon a younger earth."

When Sartre describes himself as free to "move from shore to shore," he is speaking of a creative form of homelessness. Home suggests a particular place, residence, physical structure, stable source. These are far from certain for anyone in our time. The protean impulse is both to cast them aside and to seek them (or reconstituted versions of them) out. The British actor Daniel Day-Lewis illustrates and articulates the protean embrace of homelessness. Priding himself on having no fixed address, he has become, between acting assignments, an accomplished, anonymous wanderer:

> I didn't really have a home. I'd lost my belief in what home represented. Through a passage of time, I'd seen the astonishingly rapid disintegration of two households where I grew up—my parents' house and my grandparents' house both went. The houses, which had been apparently indestructible became nothing. I came to think of the concept of home as an elaborately constructed false front.

More generally and absolutely, if a bit tongue-in-cheek, a Don DeLillo character tells us: "Home is a failed idea."

Particular family arrangements can contribute to feelings of homelessness and fatherlessness which further one's protean tendencies. Michael W.'s "deprived" family background (pages 51–52) permitted him "very little contact" with his father either before or after his parents' divorce, and during his childhood he felt himself to be "a nobody from nowhere"; but he later came to recognize a certain "ability to kind of react to [circumstances], . . . grasp them, and function in them." His fatherlessness contributed to his relatively unencumbered and highly effective movement through environments and experiences as divergent as they were demanding. To have been able to take advantage of the fragility of his sense of home and family, he undoubtedly required the love and support he received from his mother. He went into the world as a young man able to respond to a series of temporary mentorships and, in his maturity, to remain flexible—both receptive and principled—when himself in positions of authority.

A parallel pattern in a longstanding social activist, Andy H., interviewed in his seventies, goes back to his precarious upper–New York State family origins. Both parents were alcoholic and always seemed inadequate, his father emotionally distant and his mother imposing on the family a narrow, guilt-dominated form of Catholicism. A wealthy, paternal grandmother "owned everything" and dominated everyone, but held things together and evoked Andy's love until "everything fell apart" with her death. Eventually both parents were to kill themselves, as had Andy's maternal grandfather. In his subsequent struggle, as an adult, to cope with his pain and confusion, Andy was helped by the realization that "I was raised by drunken children." Though they were "busy wrecking their lives," he could come to forgive them because "I forgive children everything." While he was aware of damage done to him, he felt in some ways well served by their negligence: "I was raised in some half-assed way . . . [or else] the damage would have been deeper than it is." Emotional scars and all, Andy has been able to go far in liberating himself from family constraints: he functions reasonably well in New York City's artistic and political subcultures, engages in social and sexual experimentation, and has become widely recognized for his antiwar activism.

There can be the seemingly opposite situation where family origins loom large, and overcoming them, at least in part, becomes necessary to the protean process, as was the case with Rosalyn K. (pages 55–58). She described her parents as "really a great couple" with whom she always "loved hanging out" and "doing everything": "Their friends were my friends." Her mother in particular, an educator and widely respected civil-rights activist, set the standard for Rosalyn: "In the sixth grade she made me do a report on Engels." Rosalyn could say of her family, which

included a younger brother, "We always had a big social conscience, and
. . . I agreed with them." But during her early twenties, Rosalyn felt the
need to separate herself from family influences, and did so partly by
diverging from them culturally. Her reading Camus and Sartre was all
right, but her parents strongly objected to her passion for Andy Warhol's
"nihilistic monotone." She came to realize that "as you get older, you
don't follow your mother around doing everything." There were bitter
arguments, and she was later to view her own behavior in them as having
been "terrible" and "disgusting." Coming to realize that "my mom and I
are very similar," she determined that what she did "would be my own
thing and not hers"; she would even, with some embarrassment, "check .
. . back into the family tradition" to make sure that was the case. Where
in the past she thought that, if her mother had been unable to do something, "I . . . didn't dare to venture into those realms at all," now "I'm
able to see that I can do things that she can't." Her present family balance enables Rosalyn K. to "work on many levels at once," to feel able to
"do anything" and "go anywhere." Part of that balance is her involvement
in painting and her continuing dialogue on art with her father (who is an
artist); and her involvement with baseball which includes frequent, amus-
ing telephone conversations with her father and brother (both of whom
are also fans).

One can—like George R., the successful management consultant
(pages 58–60)—engage in elaborate combinations of identification with
one's origins and movement away from them. He recalls his father as
"tough as nails and loving," and the work they did together on building a
summer house was as primal in cementing the father–son bond as it was
exhausting. But during adolescence, George underwent an intense rebellion, undermining the values he had been taught, and aimed mainly at his
father. It included slothful behavior ("I was a lazy bum at age thirteen")
and provocative dress and manner—a ducktail haircut, contempt for work
and study, and general disobedience. While the rebellion was only temporary, it was important to George's developing sense of self and to his decisions about his future. That included his ability to mobilize his mother's
sympathy to "help mollify my father's vision of what I ought to do" as
George gave up baseball for accounting and money management. But he
sees himself as having incorporated much of his father's commitment to
hard work and some of his ingenuity in approaching difficult problems.
In that second-generation immigrant pattern, one draws upon family
identifications while extricating oneself from the family's narrow world to
seek wider ground not available to one's parents. But George R.'s continuing restlessness about his work and his life can be said to express a sense
both of continuing possibility and of loss.

When families are experienced as profoundly nurturing and supportive, the movement away from origins can be particularly difficult but no

less necessary. Nick L., a social activist in his late thirties, grew up in a large Italian family brimming with love and opinions. Through much of his childhood he lived in a large house with thirteen other people, and a medical problem that kept him at home over much of his childhood intensified his involvement with three women—his mother, aunt, and grandmother. He felt that the varied but essentially open-minded viewpoints in the family were "a good modeling situation for me" as a future activist, and a few family members even accompanied him on his first demonstration protesting racial violence. He lived at home, at least periodically, well into his thirties. But during his adolescence and early adulthood, his increasing political intensity led to strong disagreements with family members, especially bitter in the case of his father, having to do with both "external trappings" (dress and social attitudes) and radical advocacies (particularly civil disobedience). When Nick would organize or participate in a demonstration resulting in his arrest, family members would help pay his bail and then argue vociferously against his actions. He sought their understanding and approval, but went ahead even when he knew "they were gonna be unhappy about [it]," and that "there might be . . . subsequent anger"; and then, "generally speaking, the argument . . . ended." He continued to view his family background as a vital source of his social conscience, seeking to convert the dogmatic Catholicism to which he was exposed into a nondogmatic "sense of the sacred" animating much of his social activism. The importance to him of holding onto his family while at the same time defying it, and to the idea of home in general, was revealed in his haunting memory of someone at a demonstration shouting to him and fellow marchers, "You're the wanderers of the earth and you'll never have a home!"

A more characteristic protean pattern perhaps is that of rejecting much of one's origins even as one draws significantly upon them. Carol C., who turned away from the Crucifixion imagery of Lutheranism (see pages 52–55), also rebelled against her father, a factory worker who had been instrumental in establishing the consistent family message Carol characterized as "Don't question authority!" Yet, as she came to recognize, her father did question authority in his own way, had been excommunicated from their church because he was a Mason, and had received a number of death threats because of his resistance to unions. Carol later drew upon her father's idiosyncratic capacity for opposition, though reversing its content, as she became first a Marxist and then a social activist, an ardent feminist, and an artist. She also drew upon his Greek Orthodox background in associating powerful memories of the religious rituals accompanying her maternal grandmother's death (Greek chants, solemn music, black dress, musty and exotic smells) with her own subsequent spirituality.

But the rejection of background elements can also be a powerful spur to protean movement away from them, as happened with Edward G. and his father and grandfather's conservative military connections. He refers to his "anger at my father" as "undoubtedly . . . one of the things that shaped my ship into the pacifist position" and fueled his opposition to American military policies. Years later, however, he burst into tears while watching a performance of Arthur Miller's play *Death of a Salesman* (which depicts the cruel behavior of the protagonist's sons toward him) and berated himself for having been so "harsh" with his own father. Looking back philosophically at his struggles with his origins and his subsequent unexpected directions, he concluded, "People don't really know why they've arrived where they've arrived." He said further, "The past is at least as flexible as the future," thereby recognizing the presentness of memory and the reordering of earlier experience.

Finally, one's family background can encompass both a form of fatherlessness and an invitation to proteanism. Ken F., a thirty-three-year-old self-described "free-lance peace activist," came from a family with diverse political views—his grandparents "very conservative," his uncle and cousins "quite liberal," his parents "more or less liberal but not so vocal about it"—leading to "a lot of political discussions and arguments." He would "fight a lot" with his father, who was distant, frequently away from home, "a bit of a disciplinarian," and who died when Ken was nineteen. Ken then turned to his liberal uncle who headed a small peace group in their town. The uncle initiated the shy youngster into his first peace activities and helped him to gain the knowledge and confidence that contributed to his subsequent pattern of effective experiment and action.

Clearly, such family arrangements are themselves products of historical dislocation and of American "generationalism," the expectation that each generation will move beyond and away from the previous one. A sense of homelessness and fatherlessness can serve to release the self for further explorations, even when father and home are very much present. For no father, no set of parents, no arrangements of family and home, can maintain static authority in the face of the power of both our era's psychological dislocations and the mass media.

No society has exceeded ours in ambivalence about personal roots. On the one hand, the writer Jamaica Kincaid's West Indian immigrant protagonist, Lucy, declares her liberation from the perceived tyranny of roots (all the more so when that tyranny is backed by love) as a prerequisite for unencumbered experience:

> The object of my life now was to put as much distance between myself and the events mentioned in her [mother's] letter as I could manage. For I felt that if I could put enough miles between me and the place from which that letter came, and if I could put enough events between me and the events

mentioned in the letter, would I not be free to take everything just as it came and not see hundreds of years in every gesture, every word spoken, every face?

In similar spirit, Harold Rosenberg has characterized the abstract expressionist school of painting as cultivating a self that sought "to nullify its promissory notes to the past"; earlier Paul Klee declared, "I want to be as though newborn, knowing nothing, absolutely nothing about Europe"; and even earlier, Karl Marx wrote, "The tradition of all the dead generations weighs like a nightmare on the brain of the living." The contemporary artist Budd Hopkins describes the wonder of feeling free from that burden and viewing one of his own sculptures as "a strange 'thing,' an object of unknown origin, function and history."

Equally American, on the other hand, is the insistence of Saul Bellow's Herzog on being a fierce guardian of the past: "[W]ith *my* memory—all the dead and the mad are in my custody, and I am the nemesis of the would-be forgotten." And William Faulkner, creatively obsessed by the past, once said that his ambition was "to put everything into one sentence—not only the present but the whole past on which it depends and which keeps overtaking the present." But whether one dismisses family and past (as Kincaid does) or takes both constantly into account (as Bellow does, and Faulkner even more), one does so in order to transcend them.

The reversals in mentorship associated with homelessness and fatherlessness can run a gamut from the questioning of "experts" to the bitter rejection of virtually any authority in favor of one's own immediate views. In America in particular, increasingly intense questioning of existing scientific, medical, cultural, and political authority has culminated in widespread lawsuits against physicians and even more widespread rejection of political leaders. Given the flow of historical and cultural forms, it is difficult for anyone to sustain authority over others for any length of time—difficult for the rest of us to view such a person or group as possessing a *sustained* form of truth and reliability. The problem of choosing and holding on to models and heroes was expressed by Rosalyn K.: "At times I've had them, and I guess I have them now, too. But . . . in terms of having a model, . . . I actually try to avoid that. I just like to think of things more in motion toward . . . an ideal, . . . not in line with having things figured out." She did express her admiration for people who manage to "approach situations with an open mind, . . . don't have a pat answer, and somehow go through this world with a sense of optimism and hope . . . [while] they take care of their family and are still involved with their community . . . [and] with international politics." But about heroes, "I'd have to think about that."

# Surviving

*We are survivors in this age, so theories of progress ill become us, because we are intimately acquainted with the costs.*
                                                                —Saul Bellow

Death and renewal—the self as survivor—is, for proteanism, both metaphor and psychological principle. A survivor is one who has encountered death, literally or figuratively—one who has witnessed and been touched by it—while remaining alive. Over the twentieth century, human beings have survived extremities of not only mass killing and dying but also spiritual assault and dislocation. Either way, survivors are haunted by death, not only its actuality but by the immediate death equivalents I have mentioned: feelings of separation (from nurturing communities, individuals, and principles), of disintegration (of falling apart or fearing that one will), and of stasis (of being stymied, static, immobilized). At the ultimate level, one may feel divested of larger connectedness, of the various modes of symbolic immortality. Pervasive in all these feelings is a sense of loss.

The ethos of the survivor can also contribute to reconstituting the self in the face of that loss. But the road is not easy. To realize that survivor state, Bellow tells us, is a "shock": "You feel like bursting into tears [because as] the dead go their way, you want to call to them, but they depart in a black cloud of faces, souls." Bellow's hope lies in the possibility of illumination: whether the "smoke from the extermination chimneys," "revolutions," "engineered famines directed by 'ideologists' [has] instructed [us] in our brutal stupidity"; and "Perhaps we, modern humankind (can it be!), have done the nearly impossible, namely, learned something." At best, of course, just *something*, not everything. But whatever our reactions, Bellow is saying, we all bear some relationship, psychologically and morally, to the holocausts of our era.

Through my work in Hiroshima—and subsequently on disaster, the Vietnam War, and Nazi genocide—I came to recognize a number of patterns that characterize the experience of the survivor. These patterns, intensely evident in people who have been through such disasters, filter down to the rest of us as well—because the media bring us into these disasters (or reconstruct earlier ones for us), and because our personal lives include survivorlike feelings associated with separation and threat. While each of these patterns can be deeply problematic, each also contains the possibility of "learning something." First, a lasting *death imprint* can be associated with anxiety, and also experienced as a form of "knowledge" of death that informs a commitment to life enhancement. Another pattern is the *death guilt* that one feels from having survived where others have died, and that involves a sense of "failed enactment," or inability to behave ideally in either rescuing others or combatting a destructive force. Under certain conditions, death guilt can become animating and transformed into various expressions of responsibility and moral concern. There is also *psychic numbing,* or diminished capacity to feel, a useful defense mechanism for dealing with immediate threat but subsequently a problem in living. For some people, the numbing can be at least partly adaptive, sufficiently limited to enable one to conduct most of one's life with adequate energy and feeling. Still another pattern is *suspicion of counterfeit nurturance,* a general impairment in human relationships that includes distrust of help offered by others because it is perceived as a reminder of weakness; this pattern has a positive potential for sharpening one's sensitivity to what is inauthentic and hypocritical. Finally, there is the *struggle for meaning,* for a sense of inner form that can give significance to one's survivor experience and to the remainder of one's life. One may seek meaning in a mission to combat the forces that gave rise to the disaster one has survived—war, nuclear weapons, dangerous industrial procedures, or lax preparations for emergencies. All of these survivor patterns are drawn upon by the protean self.

A survivor, fundamentally, has two psychological possibilities: to shut down or to open out. Usually the survivor does both. Shutting down is the reaction of the constricted self and the fundamentalist self, as I shall discuss in chapters 8 and 9. The protean self, in contrast, opts for opening out, but always with some compromise about how much to do so, and never without vulnerability to painful survivor feelings. In the process, the protean self is helped by certain affirmations that can accompany the experience of surviving. These include the basic satisfaction, even joy, in being *alive,* in not having died, along with the sense of having undergone an experience that is illuminating in its pain. Survival also implies persevering, holding on, maintaining one's existence, and ultimately bears some relationship to symbolic immortality. Survival can contain individual or collective pride in triumph and imply physical and mental strength, as well as intelligence and even a certain amount of organismic wisdom. That sense of victory over the forces of destruction is evident in gatherings of survivors from both Nazi camps and American atomic bombings, where one hears clearly the words, even if actually unspoken: "We are here! We're alive! We have won!"

In his exposure to some of the most destructive events of the twentieth century, Michael W. illustrates certain possibilities of survivor-related proteanism. He first survived his deprived and near-fatherless childhood, with the help of a devoted mother and subsequently of sympathetic teachers. Later as a naval officer during the Second World War, he surprised himself by his own effective behavior in severe combat ("I think I was . . . very good . . . Hell! I manned the guns and the radar and so on. . . . Planes coming, machine guns spitting. . . . Incredible"). He attributed his performance to fatigue ("You were kind of sleepwalking all the time") and numbing ("If I had had more sensitivity, . . . more imagination, I would have absolutely been paralyzed with fear"), suggesting an adaptive blend of dissociation and alertness which he was able to carry over into subsequent survivals. There was no doubt about the indelibility of the experience ("Death was very, very, real to me then") or his sense of awe at having survived ("I was one of the lucky ones—I came out in one piece.")

Sent not long afterward to Hiroshima as part of the survey team arriving eight days after the dropping of the atomic bomb, he was struck by how the city had become "like a wide field, . . . an absolutely barren, devastated, flattened area. . . . I mean you thought, 'Holy God, what could that thing have been to do this?' " Among his retained images ("still very vivid in my mind") are the extensive burns and facial disfigurements he saw and the descriptions he heard of "the howling, terrible, unbelievable wind" of the firestorms. Much of his pain, awe, and confusion was symbolized by his preoccupation with a small terra-cotta statue of a household god which, although so badly damaged that its "head [was] melted by heat," somehow retained a "cheerful, happiness smile." He was troubled in retrospect by his and other people's resistance to information about radiation and by their dangerous poking about in the ruins. He retained images of Hiroshima "too horrifying" to permit him ever to return to the city, despite his five or six trips to Japan in subsequent years. I sensed that he saw himself in that damaged terra-cotta statue, with his own version of a double-edged "cheerful, happiness smile."

In any case, his survivor feelings and images contributed greatly to his sustained awareness of suffering in various parts of the world and to his energy in working to alleviate that suffering. Hence, his involvement over several years in government work with the Marshall Plan in Europe, "an intense, constructive, and wonderful experience"; and in relief work many years later in Africa during the genocidal war in Biafra. The latter survival experience was probably even more devastating to him than Hiroshima because of his more immediate immersion in human suffering, including "six or seven hundred people [he saw] who had lost one or both legs or part of a leg. . . . I was deeply, deeply affected."

These survival experiences left him, as he pursued government and foundation work, increasingly committed to peace. He found himself "more of an antinuclear activist than I realized": he was stunned and chagrined at those who laid out nuclear-weapons scenarios of millions of dead, and insisted (with a mixture of pride and self-derogation) that he was too "emotionally crippled" to attempt such "rational," "detached" approaches to matters of mass killing. Later he was to find it "baffling and infuriating" that, during the Vietnam War and the cold war in general, "talented and intelligent, decent Americans" could press ahead with policies that took no account of human suffering; and "for the dean of humanities of Harvard University to be of that mentality really is scary." In his own idiosyncratic career, Michael W. made constant use of his survivor experiences in pursuing innovative approaches to enhancing human life.

And in celebrating the ending of the cold war between the United States and the Soviet Union, he spoke as a man familiar with death and disaster: "It was like the lifting of a great famine in China of the past or the end of the Black Death [the plague of the Middle Ages]." During his semiretirement years, he has been able to engage in consultations in which "death is often the third party," as he sits with philanthropists seeking advice on how best to set up their wills to maximize their contributions to human betterment. He remains sensitive to the world's continuing dangers ("the possibility of enormous disintegration") and committed to utilizing his survivals in combatting those dangers.

The more ordinary survivor experiences of other people interviewed also became part of their protean style. Rosalyn K., for instance, told of the recent death of her grandmother who had become "like a vegetable brain for years," causing Rosalyn herself to feel: "I don't want to go this way. I'd rather fall off a cliff." The experience in turn made her think of the indignities experienced by elderly people ("being treated shitty on the streets of New York") and of more general questions of reasonably decent forms of living. Acute illnesses of her own have caused her to be "paralyzed with the idea that I'll only be able to move a little bit at a time"—to be, that is, paralyzed by the possibility of a paralysis that would interrupt the protean flow.

Alfred F., an antiwar activist in his mid-thirties, experiences frequent anxiety dreams which include landscapes of nuclear holocaust, of "being in war situations" in general, and sometimes a personal sense of having been "accused of murder or . . . all sorts of things that are just very bad." Upon awaking, he has the sense that he has survived a painful ordeal. He says, "In some ways I like them [the dreams]" because afterward he can experience "relief that it didn't happen." The dreams serve not only as an expression of general anxiety but as a means of reconnecting Alfred with the apocalyptic dangers he works against. Elements of self-accusation from earlier guilt patterns infuse continuing struggles with his own "failed responsibility" for acceding to, or not doing more to oppose, destructive forces in the world. In these ways, the dreams help to mobilize a survivor energy in working for social change.

Feigned survival can become part of a public protest. Ken F., for instance, told of how he and a group of fellow activists "just laid ourselves out as dead bodies in front of the door" of a company long involved with mining. At the same time, they displayed names of Native American uranium miners who had died from radiation effects. Prior to that demonstration, he said, "We had practice sessions, basically to figure out how to lie stiff." Such actions are meant both to confront onlookers with the specter of death in relation to certain policies, and to provide demonstrators with a semblance of a "survivor mission." Over several protean shifts, the self may hold on to certain death-saturated images that serve to anchor it in profound and dangerous truths—as happened with Michael W. in connection with both Hiroshima and Biafra, and with me in regard to the searing images of Hiroshima, Vietnam, and Auschwitz, even though I obtained these second-hand.

An extensive literature of survival powerfully evokes such images, often in combination with protean forays. Kurt Vonnegut, for instance, in identifying himself directly as a survivor of holocaust (he witnessed the destruction of Dresden as a prisoner of war), brings a special bite to his proteanism. His two great external themes are Dresden and Hiroshima; his more general themes, death-dealing stupidities carried out by human beings and, beyond those (as he puts it in his introduction to *Slaughterhouse Five*), "plain old death." "Duty dance with death," part of the sub-subtitle of *Slaughterhouse Five*, is an accurate description of Vonnegut's imaginative enterprise.

Earlier, in *Mother Night*, Vonnegut powerfully recognized how impaired our postholocaust formulations of the world really are, as a character, a survivor of Nazism and much else, concludes, "I've lost the knack of making sense. I speak gibberish to the civilized world, and it replies in kind." Although in *Cat's Cradle*, Vonnegut directs his exploratory gibberish to Hiroshima, we must turn to his great survivor novel, *Slaughterhouse Five*, for a sense of the exalted and protean possibilities of survivor mockery. *Slaughterhouse Five* is less about the Allied bombing of Dresden during the Second World War than it is about the state of mind evoked in Vonnegut by our total destruction of that city. He is therefore talking about war and holocaust, and about the human tendency to accelerate the arrival and demean the process of "plain old death." The novel is a survivor's effort to make sense—or anti-sense—of a world dominated by every variety of holocaust and every variety of numbing. The key to the "telegraphic schizophrenic"—that is, the condensed, mad style and content of this book—is the recurrent phrase "So it goes," which, with its note of combined gaiety and terror, is a mocking witness to our unfeeling murders, to our equally unfeeling survival of those murders, and to precisely the resignation the phrase suggests. *Slaughterhouse Five* is about feeling and not feeling, about remembering and not remembering, about looking back and not looking back, about dying and not dying, about living and not living. Vonnegut is angrily demanding that all of us come out from beneath our tombstones and do something—at least, *feel* something—about the forces of absurd death that stalk us.

Whether or not Vonnegut's work has been influenced by Günter Grass's *The Tin Drum,* spiritually the two novelists have a great deal in common. Instead of Vonnegut's clipped, bittersweet apocalypse, Grass gives us an elaborately convoluted—even epic—form of the mocking grotesque. The protean journey I have identified in this early classic in the post–Second World War literature of mockery is juxtaposed with Nazi evil in a series of quintessentially twentieth-century survivals. Those survivals bring about release and new beginnings, so that at the end of the book the journey is only starting: "[S]o many possibilities are open to a man of thirty."

Over the decades, Grass has made Auschwitz his starting point, writing as late as 1990, "The crime of genocide, summed up in the image of Auschwitz, inexcusable from whatever angle you view it, weighs on the conscience of the unified [German] state. . . . Anyone thinking about Germany these days . . . must include Auschwitz in his thoughts." And any German writing after Auschwitz "had shame, shame on every white page as its prerequisite." Grass himself had been a member of the Hitler Youth, a soldier in a Panzer division, and an American prisoner of war, all by the age of nineteen. Grass draws upon the German survivor experience and transmutes it into bold imagination on behalf of ethical knowledge. German guilt and shame become animating sources of the anxiety of responsibility. And in advocating (in 1990) cultural rather than political re-union of the two Germanies, Grass became a survivor-prophet, politically unheeded but a continuing influence on everyone's consciousness. All this requires that he remain insistently protean: "Something remains to be said that has not yet been put into words. An old story wants to be told altogether differently."

A talented visual artist before becoming a writer, Grass describes himself as "addicted to images." Protean survivors are likely to retain such addictions. In some cases of extreme victimization, the retained images can eventually overwhelm their possessor. Paul Celan, Jean Amerie, and Primo Levi, all extraordinary writers as well as Jewish Auschwitz survivors, achieved striking forms of illumination before they killed themselves. Grass contrasted his situation with such victims by declaring himself "not a . . . criminal . . . to be sure, but in the camp of the criminals"; and his early friendship with Paul Celan provided encouragement, even a blessing, for his survivor mission as a German. Grass saw himself as struggling alongside Celan against the evil of mass killing and absurd death, and "against passing time."

A protean survivor can become what the German-Jewish social critic Walter Benjamin once called a "destructive character" who "sees nothing permanent . . . but because he sees a way everywhere, he has to clear things from it everywhere." Such a figure "always positions himself at crossroads," and if "what exists he reduces to rubble, [it is] not for the sake of the rubble, but for that of the way leading through it." Under such conditions, "no moment can know what the next will bring." Saul Bellow is aware of that uncertainty when he raises the question, "Where is that human life which is my only excuse for surviving!"

## The Struggle for Form: Integrative Proteanism

> *The dream of man's heart, however much he may distrust and resent it, is that life may complete itself in significant pattern. Some incomprehensible way. Before death. Not irrationally but incomprehensibly fulfilled.*
>
> —Saul Bellow

A continuous quest in our time is for what I would call "integrative proteanism." Not a contradiction in terms, integration here involves holding together, however loosely, disparate elements of self. It imposes priorities among these elements and the emotions they contain, and can include certain images and forms that are both enduring and energizing. The Crucifixion, for instance, has been an energizing image for Carol C., sustaining a sense of herself as one who combats all "crucifying," all forms of torture and mistreatment. For Michael W., energizing images include those of death and rebirth, rendering him one who can draw life power and special knowledge from survival; and of the mystery of China, contributing to his expectation of being able to transcend immediate environments in favor of adventurous expansion of self. George R.'s sense of self is integrated and energized by his powerful sense of efficacy, his assumption that "you can set your own destiny . . . in this world . . . [and] there is nothing I can't do."

The anthropologist Clifford Geertz is undoubtedly correct in telling us that a certain kind of self does not prevail for all: "The Western conception of the person as a bounded, unique, more or less integrated motivational and cognitive universe, a dynamic center of awareness, emotion, judgment, and action organized into a distinctive whole and set contrastively both against other such wholes and against its social and natural background is . . . a rather peculiar idea within the context of the world's cultures." But this conception of self is preprotean, and has probably not applied for some time in most of the West as well. On the other hand, the "multiple, unintegrated or partially integrated self-representations," observed in non-Western societies by another anthropologist, nonetheless enable people to "experience a sense of continuity." Protean or otherwise, the self requires a modicum of inner continuity, and of coherence as well, but on its own personal and cultural terms. That is what Saul Bellow means when he has Herzog describe "how my mind has struggled to make coherent sense." The sources of that coherence can vary. Civic leaders and social activists, for instance, seek it in very different ways. But however elusive and inchoate the effort, all are engaged in it.

Salman Rushdie, in discussing that quest, describes personal meaning as "a shaky edifice we build out of scraps, dogmas, childhood injuries, newspaper articles, chance remarks, old films, small victories, people hated, people loved"; and then adds that "perhaps it is because our sense of [that meaning] is constructed from such inadequate materials that we defend it so fiercely, even to the death." He defends in particular the writer's need to combine immediate involvements with earlier roots, as has been the twentieth-century practice of "the world's community of displaced writers," including James Joyce, Isaac Bashevis Singer, Maxine Hong Kingston, and Milan Kundera. Rushdie is saying that this hard-won cohesion is the opposite of pure form, that it is more a matter of a workable blending of disparate elements in ways that enable one to construct an inwardly believable and morally acceptable sense of one's overall being.

For Don DeLillo (through the writer-protagonist of *Mao II*), it is the *freedom* of the self, its resistance to absolute subservience, that is a source of structure: "The experience of my own consciousness tells me . . . how total control wrecks the spirit, how my characters deny my efforts to own them completely, how I need internal dissent, self-argument, how the world squashes me the minute I think it's mine." For the young Indian woman protagonist of Bharati Mukherjee's *Jasmine,* the very openness to transformation gives strength and form: "I changed because I wanted to. To bunker oneself inside nostalgia, to sheathe the heart in a bulletproof vest, was to be a coward." Her native Indian village "receded fast" as "I bloomed from a diffident alien with forged documents into adventurous Jase." For Vladimir Nabokov (as Alfred Kazin tells it), there was a "simultaneous existence in time of our different selves as that moment in which all the languages he has used, the countries he has lived in, join to make the antiworld that every novelist needs"; after that, "self-celebration slops all over the planet." Again, however odd or bizarre its components, something on the order of a coherent self comes on strong.

People (including many already discussed) can be intensely protean while at the same time holding fast to important experiences, principles, and connections. Michael W., for instance, has drawn coherence from his survivals. In entering various high-level professional environments, he kept in mind all he had witnessed in such situations as naval combat, Hiroshima soon after the bombing, and massive African starvation: "This sounds arrogant [but] I was impelled in those discussions by a hell of a lot of this . . . stuff that . . . [others in government were] simply incapable of feeling because [for them] it was a relatively abstract problem of national security policy and countering the Russian thrust, and domino theory." It became for Michael W. a consistent principle of the self that "at some level . . . of discussion, these moral, human, emotional things have got to be [there] because otherwise, it's Buchenwald all over again." Also giving form to his personal narrative was a tendency to reflect on long-term human struggle and his own contribution to modest gains, all of which could "keep my spirits up a little bit." His formed principles could contribute to critical contemporary observations: "We're a society now that's unwilling to pay its own bills, a society that's unwilling to pay taxes for the support of absolutely essential social services . . . [because] politics has passed on into the realm of fantasy and image making." A method he has used to maintain cohesion has been to husband his energies and "focus on trying to do what . . . I can do about the few things where I think I can have a little influence." He roundly asserted the coherence of his itinerant self in a curmudgeonlike declaration at the end of an interview: "I am not a goddamned bit deterred. I mean I'm going to continue to be a pain in the neck."

As for Carol C., she was speaking both literally and metaphorically when she referred to the "safe harbor" she found in her small California seaside town. She spoke of the "open space," the "physicality of it," and its freedom from the "visual bombardment" of the city's ugliness—all of which enabled her to reach "down deeper inside of myself," to find "a lot more self-acceptance" and greater ability to "put . . . all those things from the past into some sort of framework." Whereas before she had the feeling that "there was this personal life, there was this political life, and my art," now all three seemed to blend. Carol relies on continuous self-examination to sustain her integrative process. By "beginning to listen to some inner voice," she is able to render her protean combinations more coherent. Whatever her mystical flights and personal and professional experiments, she emphasizes "the need to hang on to things, . . . to ground myself."

Connections important to Rosalyn K. include her "straight job" as a bridge between her oppositional work and the larger society; her activist organizational ties at every level from grass-roots foot soldier to decision-making board member; and her close family relationships, including a modus vivendi with her mother and personal model as well as continuing bonds with her father and brother reinforced by shared interests in art and baseball. Yet the vulnerability of these structures leaves Rosalyn in a constant struggle with formlessness and despair: the feeling that her work doesn't have a focus, and that she is "sort of wandering . . . [with] nothing straightforward, . . . that sense of not having . . . ground to walk on, of not knowing anything for sure that's right, anything for sure that's wrong." When experiencing that threat of disintegration (the feeling that "I'm a speck in time . . . and if I disappear no one will notice"), she finds it necessary to "stick to people" around her and to reassert an "almost arbitrary" set of convictions having to do with justice, fairness, and a politics of participation. By focusing her work on small communities ("where you *do* see a difference") and helping to create effective forms of protest (which made "a lot of people concerned about nuclear weapons in New York Harbor"), she is able to buttress those inner structures that "reaffirm your ability as a human being to matter, to make a difference." In that way, she sustains elements of self associated with connectedness, decency, and achievement.

Civic leaders seek stability from the social institutions in which they often feel themselves embedded, but for them, too, stability is of a "rolling" or shifting, kind. They frequently experience conflict between their sense of self and the institutional function, but tend to stay in the institution and either become a critic from within or find ways of working that transcend ordinary institutional practice. Thus, Michael W. could make use of sympathetic enclaves within government and philanthropic institutions he was part of to experiment with innovative programs, while being critical of other attitudes of colleagues. George R. responds to doubts about his relationship to his large money-management firm by extending radically what can be done by that institution. While careful to avoid rapid shifts ("I think severe change would . . . scare me"), he can maintain a certain degree of authentic inner form only by a certain readiness to make changes ("keep three balls in the air"). He is characteristic of civic leaders in that the cohesiveness of his sense of self depends greatly upon evidence of efficacy, of making things happen and achieving personal success.

Social activists also seek efficacy, but find it highly elusive in terms of both external evidence and inner conviction. Their sense of cohesion depends importantly on immediate relationships, whether with family or colleagues or lovers, and often on maintaining selective ties with conventional institutions as well. The quest for authenticity and coherence can be fierce, precisely because these are perceived as difficult to achieve and sustain. Of enormous importance here is the sense of being part of something larger than oneself, something called "the movement," which encompasses activities on behalf of peace and social change that extend far beyond the individual. Thus when Ken F., the thirty-three-year-old free-lance peace activist, was asked what keeps him going, he replied, "Immersion. . . . I've been doing it so long I can't figure out how to stop. There would be too many unfinished projects and commitments." His "immersion" has to do with his experience of a larger human connectedness, of an immortalizing purpose. Ken tells of an incident in which his sister quoted his mother as saying: "Ken called and said he just got arrested and I've not heard him so happy in months." The arrest had been vitalizing as an initiation rite enabling him to overcome fear and become a true adult member of the movement. He experienced a sense like religious illumination in this new status within this collective, life-enhancing project. Such feelings can help to hold the self together in the face of every kind of uncertainty and confusion.

What are often referred to as "defenses" (maneuvers to combat inner drives or unacceptable feelings) are actually hard-won affirmations of a self struggling to pull together its component parts—a process Wallace Stevens evokes in describing how the mind "[t]urns to its own figurations and declares, 'This image, this love, I compose myself/Of these.'" This principle of active composition requires that one's "I," or active self, subsume and render its component parts as "law-abiding" in some degree.

Just how law-abiding is an important issue, having to do with the capacity of the protean self to hold together under duress, to combine staying power or "grit" with fluidity. Precisely that combination has been expressed by Carol C. and Michael W. and, on the world stage, in the achievements of Václav Havel. In carrying out the struggle against Communist suppression of people and truth, Havel was as steadfast as he was flexible. That steadfastness within proteanism requires the kind of energizing image I have discussed, one that in turn enables the "I" to steer for the self a course that is both fluid and ethically formed.

In that way, the "I" coordinates what has been called a "narrative configuration," through which we "make our existence into a whole by understanding it as an expression of a single unfolding and developing story." The self is then understood as both multifaceted and integrated, as "not a static thing or substance, but a configuring of personal events into an historical unity which includes not only what one has been but also anticipations of what one will be." And whatever the convolutions of the protean subnarratives, the self continues to be bound by that configurational principle.

To recognize that, as human beings, we are meaning-hungry creatures is to say that we are form-hungry creatures as well. The very concept of self suggests as much. And I would argue that what we call "impulse," "drive," or "drivenness" has less to do with "instinct" than with this quest for (in Susanne Langer's term) "significant form." Charles Taylor, the philosopher, tells us that self is part of our humanity; and, whatever the claim of Eastern disciplines or Western mysticism, there is no real "escape from self." Our very experience of high states in which we seem to move beyond the self are testimony to its range and possibility. And the quest (in Zen Buddhism, for instance) for formlessness is, in actuality, an effort to have achieved, upon one's "return," changes or alterations in the self's forms. Those forms always include what Taylor calls "common space" with other human beings—shared structures having to do with family, ethnic groups, society, and culture, as well as with innate psychobiological tendencies that are the "common space" of humankind. Thus, Clifford Geertz has reported on the Moroccan concept of *nisba*, in which a profound belongingness—a framework including kinship, religious sect, and occupation—enables people to be "totally pragmatic, adaptive, opportunistic, and generally ad hoc" in most encounters with others "without any risk of losing one's sense of who one is": "Selfhood is never in danger." A pattern of protean interaction, that is, can be enhanced by enduring internal forms.

Whatever its combination of fluidity and form, we seem to need the self everywhere as agency and guide, all the more so when its integrative capacity is pressed to the limit by its protean forays. We remain, that is, "a particular voice in the conversation"—the voice of an "I"—and express ourselves from "a certain perspective in moral space." And into that "I," we are impelled to absorb, however imperfectly, all that we know and are.

# Chapter 6

## POISE AND EQUIPOISE

*One of the things that has happened to us in the twentieth century*
*. . . as a human race is to learn how certainty crumbles in your*
*hand. We cannot any longer have a fixed certain view of anything,*
*. . . [but] our lives teach us who we are.*
                                                        —Salman Rushdie

THE COHERENCE I HAVE been discussing is tenuous because the protean self does nothing in a completely linear, straightforward manner. It darts and teases, its feelings and connections less than fully clear. It nonetheless seeks always to maintain a certain poise or balance—an equilibrium or equipoise—to enable it to function in the world. That poise is bound up with agility, with flexible adaptation, and is less a matter of steady and predictable direction than of maneuverability and talent for coping with widely divergent circumstances. Such poise requires a series of additional psychological characteristics, ones that are crucial to protean existence. These include strong tendencies toward mockery and humor for "lubricating" experience, emotions and communities that are "free floating" rather than clearly anchored, preference for fragmentary ideas rather than large belief systems, and continuous improvisation in social and occupational arrangements and in expressions of conciliation or protest. No wonder that protean poise is demanding, always at issue, always required.

# The Lubrication of Experience: Mockery

*Modern man must descend the spiral of his own absurdity to the lowest point; only then can he look beyond it.*
                                                    —Václav Havel

The protean self lives in a realm of absurdity, embraces a tone of mockery and self-mockery along with a spirit of irony, and often bathes its projects in humor. The sense of absurdity has to do with a perception of the world as "discordant" or "out of tune," or in some way "deaf," "mute," or "in chaos"—that is, as reflecting the dictionary meanings of *absurdity*. Important here is the absence of "fit" (mentioned earlier) between individual self and outside world. Absurdity is not only an absence of meaning but a barrier to creating it, a form of antimeaning. To express that absurdity, to make use of mockery, irony, and humor, is to take steps toward asserting more authentic feelings.

In our time, absurdity and mockery are everywhere—in popular culture, in art and literature, and in individual lives. We constantly seek new ways to convey the gap between what we are supposed to feel and what we actually do feel. So we invent endless terms for segments of life experience, terms that suggest the experience to be less than straightforward. We speak of "bit," "bite," "byte," "bag," "caper," "game," "con game," "game plan," "scene," "show," "scenario," "schtick"; or we seek to "make the scene" (or "make it"), "beat the system," or "pull it off"; or we "cool it" (or "play it cool"), "chill out," or "cop out." What is to be experienced cannot be taken at face value. One must keep much of the self aloof from it, lubricate the encounter with mockery or self-mockery, with irony or humor. With mockery, the lubrication takes the form of ridicule or derisive mimicry; the self is dependent upon that which is mocked, expressing a point of view about it but not necessarily clear separation from it. Irony, in contrast, implies an exposure of the discrepancy between intended and actual meaning, along with a separate stance of the self making the judgment. There is much overlapping of the two, and both tend to be accompanied by elements of humor, a state of mind in which the perception of discordance can be experienced pleasurably with the self affirmed in its rejection of an assumed reality. Attempts to lubricate experience are by no means new, but for the protean self they are integral, sustained, and necessary.

For example, Carol C. expressed her mocking and ironic sensibility, which pervaded our interviews, most consistently toward religion. She described with pride and laughter how she and a friend liked to break out together in a raucous rendering of the hymn "Onward Christian Soldiers" as a means of draining off tension when engaged in demanding political work. As a young child she had sung the hymn in church in a straight fashion, feeling excited by "the passion of it." Now she considers the hymn "lethal . . . [in its] warlike and imperialistic tone" and enjoys belting it out "as a joke." She also spoke derisively of other aspects of her early religious exposure: "this white-old-man-with-the-long-beard-God" and related "heavy-duty Christian images," including "the whole Jesus, Mary, and Joseph bit": so that "if it's . . . Christmas, you see [them], . . . and aren't they cute? And if it's Easter, you see a very dark, very mournful dying Christ." But she admits that, here again, as a child, "I bought it."

Her powerful transformation of the Crucifixion symbol (see chapter 4) was enhanced by her evolving mockery and irony. She spoke angrily of the way in which that cruel procedure was "so neatly presented" with "maybe . . . a couple of drops of blood coming from Christ's hands" but in no way conveying the cruelty of "flesh . . . on a stick." Generally speaking, her mocking approach to religion helped her subvert the imposed dogma while holding on to and redirecting the image and its original passions toward inclusive human concerns. Her emerging irony and humor, moreover, are a source of vitality and provide a perspective that helps her greatly in her efforts to integrate the varied components of her sense of self.

Rosalyn K. made good use of self-mockery to puncture her own ideological certainties, and later judged herself to have "felt quite righteous about it all." She could apply a similar tone toward her current feminist beliefs so that, while objecting to women being defined by men, she could add, "I really love working with women, and I love picking on men, . . . but I don't believe that there's anything inherently violent about men or nonviolent about women." Rosalyn and her colleagues could bring mocking humor to protests and demonstrations, as in their publicized invitation to Donald and Ivana Trump to a "free brunch" for the homeless at Trump Plaza, and in her spirited group of "Phillies fans for legal abortion." Her enthusiasm for the writings of Andy Warhol was an embrace of his subversive mockery, though her earnestness here suggested that the mocking source had become too urgent a matter to be itself made an object of subversion—and that Rosalyn K. was still struggling with when and how much to invoke her self-mockery.

Michael W., in contrast, learned to control his self-mockery and key it to ethical and political questions. For instance, he spoke of "a special quality of tragedy" in potential nuclear holocaust: "It not only takes the old crocks like me who are about to be leaving anyhow, but it sweeps away all those people in the flower of their life and the children and so on and so on." He had sensitive antennae for many such lethal absurdities. He told of taking a granddaughter to the White House, where he had worked for a time, and thinking of the "bizarre" contrast between, on the one hand, the "benign tourist site" on the outside and the elegance of the President's Oval Office, "while underneath—in basement 1, basement 2, basement 4, basement 6, and basement 8—all this other stuff [people planning nuclear war] is going on." He had similar feelings about a crucial summit meeting between the two superpower heads of state: "Gorbachev with his black box [containing nuclear-weapons orders carried by another man], Bush with his black box." Michael W. wondered what future historians would make of "the insanity of . . . two leaders of the most powerful nations of the world [who] tried to go for a quiet place for a weekend in order to talk [about world peace] . . . and take with them these incredible machines [geared to blow up the world]."

I have already mentioned the profusion of mockery, self-mockery, and irony in post–Second World War literature, particularly the literature of survival associated with Vonnegut, Grass, and DeLillo and the array of movements that have constituted twentieth-century art. For Grass and Vonnegut, the heart of the matter is the absurdity of twentieth-century dying; indeed, they meditate on mass murder so extreme as to destroy all possibility of straight discourse. Over time, much twentieth-century literature has come to institutionalize this deadly absurdity. For Don DeLillo, the great disasters of the century are inseparable from what happens every day; and death in the American imagination is what his novel *White Noise* is all about. The novel's protagonist, who is chairman of his college's department of "Hitler Studies," is "generous" in helping a colleague who wishes to derive similar "power and madness" from Elvis. That colleague observes, "Every advance in knowledge and technique is matched by a new kind of death, a new strain. Death adapts, like a viral agent. Is it a law of nature?"; and, concerning American society, "Here we don't die, we shop. But the difference is less marked than you think." DeLillo's mocking/ironic/comic sensibility is relentless as the novel progresses to, and beyond, its death-haunted climax.

Mockery can hone in on everyday dislocation and pomposity, as in Bharati Mukherjee's short story about an encounter between two Indian-born "naturalized Americans." One of them, the narrator, is struck by a particular head-shaking gesture of the other, meant to convey "3,000 years plus civilization" but rendered absurd in her eyes partly because the gesture was "made famous by Peter Sellers." Or the mockery can turn into self-mockery as, alone in a "rattling cab" in New York, Saul Bellow's Herzog—not without pleasure—bemoans his fate in a highly Jewish idiom:

Oh what a thing I am—what a *thing!* . . . I fall upon the thorns of life, I bleed. And then? I fall upon the thorns of life, I bleed. And what next? I get laid, I take a short holiday, but very soon after I fall upon those same thorns with gratification in pain, or suffering in joy—who knows what the mixture is!

In *Herzog*, Bellow both mocks and revels in the wildness of the postimmigrant imagination in response to the equally wild marital-legal adventures of late twentieth-century America. More brutal is the burlesque mockery of Thomas Pynchon in his evocation of a dead or dying (Thanatoid) America, populated by "Thanatoids" who do little but watch television while "advancing further into the condition of death." Pynchon's is a near-paranoid rendition of an unalterable American death plunge. DeLillo and Bellow are perhaps more protean in combining their humor with glimmers of love and hope, in mocking absurd death in ways that convey at least a possibility of renewal.

The sustained mockery in such recent art movements as Pop art, conceptual art, neo-expressionism, graffiti, and performance art can be largely traced back to those two prominent absurdist movements stemming from cubism—Dadaism and surrealism. Artists in those movements "knew perceived reality to be inauthentic, [so they] prowled around its margins, made everything over, and indeed were always just starting out: always for the first time." André Breton declared, "I have never appreciated in myself anything other than what appeared to contrast drastically with what was outside," and suggested that a true surrealist like Dali "places himself, without saying a word, in a system of interferences." There is no better way for the self to "interfere" with this inauthenticity— to mobilize a "system of interferences" against it—than to subvert, ridicule, and dismember, all in the service of creating something other than falseness. Different forms of playfulness and lubricating humor were required: "All things come and go," Dali tells us; and Breton muses, "Life is slow and we hardly know how to play it."

A politics of mockery emerged dramatically in the late 1960s and the 1970s: the sequence of the Berkeley Free Speech Movement of 1965 to a "Filthy Speech Movement"; the 1968 slogan of rebellious Columbia University students, "up against the wall, motherfucker"; and that same year, the cry of the French students, "We are all German Jews!" The black comedian Dick Gregory caught the spirit of those times with his blend of mockery, self-mockery, and protest. Much of that sensibility subsequently made its way into the mainstream of American political and social life.

In the 1980s, Václav Havel carried the banner of absurdity in blending the artistic, the political, and the existential. He drew heavily from the literary and theatrical absurdity of such figures as Kafka, Beckett, Ionesco, and Pinter, finding in them "theatrical images of the basic modalities of humanity in a state of collapse." Early in his career, Havel embraced those evolving expressions of the Prague theater, which featured "absurd humor" that could "turn . . . the real subject on its head." In his political work, he was aware that an excess of "dramatic seriousness" would lead one to "quickly petrify and become his own statue"; instead, "you must have a healthy awareness of your own human ridiculousness and nothingness." And when asked about the conflict between his "absurd plays" and "preposterous idealism," he answered, "They are only two sides of the same coin. Without the constantly living and articulated experience of absurdity, there would be no reason to attempt to do something meaningful."

That sense of absurdity enabled Havel to open himself to varied sources of rebellion, including rock music, against the oppressive Communist regime. He became close to the prominent dissident rock group Plastic People of the Universe and its leader, Ivan Jirous, in whose mocking sounds and lyrics Havel found "disturbing magic" and "internally free articulation of an existential experience that everyone who had not become completely obtuse must understand." (This reminded me of the powerful impact of various anti–Vietnam War rock music and lyrics—notably Country Joe MacDonald's "I-Feel-Like-I'm-Fixin'-to-Die Rag.")

People close to Havel whom I interviewed in Prague told me that his sense of absurdity permits him a measure of detachment and helps him "keep the human dimension." One person said that Havel views life itself as "an absurd drama" and the Czech revolution as "the biggest theater he could organize." Another said that, when Havel came into prominence as the new president of the Czechoslovakian state, she would tell him, "This is [an] absurd drama [in] which you are playing the main role." Or of the pompousness he encountered while president, she would comment to him, "It's like from your plays," and the two of them would have difficulty controlling their laughter. Before that, just about everyone in Czechoslovakia shared with Havel and other dissidents the absurdity of their sudden reversal of status—from jail or persecution to running the country. As one adviser told me with a smile, he found himself suddenly, after "running from the police for forty years," in a position of making policy on the structure, function, and future of those same (or almost the same) police. Another adviser told me she worried only when, under great duress, she found, "We are losing a sense of humor." That, unfortunately, happened all too frequently in 1992 as Havel's reign as president came to an end. But I have no doubt that we will hear more from him about manifestations of absurdity in the world.

Perhaps absurdity is inseparable from shapeshifting in general. One student of mythology claims that the *Odyssey* deals with Proteus in "a somewhat comic way" and gives him "somewhat burlesque treatment." In any case, absurdity and mockery enable the protean self to do several things at once: articulate bitterness and anger while sometimes combining these with affection; provide "interference" from every kind of inauthenticity; and establish patterns of such lubrication as a sustained inner form.

# Free-Floating Emotions

*Nobody knows how to feel and they're checking around for hints.*

—Don DeLillo

The protean self is capable of all strong emotions, but their source and target tend to be unclear. We can become angry, anxious, or guilty while having little sense of why or to what or whom our feeling relates. Frederick Barthelme evokes that disconnection in the extreme when a character in one of his novels declares, "I felt it was stupid to blame anybody for anything." There is a blurring of cause and effect, making it difficult to grasp the relationship between emotions and self—difficult to locate the self within its own emotions. But people keep "checking around for hints," looking into themselves for indications of where their emotions really are.

Rosalyn K., for instance, although so horrified by poverty and starvation in various parts of the world that she devotes considerable energy to combatting them, wonders whether, at bottom, "what I'm fearing [is], what if it happens to me?" If she is in this way "just . . . selfish, . . . really think[ing] of myself," she may, she is afraid, lack "that sort of passion I would have [if] I'm fighting . . . for my own life." Another related concern is whether her strong opposition to violence in the world is not essentially a product of "what happened in your life that makes you really fear this." This concern is influenced by the American immersion in psychology (fairly strong in Rosalyn's subculture, and she has had her share of therapy), a collective immersion that is itself a social product of widespread uncertainty about emotional cause and effect. Her own emotional uncertainties are further revealed in a sequence in which she declared, "Our lives are being taken away from us," and, when asked by whom, replied, "Maybe by ourselves in a way." She was referring outwardly to our individual complicity in militarism and bad government but also conveying—in a way reminiscent of Pirandello's "Someone is living my life"—a psychological inability to manage her own somewhat mysterious feelings.

She feels troubled by this sense of being "out of control . . . of your life"—a fear she associates with our collective inability to "control . . . our stupid technology," as with Chernobyl (the 1986 nuclear power disaster in the Soviet Union) and Bhopal (the 1984 chemical disaster in India caused by an American company), and that was more immediate in relation to plans begun in the 1980s to bring nuclear weapons into New York Harbor ("Having [them] . . . *right here*, . . . *that's* really scary to me"). She further associates nuclear-weapons dangers with "that slow creepiness of contamination," of various forms of pollution in our cities, including their water supply: "You just can't trust your own environment." She is often reminded of a scene in Thomas Wolfe's novel *You Can't Go Home Again* in which the protagonist, standing in his magnificent apartment overlooking Manhattan, feels the building shake from the subway underneath and realizes that there is no strong earth below, only more plumbing and pipes: "It's this idea of your foundation not being there, . . . this metaphor of life sort of crumbling."

Yet Rosalyn feels even worse in rural areas or in the suburbs: "There's nobody there!" She believes that "[e]verybody *should* trust nature, . . . its nurturing qualities and it being healthy and stuff," but is aware that she herself lacks "faith in nature." She connects these feelings with a "fear of that unknown," because with "those unknown things, we don't know quite where to place them, we don't quite know what the answer would be." Even in regard to immediate environmental desecration, Rosalyn feels "frustrated" by her difficulty in locating particular persons or groups to serve as targets for her anger. She adds, "If we knew what the problem was, and you could encapsulate it that way, life would be a little easier." Despite these confusing fears, Rosalyn carries on, and is able to do so because her sense of self permits her a certain confidence in human projects that *can* be grasped. With roads and lights and buildings and tunnels, as with certain decisions people make, "those are known things to me, . . . because they're human-created." The protean self, even while adrift in its own emotions, can live with partial integration and partial trust in the possibility of constructive human action.

More in touch with social and historical currents than was possible in the past, the protean self has difficulty placing its own emotional state within these currents. Michael W. told me, "I feel about myself that I have a kind of latent melancholy about the human condition," and hesitantly added, "Maybe it's an Irish [his ethnic origin] thing." He also wondered whether this "melancholy" might be "connected somehow with wartime experiences and with the nuclear thing." At the same time, he sees himself as "hopeful about humanity, . . . not bleak," and asks, again with great uncertainty, whether now that things look better (the end of the cold war), "I'll feel new energy."

Andy H., when wondering about the relationship of his personal feelings to "the chaos in which we live," went off on what seemed an odd tangent. He mentioned that having been born in 1914 means "some magical sort of thing to me," because of his understanding that it was the last year in which there was general confidence that the earth could support its human population—and, by implication, the last year of high optimism about the human future. He could then say with surprising seriousness:

"Was I the one that tilted the world? Was I guilty? . . . A single, white male that tilted the world into the chaos it's in? The sense of my own guilt is very deep, and . . . I deal with it by saying there is no guilt."

The statement is almost a caricature of guilt experienced for being a privileged white male. Or to put it another way, Andy H. articulates with grandiose concreteness a feeling that is broadly experienced, especially by activists, but usually more amorphously. The sense of guilt has to do not only with privilege in a world dominated by suffering, but with a sense of one's lacking the communal grounding, shared moral clarity, and capacity for effective action that could bring an end to this suffering.

The protean self constantly seeks to "locate" its fears, angers, self-condemnations, and losses. (Rosalyn K., for instance, associated the end of her long love relationship with her fear of "unknown things.") But all of these emotions tend readily to emerge into amorphous forms of anxiety. Anxiety has always been thought of as a nonspecific expression of physical and psychological unease, as possessing what Freud called "a quality of indefiniteness and lack of object" and a potential for "a free-floating condition." I would define anxiety as a sense of foreboding stemming from a threat to the vitality of the self or, more severely, from the anticipation of fragmentation of the self. Anxiety is always a part of other emotions: what we feel in relation to guilt or shame (sometimes called "guilt anxiety" or "shame anxiety"); or what we are warding off when we experience anger or rage. The choice of emotion, or of a combination of emotions, depends upon who or what we blame for the perceived threat. The modeling for patterns of blame begins in early childhood and can be relatively structured and bound by social institutions (having to do with family, religion, education, and authority) when those institutions themselves are stable and clearly structured. But when social arrangements break down—at least, regarding their psychological messages—everything becomes highly uncertain, and the free-floating potential of all emotions is drawn upon and extended. Hence, we lose much of the classical distinction between fear (involving a genuine threat) and anxiety (a vague foreboding). While some such distinction is still worth making, our emotions in general are increasingly fluid, open to influence from many directions, and themselves often a source of experiment.

We become uncertain about interpreting our own feelings. The experience of loss (having to do, for instance, with homelessness and fatherlessness or with shifts in relationships and groups) may evoke nagging forms of discomfort that can be looked upon as existential *angst,* as failure due to personal deficiency, or as unfair personal treatment deserving anger and resentment. Intense social, political, and religious currents can interact with influences from early life as we grope for ways of authenticating whatever emotions we experience. Saul Bellow captures this confusing struggle when he tells us that, in relation to terrible scenes witnessed in a courtroom, "Herzog experienced nothing but his own *human feelings,* in which he found nothing of use. What if he felt moved to cry? Or pray?" "*Man has a nature, but what is it?*" Bellow asks.

The struggle for clarification and even purification, as it occurs in art, is described by Robert Motherwell as "the need for felt experience—intense, immediate, direct, subtle, unified, warm, vivid, rhythmic. Everything that might dilute the experience is stripped away." For Motherwell, "[a]bstract art is an effort to close the void that modern men feel." Bharati Mukherjee also deals with emotional purification when she has a protagonist bemoan her tendency to feel different sides of things: "It's hate I long for; simple, brutish, partisan hate." That longing for simplicity in hating is understandable enough, but it can render people susceptible to despots and fundamentalists all too ready to offer that simplicity.

Jorie Graham describes the struggle of contemporary poets to make their way, past obstacles, to passions that are authentic and primal:

> Our poems promote *voice*. . . . They jazz the surface up—they let themselves be seen through—they ham it up, they are totally, tragically aware of themselves as surfaces, as media events, as punctured through with temporality (the minutes click by loudly in them as if paid for at advertiser's rates), and yet they still insist on the deep song, the undertow, the classical griefs and celebrations.

A certain emotional unclarity, however, always remains. The artist Budd Hopkins speaks of his "struggle between unedited, emotionally subterranean needs on the one hand, and a classical ordering instinct on the other," culminating in "a strangely reassuring uncertainty." However fragile the ordering of emotions, the uncertainty can have the advantage of keeping the imagination open and thereby protecting one from emotions that are monolithic, suffocating, inauthentic.

## Free-Floating Communities

> *Well, then, suddenly you . . . realize there's a hundred people in Albany, . . . a thousand people in San Francisco, . . . ten thousand people in Europe. Suddenly you realize that when you're doing it, you're not alone.*
>
> —Alfred F.

Just as free-floating as individual emotions are one's relationships to communities. In late-twentieth-century America, the traditional community—

the enduring, close-knit human group in a particular geographical area, with common purposes within which individual desires are significantly subsumed—tends to be more a nostalgic ideal than an actuality. The sociologist Robert Bellah and his colleagues contrast communities with "lifestyle enclaves": "Whereas a community attempts to be an inclusive whole, celebrating the interdependence of public and private life and of the different callings of all, [lifestyle enclaves] involve only a segment of each individual [and] . . . concern only private life, especially leisure and consumption." These researchers go on to observe that "many once genuine communities [often formed by particular ethnic groups], though still referred to as communities, may well be on their way to becoming lifestyle enclaves." But what I believe to be taking shape may be neither a traditional community nor merely a lifestyle enclave. Free-floating communities attempt, always tenuously, to combine highly fluid arrangements with some of the supportive elements of the traditional community.

For the protean self, communities are partial, fluctuating; come in odd places and combinations; are often at a distance; and vary greatly in their intensity and capacity to satisfy the needs of members. Community may well be the most grave problem facing the protean self; yet here, too, the improvisations convey the sense that something new is always on the verge of being created.

George R., for instance, as a successful management consultant, finds elements of community in a firm where he has worked for many years, in a network of professional contacts extending throughout the United States who depend upon his specialized knowledge concerning public institutions, and in a Catholic church he and his family belong to and regularly attend. But none of these constitutes a true community, either geographically or in holistic terms. Nor is George R. without considerable ambivalence about any of them. Yet each of them is importantly nurturing to him. Keeping "three balls in the air," then, is as much about juggling communities as juggling elements of the self. Similarly, Carol C., after leaving her parental home, found at least partial communities: first among student activists; then in a hospital setting among colleagues working with children; and subsequently in three different geographical areas (and then in ways that maintained connections from a distance) with feminists, art students and artists, and political activists. Despite the periodic and peripatetic aspects of these communal connections, they have served Carol well and remain integral to her sense of self.

Rosalyn K. described how, during her twenties, she was involved with "a loose, flowing" group of people, "a network of friends" with shared social commitments who "would go to meetings and do mailings and organize actions" as well as go to parties and on camping trips together. As she got a little older, however, she found herself seeking more time for herself "to be home with my cats and . . . watch more baseball games." But she still chooses "to spend time with people who are like-minded," and finds being an activist "people-oriented." Working together for social goals, as she explains (in words that suggest both necessity and fragility), "gives you the sense of, well, a community." She is contradictory about how profoundly that community serves her, saying at one time that it "doesn't really help on that deep, deep personal scary level," but at another time that being in touch with other activists, mostly women, in various parts of the United States and the world "just gives you strength. . . . You know that there are more people like you, . . . and it means everything." Musing on how "our generation has provided a lot of different alternative life styles"—meaning various forms of collectives and group housing—she adds, "I have hope that we'll . . . create communities for . . . support—communities, . . . that's what I like."

Her most intense immediate community consists of an affinity group, which has existed for about six years and consists of twenty to forty women who meet regularly and also engage in various forms of social action together, including a yearly "women's peace camp" weekend. While not an organization as such, the group means a great deal to her and provides "direct energy." She also has an informal living arrangement with another woman: each leads a separate life, but "we always come home, we have a nice little house together, we love our cat, and . . . it's like a little nuclear family." Yet although she feels "happy and content," she is aware that "another part of me" is clear that the arrangement would break up should one of them become involved with a man with whom she wished to live: "Much as we love it, we're both not committed to [its] being our primary, familial relationship forever."

Rosalyn's interest in sports has its own bearing on communal belonging. In a way, it takes her *out* of her ordinary communities ("It's an anti-of . . . everything else I do, . . . not intellectual, . . . no political causes [or] greater goals for humanity"). But when she went on to point out with some pleasure that "it distinguishes me from lefty intellectuals," and that within her women's affinity group it is a kind of standing joke, "a colorful part of my personality, . . . my little niche—I'm the jock," it became clear that this interest actually reinforces her relationship to these communities by providing a bit of flexibility and humorous lubrication. Moreover, beyond those activist groups, "it makes me a regular person, . . . a normal Joe." When working in shelters, "what I do when I get there is turn on the TV and . . . talk sports with everybody," which both helps her communicate with people and eases her own pain about the conditions she observes. Beyond that, "I can go to any bar anywhere in this country and . . . hold a conversation with anybody . . . [or] sitting on a plane, . . . waiting for a train. . . . I truly enjoy it." Sports, that is, gives her a certain sense of personal space within her activist community while providing ties to the larger American community, all of which contributes to her balancing act of multiple levels of partial belonging.

Alfred F., the activist with nightmares of nuclear holocaust, graphically portrayed the communal importance of "the movement": "When you're working with a lot of people who are committed in the same way you're committed, who think the way you think, and who are there for support, it really helps sustain you. I don't think people can be sustained like this without a movement." The community's outward extension is amorphous (the images of fellow protesters in various cities of the world mentioned in the section epigraph) but important (his realization that "you're not alone"). But his depiction of the feelings of his fellow activists—"They want to make sure they're going to live in a community where they have this sort of support because it's very frustrating to be isolated"—reveals the fragility of that community and the consequences of its loss. His ties to the movement, however fluctuating, enable him to integrate his academic world with his activism: "Well, it's personal . . . and it's political. . . . My work and my activist life are the same thing."

In contrast to these two social activists, Michael W. has maintained his communities within the American mainstream. But they have been just as varied and have required no less of a balancing act. As he moved from university scholarships to combat service in the Second World War, to the atomic bomb survey team, to State Department work in Europe and the United States, to the foundation world, he increasingly combined membership in a community with a certain detachment from it. His sequence was first a sense of being almost accidentally invited into each community, then a display of ability and vision, and finally dissatisfaction with the status quo. His integrative talents enabled him to roam widely within and among these divergent communities, contributing significantly to each even as he drew upon it in his evolving commitments and explorations.

Not surprisingly, contemporary fiction tends to be more than skeptical about community. To her statement "Towns are the illusion that things hang together somehow," Anne Carson adds another ironic definition: "Matter which has painted itself within lines constitutes a town." Thomas Pynchon caricatures the remains of a 1960s-1970s alternative community in depicting the living arrangements, in a run-down motel behind a roadhouse, of his protagonist's best friend: "His old bass player and troublemaking companion had been living here for years, in what he still described as a commune, with an astounding number of current and ex-old ladies, ex-old lady's boyfriends, children of parent combinations present and absent, plus miscellaneous folks in out of the night." In his mocking representation of the darkly dislocated underbelly of American proteanism, Pynchon reveals the intensity of the communal urge then and now.

Free-floating communities, not fully appreciated, have been at the heart of the revolutions against Communist oppression in Central and Eastern Europe. Theorist-participants in those revolutions—Václav Havel in Czechoslovakia, George Konrad in Hungary, and Adam Michnik in Poland—have all emphasized a concept of a "civic society" based on open and equitable communal relationships, either prior to, or even in place of, assuming political power. The British writer Timothy Garton Ash accurately described this principle in Czechoslovakia: "There should be forms of association, national, regional, local, professional, which would be voluntary, authentic, democratic, and first and last, not controlled or manipulated by the Party or Party-state." Konrad told of "spiritual author-ity" (in contrast to the political authority of the regime) taking shape: "In every village and every workshop there are people whom others listen to. Everywhere there are clusters of old people and of audacious youth. A network of spiritual authority exists. We know of one another. . . . [O]ur shamefaced common consciousness is beginning to raise its head." And Michnik spoke of a "civic catechism" and of the extraordinary develop-ment of the Solidarity movement in Poland: "The essence of the sponta-neously growing Independent and Self-governing labor union solidarity lay in the restoration of social ties, self-organization aimed at guarantee-ing the defense of labor, civil, and national rights. For the first time in the history of Communist rule in Poland 'civil society' was being restored, and it was reaching a compromise with the state."

Ivan Klima, the Czech novelist, has a writer-protagonist enter a church and there meditate on community:

> I had lately felt like an outcast, expelled from every community, unless I were to count the community of those who had been similarly cast out. They had tried to prevent me from addressing anyone, deprived me of my audience—and my audience had naturally not spoken out on my behalf. [So during the church service] I was aware of the presence of order and rejoiced that I too had a part to play in it, that I, too, was being addressed as one of the congregation, as a human being.

If those revolutions could be said to have been achieved via commu-nity, the difficulties in sustaining any such community have been all too evident in each of the three countries and throughout post–Communist Europe. Recent fierce ethnic plunges—on a continuum from strong group identification to aggressive ethnic nationalism to violent assault of ostensible ethnic enemies—are themselves indications of intensified communal hunger at a time of extraordinary confusion. As in our own country, people struggle with fragmented, irregular groupings. We sense that we require, and are struggling to evolve, new definitions of commu-nity, new concepts of the more flexible geographical and psychological forms it may take.

# Ideas and Fragments

*Fragments are the only form I trust.*

—Donald Barthelme

"I am not worried about ideological consistency. I do want to be coherent," is the way Jean Bethke Elshtain, the political scientist, describes her own intellectual approach. Protean shifts and doubts are nowhere more evident than in the holding of ideas. Skepticism about ideologies and belief systems has become itself an article of faith and can readily extend to ideas in general. The problem is not so much embracing a particular set of ideas at a given moment as it is holding on to them as part of one's belief system. Doubt is both mother and child of proteanism and can be a valued trait. Joyce's Stephen Dedalus, asked whether his doubts about religion are too strong to overcome, replies quite simply, "I do not wish to overcome them."

Distrust of belief systems reached an apogee during the late 1960s and early 1970s, when protestors embraced only political fragments and a few significant images on behalf of tactical fluidity, while rejecting much of prior protest ideology as well as mainstream political ideas. Daniel Cohn-Bendit, a French student leader at the time, characterized the process as "uncontrollable spontaneity" and "disorder which allows people to speak freely and will later result in some form of 'self-organization.'" While that position had its contradictions, it reflected deep psychological inclinations that are still very much with us, as expressed by people we interviewed as well as by many writers and thinkers in our time.

Rosalyn K. both distrusts leftist pieties (like "the capitalists' downfall!") and has difficulty finding acceptable rhetoric in their place. She doubts the existence of large numbers of "evil people . . . or evil systems or evil institutions," stresses that "things are complicated" without there being "easy answers to anything," and admits, "I don't have it all figured out." So she settles for the general political advocacy of a decentralized participatory self-government mentioned earlier. Having decided that "if I wanted to live, I would have to come up with some basic values," she "picked ones that were pretty close." These include a principle of "stick to people," "a sense of justice and fairness," and a policy (directed mostly at nuclear weapons and the environment) of "working against death."

Rosalyn has similar ambiguities concerning religion. She identifies strongly with her cultural Jewishness, but says "I believe in God—I mean I don't believe in a . . . God defined by anybody"; about the religious conviction of something beyond death, she adds, "I don't not believe in it. . . . I could never say no but I do not believe in any *human's* definition of it." (Once again, this is reminiscent of an attitude of Stephen Dedalus: his friend asks, "Do you believe in the Eucharist?" and Stephen answers, "I do not"; when the friend then asks, "Do you disbelieve then?" Stephen tells him, "I neither believe in it nor disbelieve in it.") Rosalyn is highly skeptical of anything on the order of "a model society or a model community or a model philosophy," preferring to see things (as stated earlier) "more in motion and working toward . . . an ideal."

Alfred F., an activist of about the same age, is reflective and amorphously hopeful in his ideas: "I don't know that there's [a] human nature per se, . . . [but] I think, given the right circumstances and . . . social setting, . . . people prefer to work together and people prefer peace to conflict and . . . nonviolence to violence." He, too, stresses flux and change: "No society, no culture lasts forever. . . . In this case, I would agree with the people who call themselves Marxists [from whom he otherwise separates himself] that there are certain contradictions within our society which [are] gonna lead eventually to the society transforming to something else. . . . We can have regression, but I think . . . humanity evolves socially as well as physically." He speaks of a "scientific evolution" as helping to eliminate starvation, poverty, and "some of the worst ills." But in order to emphasize both change and individual autonomy, he paraphrases a statement he attributes to Eugene Debs, the American turn-of-the-century labor leader and socialist: "I'll never lead you into the Promised Land because if I could lead you in, somebody could lead you back out."

Andy H., the older activist, spoke of the contemporary dilemma of wanting to know all while failing to understand much: "When you're half-ass Freudian as I am, . . . you want explanations for everything, and there are no explanations for an awful lot of things." Having weathered many political shocks and surprises, including the Hitler-Stalin pact of 1939, Andy came to the conviction that one has to "believe in [be ready for] anything," including the most bizarre developments: "All things are possible." That was in keeping with another activist's insistence that so many questions are "up for grabs."

George R., the financial consultant, also distrusts belief systems but does retain faith in the American Horatio Alger ideal that one can do anything in life to which one sets one's mind. While combining economic ambition with a concern about contributing to the public good (in his case to the financial health of educational institutions), he spoke less about ideals than about pragmatic issues in managing problems. He "worries a lot" about Latinos and blacks: if arrangements to improve their educational opportunities are "not dealt with well, then the results in the long term are gonna be a significant drain on the country's resources." He added, "I like to think people plan and think about these things— . . . leaders in our society, . . . corporate . . . or educational . . . or what have you, . . . meeting regularly on this subject." But he revealed his doubts about what he would like to believe to be happening when he said further, "I really think what's gonna make the difference is when . . . the pain threshold [on the part of the rest of the population] increases sufficiently so that people can't afford not to do things."

As someone who believes in managed decency, he expressed outrage at the extent of fraud and misuse of funds he has encountered, perpetrated "by people like yourself and myself"—that is, by members of the educated middle class. But he felt most intensely passionate about drug dealers, such as members of the big Colombian cartel, and he advocated the solution put forward in the novel and film *The Hunt for Red October:* "To actually go down and destroy them where they live." He then stepped back from this extreme advocacy as "strange coming from a person like myself. . . . I look at myself in the mirror and say, 'Gee, that's not you.'" But he asserted his position by pointing to the large numbers of "people getting killed . . . because of the drug culture, . . . good people wiping themselves out, . . . and the drain on society"—all of which makes him "pretty restless, . . . pretty violent, I guess." His violent imagery is partly related to his sense of the drug culture threatening his children ("In my little (suburban) town where my kid is in the high school, . . . they're dealing drugs out there"). It also threatens his powerful need to believe that America can somehow deal with its problems, that people in high places can manage things. This central belief about America's capacity to live up to his standard of decent management (and managed decency) is important to George R. in his efforts to cope with his pervasive restlessness and make cohere the fragmentary, sometimes contradictory, ideas he holds about most issues in his life.

Edward G., the sixty-year-old religious atheist, reflects the flux and many-sidedness of ideas that one can embrace over a contemporary lifetime. Part of his rebellion against his military/Baptist/Republican father was his objection to the "cruel and vindictive," even "genocidal" God of the Old Testament. But in his subsequent embrace of the Gospels (see pages 61–64), he came to focus especially on "the statement that Jesus had made about whoever loses his life for my sake will find it, not save, but find it, and whoever saves his life will lose it." That sense of Jesus led him to the philosophy mentioned earlier of "sending something over" (through acts of compassion and generosity) during one's life. Over the years, he struggled with such ideological principles as temperance (via the Prohibition party), socialism, pacifism, and "non-Trotskyist" anti-Communist leftism. The Cuban missile crisis convinced him that "the Russians were as crazy as we were," but he held to a "vision" he had as a young man of capitalism as "fundamentally an evil system," and finally has come to advocate a humane version of democratic socialism in which "we don't . . . have to have capital punishment, . . . don't have to hurt people, [and] . . . don't really have to have war, . . . armies, . . . racism." Because "we have not moved enough in that direction, . . . the human condition has not yet begun to emerge," and "we don't really know . . . what a human being is like."

He came to believe in every variety of protest, rather than holding to a single correct form, and applied in effect a theory of complementarity: "It would be useful if we thought about these different kinds of actions in the way you learned to think about light [which] functions both as particle, discreet separate particles, and also waves, . . . that you can meet light either way [because] it works both ways. . . . So you have to roll with the fact that Berrigan's burning draft files has a validity on one level and my alternative approach has a validity also, [as do the] wonderful spontaneous actions of the kind Abbie Hoffman performed."* This inclusive view grew out of his own evolution from early confrontational inclinations to a softer approach that is sensitive to the feelings of all parties, including policemen who may be taking steps to limit or prevent the protest. But his politics include the message to younger people "that the future really is in your hands," that "you can change, there are changes, real chances of change": "Part of my job now . . . is to let people see that the future for us finally is open."

Although Salman Rushdie tells us that doubt has become "the central condition of a human being in the twentieth century," he also insists that "everything is worth discussing. There are no subjects which are off limits." But the problem, Saul Bellow tells us, is that "[h]umankind lives mainly upon perverted ideas." And he speaks of the "dream of intellect" as "the delusion of total *explanations*." Bellow distinguishes between ideas, always available with little effort, and the process of thought itself, which many people fear as "dangerous and destructive." The poet Howard Nemerov carries that late-twentieth-century sensibility much further when he speaks of "the comic-book lightbulb of Idea" and "the idiot balloon of speech." Don DeLillo describes the confusion that can result from the dishonoring of words: "Every thought is permitted. And there's no longer a moral or spatial distinction between thinking and acting."

The path to contemporary confusion was in many ways paved by some of our greatest nineteenth- and early-twentieth-century thinkers, by what Paul Ricoeur called the "hermeneutic of suspicion" of Nietzsche, Freud, and Marx. There has been an explosion of distrust for the way words are

---

*He was referring here to either Daniel or Philip Berrigan, the radical Catholic clerical antiwar activist brothers, who have regularly practiced civil disobedience since the 1960s; and to Abbie Hoffman's staging of mocking, media-centered protest happenings, such as the floating and then burning of dollar bills on the floor of the New York Stock Exchange in 1967.

used, for received ideas, for ideologies in general. So much so that movements are described in terms of what they are not. Thus, George Konrad gives the title "Antipolitics" to his ringing essay on asserting human freedom against communist control in Hungary, and declares: "Antipolitics strives to put politics in its place and make sure it stays there, never overstepping its proper office of defending and refining the rules of the game of civil society. Antipolitics is the ethos of civil society." And Václav Havel evokes critically the mindset of "someone who subscribes to an ideology and believes that anyone who doesn't subscribe to it must therefore subscribe to another ideology, because he can't imagine anyone's not subscribing to an ideology." Much of the protean quest parallels Konrad and Havel's search for ways to clear away the debris of suppressive idea systems, to remain open to every variety of constructive idea and influence, and at the same time to take stands and risks for what is worth defending. That constellation of aims reflects the difficult struggle for protean-style conviction and commitment.

## Work Patterns

*I don't want to embark on one direction and not deviate, and that's what a career does to you.*

—Alfred F.

In work patterns, the protean self seeks alternatives to the lockstep of narrowly conceived "career." Economic necessity, of course, can loom large, but so can the fear of entrapment in inauthentic work, as depicted by Frederick Barthelme: "fighting with clients, shrugging off what we did when we did bad work, which was more often than not.... If you take away the hope of doing something interesting, work becomes intolerable." And that work entrapment, at least in American life, can be equated with a larger, middle-class entrapment in the spiritual and financial chaos of consumerism.

An alternative of protean fluidity is epitomized by the protagonist of Penelope Lively's novel *City of the Mind*, the "English architect stuck in a traffic jam" (see pages 20–21). A member of a small firm specializing in renovation of old buildings, he is attuned to the city's own transformations, to its "turbulent areas of metamorphosis": "Gaunt shells of nineteenth-century buildings, delicately shrouded in green netting ... alongside huge spaces bright with machinery of construction: yellow cement-mixers, orange bulldozers, immense elegant cranes in yellow, red, green, blue—

dinosaurian monsters unleashed to wreak their mechanical will upon the London clay." The multiple layers derived from the city's history, it is implied, parallel those of the architect's mind—as does the description of a particular area as "a landscape of simultaneous decay and resurrection . . . [where] glass, steel and concrete rear from the mud and rubble and excavation."

Lively's architect thrives on the bombardment of images he receives from the structures around him ("buildings that ape Gothic cathedrals, that remember Greek temples, . . . Victorian stucco, twentieth-century concrete, a snatch of Georgian brick"). He is energized by this "[k]aleidoscope of time and mood," by the very multiplicity that enables him to see beyond the structures to the cultures and histories that formed them. In this dialogue between a protean person and his equally protean surroundings, "[t]he city feeds his mind, but in so doing he is manipulated by it, its sights and sounds condition his responses, he is its product and its creature. Neither can do without the other." Struggling for a balance of order and disorder, he extends his own imagination, expands "the landscape of the psyche," finding there "a coded medley of allusions in which the private and the universal are inextricably entwined." In attempting to combine steady technical skills with this form of fluid professional imagination, the architect not only adapts to his environment but asserts his larger human connectedness—providing a vivid example of the expanded possibilities, along with the vulnerabilities, of protean work patterns.

For Carol C., work has become a matter of balancing, with changing emphasis, two different professions. In her shift from speech therapist to sculptor, she was neither taking on a completely new occupation nor entirely surrendering her earlier one. But she was making a profound change in the conduct of her life and the ordering of her self. During our first interview, when I asked whether she earned a living as a sculptor, her answer was, "Now I can say that, but six months ago I was doing another job." That is, she had resumed part-time work in speech therapy, and even now considers that professional skill to be "my insurance policy," to be drawn upon "only when my money runs out." Her sense of self continues to include both sets of skills and both areas of work. But her direction is to commit herself increasingly to her art, to "restructure its groundwork" into more lasting inner forms, while her work in speech therapy has receded to a quiet corner of the self and participates less actively in the energies of self-process.

Although Michael W., the foundation consultant, came to feel "scattered around" intellectually and organizationally among such entities as social science, international affairs, and philanthropic work, when he commented, "I'm not quite anything" and, "Whatever the hell it adds up to I'm not all that sure," his irony contained a certain pride in what he had achieved. Indeed, I found no more affirmative expression of work satisfaction than his characterization of his post–Second World War involvement on the Marshall Plan as "an intense, constructive, and wonderful experience." And even when becoming, in old age, less outwardly protean, undergoing that "narrowing down of my interests [in order to] . . . apply whatever energies I have more efficiently . . . [to] work . . . on these dinky little problems," there was again pride behind the self-mockery. Clearly, the larger ethical and political concerns that had governed his life "are still alive and smoldering . . . there somewhere." All of his variations in professional function—in terms of intellectual address, workplace, breadth and focus, and personal and public levels—are characteristic of the protean self.

So are efforts, like those of Alfred F., the graduate student and social activist, to blend professions into a functional whole. Alfred has been juggling his talents since his high school days when he was both starting quarterback and editor of the school newspaper. When asked about what he might be doing two or three decades from now, he quickly replied, "I'll be too old to play for the Mets," and explained, "I'm sort of kidding about that because that's how I measure my age." In recent years, he has done various forms of part-time writing and research to support himself, but his "only real full-time employment" has been with activist organizations. He is determined that he will not confine himself, in the future, to an academic department because "to end up like that, that's [as] close to hell on earth as possible." He therefore seeks his own "middle ground," while avoiding "the sort of traditional twentieth-century model which is you pursue a particular career, you work for thirty or forty years, and you retire." Rather than struggling "to move up the academic ladder," Alfred F. seeks to find an idiosyncratic arrangement in which, having obtained his Ph.D., he will be able to "write and most likely teach because that's the way you write," so that he will "be in academia" and at the same time "still be active, . . . work on particular projects," but "I won't be a full-time political activist." I sensed that his goal of rendering "my work and my activist life . . . the same thing" requires continuous forays and retreats and constant effort at vocational equipoise, but is by no means unattainable.

Andy H., the respected older activist, has experienced considerable pain in his career struggles. He began to study art while in high school and at first was fond of painting dramatic subjects, such as "nuns being watched by fallen women, . . . exotic people, black folks, Polynesian people." Coming to New York in the 1940s to pursue his study of painting, he met some of the great writers and artists of the time, attended opera and ballet, all "a wonderful liberation" in which "the city was yours." Upon being exposed to great art, however, he began to recognize the limitations of his own talent and destroyed most of his work. Although abandoning an artistic career was a "crushing" disappointment, a chance meeting with a talented photographer introduced him to a new profession. In the casual style of those circles at that time, Andy was invited to "hang around the studio if you want to find out if you can use a camera"; and before long, Andy was able to support himself as a photographer. He could "enter the commercial world," do extensive work for popular magazines, travel to Europe and Africa where he met people "who were different . . . [and] who didn't come from Cincinnati or St. Louis." He found it exciting for a period but "never . . . artistically satisfying," and sometimes felt "trapped" by commercial requirements. Along the way, he did other work, decorating interiors of department stores and even, for a period, running a restaurant with a friend. He was not to find his vocation until he became a full-time peace-movement leader. And although highly successful in that work, bringing to it some of the aesthetic sensibilities of his earlier professions, he cannot entirely eradicate a somewhat sad sense of himself as a failed artist.

Finally, Ken F., the free-lance activist in his early thirties, avoids full-time work with any peace groups "unless that organization will let me do what I want." That means, in essence, that he works only at jobs he himself creates—a pattern not uncommon in activist organizations and in experimental groups of various kinds. But Ken often finds that such self-created jobs are economically unfeasible. Although he had been a good student, he did not bother to finish college and seems to resist acquiring a profession, content to drift occupationally in the fashion of what Jung called the *puer eternus,* or eternal youth. Yet Ken continues to be sought after and to function effectively as a member of a loosely drawn activist work community.

Work entrapment means very different things to different people, of course, but it is regularly perceived by the protean self as a serious threat to its psychological lifeblood of flexibility and fluidity. Entrapment can also become associated with demeaning absurdity, as in the case of Frederick Barthelme's description of "an ape concept promotion," in which a protagonist has to arrange for "thirty-five tiny red wind-up apes" and "the jokers at the office were proud of me for finding those apes." Both entrapment and absurdity extend to the economic quicksand of middle-class American existence—as suggested by the bills (themselves protean in their reach) that had to be paid:

> doctors, dentists, groceries, department stores, car people, insurance freaks, oil and gas guys, telephone bills and bills from the yard man, bills for dirt bought and bushes planted, bills for bathing suits and Mexican food, for heat and cooling and air to breathe, for clothes, toys, makeup, bills for the state, the city, the nation, for the enterprise. So I paid the bills, no more no less, in my sea of little failures.

Saul Bellow brings a liberating absurdity to his view of the American work scene as Herzog recalls that, after a period of widespread unemployment, jobs finally appeared, "but somehow my consciousness remained unemployed." A job with unemployed consciousness is Bellow's version of work entrapment. Herzog goes on to reflect that as "one of the great forces of the universe," the human intellect "can't safely remain unused." He expresses a slyly mocking suspicion that "the boredom of so many human arrangements," notably those of middle-class family life, might have "the historical aim of freeing the intellect of newer generations, sending them into science." Bellow here is relating inauthentic work to lifeless living and, at the same time, playing with the idea of generational emergence from the bind.

Every aspect of protean restlessness, confusion, and combinatory possibility goes into the work experience. But work is crucial in its function of "making a living," a phrase that here includes not only the economic dimension, important as that is, but also the meaning and coherence of the life at issue.

## Protest and Change

*You never can stop. It's an ongoing thing that never ends.*

Andy H.

Proteanism does not necessarily mean protest or activism. One can be, like George R., politically or socially conservative while in many ways individually protean. But as has been apparent in the protests of many people described, the struggles and shifts within the individual self are likely to be associated with a sense that society, too, is changing or requires change.

Alfred F.'s vision, basic to his protest, is infused with a protean spirit: "The only thing I'm one hundred percent sure of . . . about the future is that it won't look like the present. . . . There's no such thing as a status quo. Change is natural to everything, to every . . . organism, to nature, to societies. . . . Change is constant. There's just no guarantee as to . . . where the change is headed." He went on to discuss the importance of the protestor's imagination: "In my mind I can imagine what would produce an immediate change," and further: "What I think is possible to accomplish and how things would change [is] what my activism is based on." He described having a certain detached theory about a "structural basis [to a] whole series of wrongs, [which provides] a general direction you'd like to see things go and that you believe things can go." But rather than hold strictly to any theory, "you move, and where openings occur, you step in": the activism itself "becomes part of your experience, . . . part of your learning, . . . your belief system"—that is, part of the ever-evolving self. One must then "absorb" what happens and "try to make sense of it," always keeping an equilibrium between "moral outrage" and a reasoned tactical approach that avoids "quick, emotional responses to events." As part of this care for the activist self, "you don't let [the struggle] eat you and you don't let it kill you." But Alfred admitted that he is not immune from violent feelings as part of "an animal instinct, call it revenge," which he works hard at limiting to a "quick fantasy" in order to maintain his psychic balance.

What troubles Alfred most ("makes me depressed more than what the governments do") is general apathy and acceptance of wrong policies, which give him the sense that "nothing's gonna change . . . no matter what we do. . . . More misery and more poverty and more death and more people being unhappy and more selfishness." The collective loss of energy and movement, that is, undermines his psychological equilibrium—his poise and equipoise—and leaves him with feelings of meaninglessness and personal stasis. But he overcomes these feelings by reasserting his combination of scholarship and activism and probing for what he believes to be "openings" to effective results. He returns always to his guiding principle: "My belief [that] people ultimately change . . . [and] things are ultimately gonna [be] change[d] by people." But the process is difficult: "Sometimes you wanna just shake people and say, . . . 'What's wrong with ya?'"

Rosalyn K. can maintain much of her protest energy by experiencing the humanity of social outcasts, such as the homeless, to the point of imagining herself in their situation: "There are too many people on the streets. You just have to work in a shelter and realize [when you talk to people] . . . how much you have in common with them. They're not some deranged, drug-addicted people. They have kids. . . . This could happen to me." She can then accuse herself of being "selfish" in clinging to her comparatively privileged life and not doing more for them. Rosalyn is also capable of fierce anger, as when the movement to prevent nuclear weapons from being brought into New York Harbor had, after enormous effort, achieved considerable success in paving the way for a referendum on the subject ("We turned the congressional delegation around!"), an unexpected judicial decision, on the basis of a technicality, removed the issue from the ballot. She and other protestors concluded bitterly that "democracy does not work." But rather than withdrawing, they dealt with their anger by mounting, on the day of the voting, a new demonstration in which protestors dressed as the Statue of Liberty, wearing stickers saying

"Democracy Denied," attempted to block the mayor of New York City from casting his ballot.

In a personal sense, Rosalyn was following a longstanding pattern of reasserting her activism as a way of "feeling more like a human being" and fighting off the "despair I feel at night." She is greatly helped by interpretive formulations made within her women's affinity group concerning much that she witnesses around her: "We really make the connection between violence . . . on an individual level and the global level, . . . [including] rape against our bodies, against our land, against our water, against our city and our resources, and against our people and our houses." As she and her colleagues continue to struggle and improvise, she is able to counter her fear that "you can sort of fool yourself that you're doing something [effective]" with a willed conviction both that "we do make a difference," and that even failures such as the canceled referendum represent "a tiny step" in the direction of positive change.

Andy H., after decades on the activist barricades, has come to an increasingly complex view of his and others' protest. As an example of moral paradox, he told of a revered woman activist, a person he and others thought of as a "true saint," who made a decision to accept an eighteen-year jail sentence rather than promise a judge she would not repeat her act of civil disobedience in a missile factory. But that decision, Andy believes, infuriated the friends and neighbors with whom she had left twelve adopted, disabled children. He was not being critical of her so much as insisting that we need to look at all sides of these issues because everyone is groping, "trying to get hold of something." He also came to realize that sudden, exciting reversals are possible. Thus, the events of the late 1960s and early 1970s especially moved him because "[in] the history of the United States and the world, everything was turned upside down." At the time, he now says sadly, "you really couldn't see that things would go back to what they've gone back to." From that reversion he learned the "terrible lesson" (as expressed in the section epigraph) that "you never can stop" and that the protest struggle is "an ongoing thing." Similarly, when he visited Cuba decades ago, he had been deeply impressed by many revolutionary developments there, including the training of "barefoot doctors" to help the peasants and the general sense of responsibility "to take care of your brothers and sisters." But he is reluctant to make a return visit because he knows that he would no longer find things to be that way. He comments philosophically, "Rather than the world being black and white—this is something I always knew it wasn't—it [is] . . . variously hued."

He ends up with a gentle and amorphously protean vision: "I can see somewhere along the line, it's going to be a spiritual awakening. . . . It's going to happen in a mysterious way because . . . it has to happen fast, . . . in a few generations, . . . if we're going to save ourselves. A new man and

118

THE PROTEAN SELF

a new woman [are] going to come along, and it's going to be one of the miracles we call penicillin or ... whatever, ... and it's going to happen to us, and we are going to save ourselves. Now that's one way I feel." But he is also aware of a more paradoxical sense: "I don't see there's any hope, and yet I have [an] enormous amount of hope. . . . This mystical thing that I don't believe in is going to do it. A change is going to happen."

Civic leaders can also have strong adversary feelings. But as they do not tend to engage in collective acts of public protest, those feelings can have difficulty finding expression. Both Michael W. and George R. asserted critical views from within the mainstream institutions they have served. Michael W. tried actively to make use of his institutions—the American State Department and various philanthropic foundations—in his opposition to injustice and militarism. His comment that "I was more of an antinuclear activist than I realized" suggests the weighting toward propriety that civic leaders' inner balance seems to require. In a parallel way, George R. is vehement about the criminal practices he has encountered within the world of nonprofit organizations. But rather than emerge as a public crusader on that or any other issue, he works hard and innovatively in ways that combat such crimes and establish new procedures that benefit the institutions concerned and the large numbers of people they serve.

Václav Havel defines the intellectual as one who engages in perpetual protest:

> I too think the intellectual should constantly disturb, should bear witness to the misery of the world, should be provocative by being independent, should rebel against all hidden and open pressure and manipulations, should be the chief doubter of systems, of power and its incantations, should be witness to their mendacity. For this reason, an intellectual cannot fit into any role that may be assigned to him. . . . An intellectual essentially doesn't belong anywhere; he stands out as an irritant wherever he is; he does not fit into any pigeonhole completely. . . . To a certain extent an intellectual is always condemned to defeat. He is like Sisyphus in that regard. . . . And yet in another, more profound sense the intellectual remains, despite all his defeats, undefeated—again like Sisyphus. He is in fact victorious through his defeats.

Havel's Sisyphean principle is consistent, as we have seen, with the feelings of several American activists. But Havel goes further in this sketch of the committed intellectual as not just Sisyphus struggling to push a boulder up a particular hill but a roving Sisyphus who has no hill of his own and is responsible for all hills and all boulders. It is an impossible requirement, one only Havel has perhaps truly undertaken, and one imaginable only in our protean century. To be sure, Havel's vantage point changed when he became president and ex-president of Czechoslovakia and president of the Czech Republic, but in his successes and failures he has by no means abandoned that model.

When Havel's imaginative flexibility enabled him to join forces with forms of protest very different from his own, such as Ivan Jirous's Czech rock group, he came to understand that the suppression of the Plastic People of the Universe's music would be even worse than the imprisonment of political dissidents: "It was . . . an attack by the totalitarian system on life itself, on the very essence of human freedom and integrity, . . . [on] young people who wanted to live in their own way, . . . make music they liked, . . . express themselves in a truthful way." Although Havel and Jirous were at first mutually suspicious, they were able, as they became friends and collaborators in protest, to learn from one another: Jirous, about public political commitment; and Havel, about moving beyond "the confines of 'established opposition'" to a broader experiential basis for resistance.

Rock musicians have a long history of protest in the United States, England, and elsewhere—witness the Beatles, the Rolling Stones, and Country Joe and the Fish in opposition to the Vietnam War. But these cannot approach the protest tones of subsequent "punk rock" groups. Johnny Rotten of the Sex Pistols has been seen as "something new in postwar popular culture: a voice that denied all social facts, and that in denial affirmed that everything was possible." For "the Sex Pistols were a commercial proposition and a cultural conspiracy, launched to change the music business and make money off the change—but Johnny Rotten sang to change the world." Rotten and the Sex Pistols were influenced, directly or indirectly, by Dada, surrealism, and various of their offshoots. Their lyrics spoke of Nazi camps and the Berlin Wall with music that "drags you into its absurdity and strands you there." During its brief life (after one year in the limelight in the mid-1970s, the group broke up with sensational "followup news [of] dissolution, murder, suicide"), its slogan was, "NO FUTURE," and its members seemed to wish to "put an end to the *dead time* that has dominated this century," and—like a group, known as "The Situationists," thought to have influenced them—to find a way to "*get out* of the twentieth century."

But as Havel and the American social activists know well, the only way to "get out" of the twentieth century is to preserve things into the twenty-first, to maintain that principle of the protean Sisyphus along with the recognition, expressed by Andy H., that the chaos in society and in people, as well as the need to confront it, "never ends."

# Chapter 7

## ENDURING CONNECTIONS

*People need to manufacture some structure in their lives.*

—Lucy G.

In THE MIDST of flux, the protean self seeks connections that last. These connections are expressed in intimate bonds with other people, in the life cycle, in larger links to history and nature, and in enduring ethical and religious principles. Yet these same sources of larger connectedness can be viewed as traps, as barriers to experimentation; they tend to be sought in ways that leave openings. More than that, claims to ultimate value or truth are themselves in disarray. Thus Don DeLillo both asks, "When the Old God leaves the world, what happens to all the unexpended faith?" and also answers: "When the Old God goes, they pray to flies and bottletops." DeLillo is telling us that principles of permanence and immortality are up for grabs, and best approached with elements of mockery and absurdity. Still, the hunger for such principles persists, the hope that (as Saul Bellow puts it) "you get one last chance to know justice. Truth."

Whatever the skepticism, the contemplation of these ultimate matters can be freer than ever. In Vladimir Nabokov's writings, for instance, "life and death are fascinatingly patterned phenomena, endlessly foldable and unfoldable, the beautiful variousness of nature: the thing-in-itself." Those "endlessly foldable and unfoldable" patterns can propel one in various directions, including that of larger human ties and a species mentality. There seems to be no gender distinction in the overall quest for such ties, but our interviews suggest that, to a degree, women seek them more consistently (though by no means without ambivalence) through relationships with other people, and men (also with frequent uncertainty) through relatively abstract symbolizations. But for all people in this era, connections that are both enduring and authentic become as elusive as they are necessary.

## Intimate Bonds

*I construct myself continually and I construct you, and you do the same. And the construction lasts as long as the material of our feelings doesn't crumble and as long as the cement of our will lasts.*

—Luigi Pirandello

The protean self guards against, but is attracted to, what Saul Bellow once called "potato love"—the steady, dependable, nurturing love that threatens suffocation in its very anchored and anchoring reliability. While this ambivalence is hardly new—indeed, it echoes sentiments, mostly suppressed, that are probably as old as the family—it is now overtly articulated and infused with newly intense fear of arrested motion.

Rosalyn K., for instance, is focused on personal ties but states, "I don't really see a family [for myself] necessarily. . . . That's not one of my goals." She fears that such a development in her life would be incompatible with her commitment to social activism, and points to examples of people she has known who were, like her, "very, very active" until, with new family ties, they came to see themselves as having "outgrown" that activism. She is also troubled by the idea of becoming a mother, because it means being "responsible for another life" rather than for the kinds of things she loves to do ("I paint banners, I do flyers") in her activist work. Yet she is also aware of the advantages of having a family in that it "forces you to be involved with local issues more," with "the neighborhood and your community." And she is, of course, especially admiring of those who combine loving family life with continuing activism.

Rosalyn's attitudes toward intimate bonds reflect her general tendency (frequent enough in the protean self) to experience emotionally both sides of any such equation. She speaks in glowing terms of her parents' loving relationship and of her early family life, conveying an impression of an idealized model she has constructed, one impossible for her to realize in her adult life. In any case, Rosalyn describes the ubiquitous divorces around her as "more of a reality." In her own sustained relationship with an older movement leader, "I really loved his kids, too," and "we were definitely a family." During this period, she had considerable happiness: "When you really love somebody, . . . you do start to care about yourself." The breakup caused her to experience disturbing feelings of loss ("Oh, God, it's awful! I'm without him, what can I do?") and what she described as a "deep" sense of loneliness. She further commented that in such situations, all one can do is "eat a lot of ice cream and . . . try to go out on dates," her uneasy laughter combining pain and gently affirmative self-mockery. Rosalyn does not seem to have an aversion to family life so much as a sense that love relationships, even "really good relationships, . . . these days . . . don't last that long," that "it just doesn't feel possible [for them] to last . . . more than a couple of years." That expectation, not entirely negative but surely limiting, becomes factored into Rosalyn's psychic admixture.

Alfred F. reveals a parallel ambivalence, along with less emphasis on intimate ties in general. His disdain for career includes retirement and "kids and grandkids." But in rejecting that package, he does not rule out all of its elements: "I always see myself as being involved in relationships, but . . . I may or may not have kids. I don't feel a drive . . . to bring up a family in the traditional sense, but I'm not against it. I just don't have feelings one way or the other." He may well be struggling with his limited capacity for precisely the "feelings" required in a sustained love relationship, and is clearly worrying about the possibility that family life would result in personal stagnation. He is uncertain about how a family could combine with his projected combination of academic and activist commitments, but keeps this possibility, like most others, open.

The protean self can undergo profound confusions in its intimate relationships and otherwise, over time, function well. Andy H., the elderly activist, was involved in his mid-twenties with a woman who became pregnant, frightening both of them. Despite his insistent revelations to her about his homosexuality and his "total unreliability as a partner," she rejected his suggestion of an abortion and insisted upon having the child. They then decided to get married, but he proceeded to live out his own confusions, went off at night with other men, and was rarely with her: "[The marriage] didn't work, and I had no intention of letting it work." She left, returned to the South to have her child, and initiated a divorce. Although he did not see his son for many years, he eventually formed a warm relationship with him. What disturbed Andy H., however, was a question his son asked that he never felt he could adequately answer: "Why did you two ever get married?"

In connection with that question, he spoke of "my ambiguity about things to be" and "a refusal to face certain things." That ambiguity is strong concerning his sexuality in general: "I never think of myself as being homosexual. I never think of myself as being bisexual. I think of myself as being unresolved." He is drawn to an observation of the art historian Bernard Berenson who described having lived his life as a heterosexual but (in Andy's remembered version) "in his old age found young men, babies, roses, young women, everything as equally attractive." Andy H. has had sexual relationships, over the years, with both women and men, but has been with a male partner for three decades. He states that, with the help of psychotherapy, he gradually "liberated myself" from much of his sexual ambiguity. But clearly not all: here, as in all other areas, he thrives on seeing life as "full of questions that don't have answers to them."

George R. exemplifies a very different tendency to remain committed to intimate family ties, but also manifests restlessness and ambivalence. His family is clearly an anchor for him, and we recall his profound fear of any family breakup. At the same time, he chooses to travel extensively, knowing that it strains his family bonds and makes him feel remiss in maintaining his part of them. His immersion in "potato love" seems to outweigh his sense of being trapped by it. Both sides of the potato, so to speak, are necessary to his version of protean creativity.

Lucy G., an unmarried foundation executive in her early sixties, spoke of a familial network including both relatives and nonrelatives: "I have a youngster [a younger friend] who is now in her thirties, who's very close to me, and her daughters. Her baby is my godchild. . . . People make up families if they don't have them. . . . I've always had extended families." She further commented (as in the chapter epigraph), "People need to manufacture some structure in their lives."

Intimate bonds can be complicated by uncertainty about expectations and assumed rules, resulting in ad-hoc attitudes and behavior. Those problems are perhaps most glaring in contemporary parent–child relationships, as burlesqued by Frederick Barthelme in describing a scene between a forty-year-old father and his ten-year-old son. The father is apologetic about having bought radio-controlled toy cars for himself without inviting his son to play with them, and the son reassures him, "That's O.K., Dad. . . . I've got my stuff and you've got your stuff. That's the way it is. That's the way it's supposed to be, isn't it?" The father replies, "I guess so. I don't know, really, how it's supposed to be, I mean. I don't think anybody knows how it's supposed to be. You know what I mean? I mean, it's just a certain way, and that's how it's supposed to be. Between fathers and sons, I mean." To which the son replies, "Yeah. That's what they say on TV."

That same father also muses on the subject of male sexual restlessness: "Let's face it, a new woman stands for a new life, that's why men are always after them." A question for the protean self is whether the "new life" is a temporary manifestation of a serial quest or something more enduring. For strong involvement, as F. Scott Fitzgerald's Jay Gatsby surmised, can threaten the protean process: "He knew when he kissed this girl, and forever wed his unutterable visions to her perishable breath, his mind would never romp again like the mind of God."

Saul Bellow usefully mocks this male-revival-via-woman theme when he has Herzog settle into a highly erotic affair "at least until such time as the new life that is being offered to him starts to feel like a form of bondage." In the same spirit, Herzog expresses the conflict (an old one, but exacerbated in our time) between private erotic pleasure and larger moral endeavor: "What am I doing hanging around with all these women? Isn't there something better, more productive, more valuable to the larger public world, that I should be putting my time into?" Bellow goes on, through Herzog, to raise various questions about maleness and its susceptibility to female influence. Herzog suffers from what Bellow himself once called "the persistent American feeling that the intellectual life is somehow not virile," that "artists and professors like clergymen and librarians, are thought to be female." Yet Herzog values certain "feminine" qualities in himself, feels he has inherited his mother's "good heart [and] . . . gentle spirit," and clings to principles of love and feeling as opposed to cynical "Reality Instructors around him." While both devaluing and valuing women, Herzog enables Bellow to anticipate recent inclinations, especially in America, toward expanding the sense of maleness to include gentleness and open expression of tender emotions. Characteristically for himself and for proteanism, Herzog is emotionally all over the place in his struggle to achieve the virtually impossible combination of sustained sexual love and intimacy, on the one hand, and continuous experimentation on behalf of renewal, on the other.

## Life Cycle

*Humans have a capacity for change across the entire life span.*

—Orville Brim and Jerome Kagan

However protean a self, it must come to terms with the life cycle. The physical and psychological person must move through childhood dependency to puberty and adolescence, through adult responsibility to old age and death. But, as I have emphasized, these psychobiological universals can be stretched, rendered less determinitive and more psychologically negotiable. The protean self presses the limits of the life cycle, looks for ways of surmounting its constraints. Along the way, it must confront death, the most irreducible of life-cycle stages; and even there, it has various modes of attempted transcendence. Recent psychological work, itself emerging from our protean times, substantiates this view of the life cycle. Two leading developmental psychologists, Orville Brim and Jerome Kagan, reject the traditional psychoanalytic assumption that experiences of early childhood determine and "constrain" what happens in adolescence and adulthood; insist that significant growth and change occur "from birth to death"; and that what happens in early life can be "transformed" by later experience in ways that render the entire life cycle more open than has been assumed.

This openness of the life cycle was evident in many people interviewed for this study. The series of crucial shifts Carol C., for instance, made during her early thirties (changing from speech therapist to artist, moving to a different city, publicly acknowledging her lesbianism) had surely been influenced by her earlier life but were in no way narrowly prefigured by it. She still claims considerable leeway in further evolution of her sense of self as she moves through middle life.

Yet, as Michael W. makes clear, much that one does and feels in relation to living and dying has to do with where one is in the life cycle. Looking back on his Second World War experience when his ship was torpedoed and sunk, he reflects on the capacity of very young men to call upon useful psychic numbing that excludes the idea of death: "If I ever have to go to war again, I want to go only with a crew of seventeen- and eighteen-year-olds and I only want to be twenty-one, . . . it is only three things, . . . unawareness, ignorance, . . . inexperience, . . . maybe a fourth one, a lack of imagination, that enables you to survive in a war situation. . . . Because if I had . . . the imagination or the sensitivity or the intelligence or whatever the hell to imagine what it would be like when one of those torpedoes really went off, I suppose I would have had a total complete psychological breakdown. . . . But I was so dumb and unaware that . . . I suppose . . . people like me were brave and functional through all kinds of battle situations."

Yet the deaths he witnessed during this wartime experience and subsequently in Hiroshima remained in a sense removed from his own ongoing existence: "I think death didn't really come into my life until my mother and my sister died. And I was by that time in my thirties or forties . . . [when] death as a reality, as something that you know directly, touched me." He was later to become an astute observer of death-related issues: "In American culture, . . . we kind of keep it back, a little bit out of the line of sight." While helping people to set up foundations, he has observed, "Several of these fellows, . . . I think, honestly felt they were eternal . . . because they never could face the matter of making decisions that implied or were premised on the fact that they were not going to be around after a while." He went on to observe that "from the . . . angle of vision that I have on these things, [death] is the constant third-party participant in the conversations that I have. It is there . . . looking at him [the person setting up a foundation in his will]. . . . It affects, either positively or negatively, everything that he says and everything he does, consciously or unconsciously. . . . It is a palpable factor in these situations." Michael W.'s protean imagination enters actively into this evolving relationship to death: in his capacity to step back and reflect on his own behavior, on American cultural attitudes toward death, and on death as a "third party" in his professional relationships with philanthropists.

Andy H. suggests another pattern, a sense of self that remains bound to youthfulness and the young themselves. Reminiscing at the age of seventy-six about the events of a long and complex life, he spoke animatedly about his young adult years as a bohemian pacifist. He saw beauty in the subsequent rebellion of the young during the late 1960s and early 1970s—so much so that he joined it: "I was probably the oldest person at Woodstock!" (He was in his late fifties.) He has been cutting down on his work over the past few years, recognizing that he is getting old; that although "I'm still not decaying, . . . it's going to happen"; and that to fail to cut down would mean being "complicit in your own death, . . . party to my own murder." But equally important is his feeling that "I don't want to be complicit in the madness of the old who dominate," meaning that one has a duty to give way to the young.

The life-cycle patterns of Carol C., Michael W., and Andy H. include moments of radical decentering of the self, of suspension of its existing integration in order to open out to new influences which alter that integration. There can be an inner shuffling of emotional emphases, of proximate and ultimate levels, and of images of past and future. Radical decentering can enhance protean defiance of the life cycle. The literary critic Terry Eagleton refers to such decentering in another context as "revenants and redoublings, loops of time which leave you lagging behind or out ahead of yourself," and may produce an "ontological vertigo" but can also be the source of a "bolder, more recklessly exposed imaginative reach." Though describing the work of a British poet, Eagleton was also talking about the life-cycle-related struggles of the protean self. (That the poet's name was Andrew Motion seems somehow more than coincidence.)

## Ethics, Spirituality, and Ultimate Concern

*I suppose I could still say I believe in God, but . . . I think there are
ways of explaining . . . the conditions of human existence with an
infinite variety of stories.*

—Francine C.

The protean self seeks ethical commitment, whatever the difficulty in
finding and sustaining it. People we interviewed could find lasting commitment in improvised forms of spirituality as well as in family and generational sequence; and, in the case of social activists, in maintaining the
planet and its inhabitants by opposing nuclear weapons and war making
and by embracing principles of ecology, pacifism, and justice. In its aversion to dogma, the protean self tends to settle for a pluralistic spirituality
that allows for doubt and uncertainty and includes a stress on personal
responsibility. Lasting commitment brings one to larger human connectedness or symbolic immortality, but that ultimate dimension, too, has its
ebbs and flows.

Andy H. exemplifies those ebbs and flows in connection with a secular
spirituality derived from many sources. Despite his rebellion from his
parents' Catholicism, which he associated with intolerance, rigidity, the
Inquisition, and Dante's *Inferno*, it contributed considerably to his subsequent spiritual inclinations. At the age of twenty-four, just after America's
entry into the Second World War, Andy was on a hilltop near the ocean
and had a mystical experience during which he realized, "I'm not going
to die"; he experienced at that moment a sense of himself, both troubling and liberating, as "an outcast [with] . . . no debt to pay to society."
(As it turned out, his homosexuality prevented him from being drafted.)
More than a decade later, he took LSD on a few occasions and experienced "the absolute gloriousness of the life we lead and our blindness to
see it"; and when walking through Central Park, felt the seals "singing
their songs and whispering to me." These LSD experiences contributed
to his emerging spiritual commitment to pacifism and to the view that
"crappy as life can be, . . . [it] can be so marvelous. Everyone has a right
to stay alive. You have no right to kill anybody else or be killed." He
became clear in his view that war making is an example of the "incredible
arrogance of the rich and powerful sending in the young and the helpless to do their dirty work for them," and drew sustenance from the poet
Edna St. Vincent Millay's famous line, "I shall die but that is all I will do
for death." To his continuing opposition to those who contribute to
potential nuclear holocaust or environmental destruction, he brings an
affirmation of the great chain of being: "They know what I know. Their
grandchildren are as vulnerable as my grandchildren."

128                                      THE PROTEAN SELF

Reflecting on the experience of the spaceship *Voyager* "not finding anything out there," he spoke of the "enormous feeling of being alone, . . . that God had indeed abandoned us, and that somehow or other we cannot live the lives we're leading without killing ourselves." He added, "God abandoned me very, very early on." Here Andy H. was articulating a sense of spiritual loss common to the protean self, though often inchoate. Andy prefers to identify himself as agnostic rather than atheist because, as always, it is for him "terribly important to be able to live without an answer."

But he has sustained his fierce social conscience from young adulthood through old age. He remains appalled that the physicists, in making our first atomic bomb, thought that there was a chance they would ignite the atmosphere and destroy much of the world: "But they went ahead and did it anyway." His outrage at human destructiveness is fueled by images from the Battle of Marne in the First World War: "a million men killed within six weeks, . . . sloughing along in the dirt with the stench of human beings, and it went on and on, and people went out and sold bonbons and sang pretty songs about raising money to kill more people." Reading about that war contributed to his deep distrust of governments and his evolving philosophical anarchism: "You could trust in yourself. . . . You've got to do it on your own. You are responsible, and only you are responsible, and you can betray yourself. You must somehow learn not to." He associated that commitment to autonomous individual responsibility with reading Nietzsche and being deeply impressed by "the right to commit suicide, the last [act of] free will"; but, he added, "I'm also free not to kill myself."

Equally fiercely, Andy H. insists on hope. Though angered by a friend who—in saying, "It would be fun to hang around to see the end of the world after the bomb went off"—seemed to take lightly the self-extinction of our species, Andy also realizes that the friend was expressing "the flip side that all of us have of dealing with that possible situation." He prefers a more dialectical, and perhaps mystical, sense: "It's going to happen, but we must not allow it to happen." His connectedness and social conscience extend even beyond humanity. He told of a recurrent dream of nuclear holocaust in which he wanders to the Central Park Zoo and releases the tigers and snakes, even though it is likely that he will be killed by them. Indeed, in Andy's postnuclear holocaust image of ultimate desolation, "there's no people on the earth, . . . no animals." But he added, with cautious intensity, "I suppose the earth will heal itself and eventually will come [to live] again. I suppose that's my sense of immortality." That sense of immortality has to do with his ties both to the planet and all its forms of life and to his own family-centered, biological chain: a vision he has, which he knows is not literally true, that, even in total destruction, his grandchildren are "exempt from it in some mysterious way," especially the youngest one, who is "the perfect golden child."

Francine C. also considers herself an agnostic. When asked about her religious beliefs, she replied: "I really don't know. . . . In my work I have . . . spent time with Buddhist monks from Sri Lanka, . . . so I'm very familiar with systems of belief, and I just cannot give one system of belief more credence than another system of belief." That attitude is consistent with a hesitant belief in God along with her insistence on the "infinite variety of stories" that explain the conditions of human existence. But although she insists that she does not adhere to any one of these stories, her spiritual plurality is anchored in the clarity of her Jewish identity: "Historically I identify with the Jews. . . . I would never become anything else."

Michael W. developed his secular ethics in rather even fashion. Recognizing the dangers posed by fascism in general and Nazism in particular, he altered his prior opposition to all war and, despite the opportunity for a deferment, enlisted to fight in the Second World War. As his retained images of combat and of Hiroshima energized his lifelong opposition to war making and militarism, he extended that ethic in every conceivable direction—to compassion for "more than twenty thousand crippled children" in Angola maimed by bombs the United States supplied to the rebels there, to disdain for decision makers who are "lost in the depths of technocracy" in their lethal nuclear scenarios, to insistence upon "a humane and moral component" of political action in general. Indeed, the protean reach of his conscience subjects him to perpetual unease. He bemoans our society's "demotion of . . . humane values and . . . elevation of the role of purely the market and material things," and hopes "that I have enough time to swing back some of that." He speaks of Hiroshima and Auschwitz as "having this connection that they are human calamities of a scale . . . you can't grasp," especially in terms of their "implications for human society and human survival." He, too, personalizes his commitment to the larger continuity of life, wondering "what kind of world . . . we're going to hand over to the next generation," and whether what we leave it will "make it possible for that generation to cope with its own problems." He revealed his concern about his personal role in the enterprise when he asked me to send him a copy of the transcripts of our interviews so that "my grandchildren would have a record of my life." For him the end of the cold war meant not only "the end of the Black Death" but the beginning of his ability to "think of my daughter and granddaughter with a more hopeful feeling and a more hopeful world."

Edward G. identifies the atomic bomb as a powerful source of his lifelong activism. As a teenager, he had read a Ripley's "Believe It or Not" cartoon describing an explosive "so powerful that one pound would destroy the entire city of London." As soon as he heard about the atomic bomb, he knew it was the bomb he had read about; he felt "exhilarated by it" because "the war was ending"—a response typical at the time, although one he now views as "indeed . . . strange." (We recall his subsequent dreams about atomic bombs and buildings collapsing to the "molecular level," and his impassioned high school graduation speech warning against such weapons.) During the Cuban missile crisis of 1962, he responded with "absolute terror" and a feeling of being "paralyzed that whole week [as] . . . I sat there near the window waiting for the flash of light during that . . . insane crisis." But not so paralyzed as to prevent him from organizing, with others, a large demonstration against any use of the weapons, or from participating in a joyous party with his friends to celebrate the end of the crisis. He sees fear of the bomb as having shaped much of American social behavior and literary expression: "If you want to know the origins of the Beat generation,* look at the atomic bomb, look at the end of the world. What is Ginsberg writing about, . . . Kerouac writing about, except . . . the existentialism of a world in which tomorrow suddenly becomes optional."

Edward G. combines this nuclear-weapons–centered commitment to the human future with a mystical view about individual death. After a peyote experience (during which he was convinced he was dying [see page 63]), he felt at the same time "extraordinary, . . . profound, boundless, . . . marvelous"; he decided to change his life, cease to be a slave of "all the meaningless [peace] meetings, the meetings and meetings and meetings, and the minutes and minutes," and began instead to be more reflective about his pacifism and social activism and to open himself more to the world and its complexities. He came to look upon death as "leaving this room for something else altogether," so that "if [people] die young, they die because they've chosen to leave this room." And more generally, "if the [human] race dies young, and we're very young, it will be because we've not been able to fulfill the extraordinary promise of perhaps being the only group like us." (In coming to look upon dying as "dissolving like a sugar cube in water," he would thereby become part of something larger than himself.) But while remaining focused on the nuclear threat to human continuity and on the metaphysics of individual death, Edward G.'s impulse in practice is to discuss such matters only "for a limited period of time": "Then I want to get on with what it is we're going to do."

Other activists have different expressions of lasting ethical commitment. Rosalyn K. sees it in terms of a basic definition of humanity: "It's important for people to be active in things that matter, . . . to take responsibility [because] that's what a human being is." And: "You have to

---

*The literary movement of the 1950s and 1960s that saw itself as radically alienated from American society and the Western cultural tradition in general. The novelist Jack Kerouac was its scribe, and the poet Allen Ginsberg an active participant (see pages 42–43).

fight against mortality [or] . . . why bother living, . . . whether it's your own death, or society's death, or injustice." In all this, she functions from doubt and from "as if": "You have to pretend there's some order, . . . [that] something makes sense and [then] work toward it."

Ken F., although seeing himself as a "free-lance peace activist," stresses the importance of "being around for a long time"—that is, of sustaining one's commitment. Alfred F. came to focus on principles of empathy, even toward adversaries, as illustrated by a set of feelings he experienced at a large demonstration when he heard a captain in the National Guard stutter as he yelled at the demonstrators: "I realized at that point it's a very human thing to hear someone stutter. It's a frailty, and you realize when he doesn't have his uniform on people probably make fun of him. I mean these are quick things that go through your head. It really humanized the situation very much, and I really felt sorry for him. . . . He's a captain in the National Guard, but he stutters." That kind of "humanization" enabled Alfred to connect his protest to species consciousness (see chapter 11). The same is true of Andy H.'s concern about his adversaries' grandchildren and of Carol C.'s sustained opposition to all who torture or cause others to suffer.

## A Sense of History

*The most dangerous of all the lies we are fed in our lives [is] . . . the idea of the continuum.*

—Salman Rushdie

History records the flow or movement of events and experiences. It includes, in a contemporary view, "moments that seem to leave nothing behind, nothing but the mystery of spectral connections between people long separated by place and time, but somehow speaking the same language." This is a view of history as a context for proteanism. That restless context also includes a sense of all the unsettled debts of history that may come "back into play." In the twentieth century, many of those debts are inevitably violent.

But whether violent or not, these historical "debts" epitomize more general discontinuities. One should be wary of any claim of order (that it all "adds up"), "continuum," or of homogeneity: "The world is incompatible, just never forget it: gaga. Ghosts, Nazis, saints, all alive at the same time; in one spot, blissful happiness, while down the road, the inferno. You can't ask for a wilder place." Rushdie tells us that in our century "[h]istory stopped paying attention to the old psychological orientation of reality," so that "character isn't destiny any more. Economics is destiny. Ideology is destiny. Bombs are destiny. What does a famine, a gas chamber, a grenade care how you lived your life? Crisis comes, death comes, and your pathetic individual self doesn't have a thing to do with it, only to suffer the effects."

But Bharati Mukherjee sees history as protective, as (in the eyes of one of her characters) "a net, the kind of safety net travelling trapeze artists of her childhood fell into when they were inattentive, or clumsy." Somehow, she implies, this amorphous constellation of human connections will rescue us from personal collapse and prop us up once more. But whether as blind and relentlessly destructive force or reliable safety net, history is perceived as there in our lives, as not far away from us. We experience ourselves as permeated by historical events.

Michael W. is especially likely to invoke the currents of history in connection with his individual life—the Depression years, the Second World War, Hiroshima, the American role in European recovery from the Second World War, the cold war and nuclear threat, recent wars and conflicts throughout the world, and America's faltering leadership during recent decades. He speaks of himself as a "broken-hearted liberal" who has profound doubts about his country's capacity to cope with "its own deepest problems." And he is thinking historically when he states that America "just isn't living up to what it seems to me it reasonably could and should be expected to perform." He looks back to an era when "at least it seems to me there was an American life in the years when I was old enough to vote and young enough to have a little energy." In contrast, he sees a contemporary society "in which politics has passed on into a realm of fantasy and image making." He is aware of historical upheaval and future danger, seeing in the international events of the late 1980s and early 1990s "a set of changes [so] rapid and profound" that they contain "the possibility of enormous disintegration in the world, . . . [in which] the worst scenario would be that three or four years out, we have a world in the southern hemisphere really ablaze with civil wars and instabilities, and then those damned nuclear weapons . . . at least in some degree available." Yet he can also see, in historical flux, the ever-present possibility of renewal, as with the end of the cold war and with the revival of the human spirit in suppressed Chinese artists (see page 52).

Andy H. also saw himself as being in the thick of powerful historical forces, specifically of dramatic social change: "Oh, I was very excited by the early 1970s, late 1960s. Nineteen hundred and sixty-eight, you know, was an extraordinary year. . . . I used to think it was worth getting up in the morning." Not only was "everything . . . turned upside down" in the United States and the world, but one was *conscious* of these historical shifts: "It's really quite extraordinary to get into the awareness. I was so glad that I was aware that I was in the [historical] moment." A conclusion for him is that, given the historical flux and unpredictability, "nothing, *nothing*, was impossible."

History was personally liberating to Andy but eventually problematic. Traveling around the world as a photographer, he was "dazzled" by the array of interesting people he met, and drawn especially to Jews because of a "mysticism" he has experienced toward them as "the savior[s] who liberate . . . us from the restrictions of the world" as imposed narrowly and coercively during his childhood and "from the horror of the life that was laid out for me." When Jews were being murdered in vast numbers by Hitler, Andy had to struggle with the relevance of his attraction to pacifism. He was later to be troubled by a reversal of his sense of historical developments in Cuba, first moved by the revolution and its vision of a "new man," and then appalled by "the horrors of the concentration camps . . . and what they've done to homosexuals and how they threw their intellectuals out." But in the end, he reasserts his pacifism and sees in the flow of history the hope "that . . . life is going to go on, that we have resources, that we have love, a lust for life, an eagerness to stay here and wait for next spring."

Alfred F. told us, "Since I was probably twelve [I have] considered myself a radical," suggesting that from that age he has felt himself part of a historical process. Though he added, "I didn't fully understand why until I got older"—that is, his later explanation to himself had to do with his understanding of the historical process in which he found himself. As a younger activist, he experienced the "height and tail" of the anti–Vietnam War movement; and during the 1970s, he encountered important currents of feminism, pacifism, and opposition to nuclear weapons and to nuclear power, currents bound up with his sense of history. Rosalyn K. experienced a similar sense of historical connection to the Three Mile Island nuclear accident in 1979 while still a college student. "Rosalyn, you just can't sit here," she remembers thinking. "You have to do something." And in that way she came to define an adult as "someone who just takes responsibility in this world"—responsibility, that is, to affect important historical developments: "I just couldn't think of the world's events as having nothing to do with me."

The collective human narrative seems no more predictable than the individual one. Or as Isaiah Berlin more reservedly puts the matter, there is "no reason to see history as an autobahn from which major deviations cannot occur." History itself, it would seem, provides much of the protean constellation—ever threatening, ever confusing in its shifts and juxtapositions, ever a possible source of new combinations.

## Self and Planet

*There's a little struggle going on all the time as to whether we're going to survive or just fry ourselves and I think it's a collective struggle.*

—Edward G.

Widespread awareness of our capacity to destroy our planet, whether through weapons or environmental poisons, has, for many people, become inseparable from stronger planetary identification. More often than not, ecological concern merges with nuclear threat. Edward G.'s declaration of the collective struggle "as to whether we're going to survive or just fry ourselves" is an example of that merging. In connection with that struggle, he spoke of avoiding "a very earth-centered position" and considering "the enormity of the galaxy and the conditions that lead to life." He spoke bitterly of the "poisons" we release in our environment; then insisted that, as human beings, "our consciousness . . . makes it possible for us to see one future [self-destruction] and to substitute an alternative future for it," but cautioned, "We haven't done that yet."

Morris A., a prominent journalist and political conservative, told me that until recently he was disdainful of environmentalism as a kind of "sixties . . . preening," a form of "political faddism" associated with "the Abbie Hoffmans of the world and all that." His mind changed when he was "rocked" by seeing a strip mine in West Virginia, and by such events as Chernobyl and the chemical disaster at Bhopal, as well as by his awareness, as a New Yorker, that "I'm living in the greatest environmental disaster in many ways, which is the modern city." He went on to say, "You can't breathe. . . . There's filth in the streets. . . . And where people attack each other, . . . beat each other up, mug each other, [it is] partly out of environmental reasons. You can't tell me that housing has nothing to do with mugging." His "worst case" environmental image is contemporary Ankara, where the pollution was so extreme that his newspaper had to close its bureau because it "couldn't get anybody to go there." At first aloof from ecological issues, Morris came to involve himself increasingly in them as central, in his changing judgment, to all human problems.

Andy H. likens people's callousness in destroying the earth to carelessness with one's own body: "It's like the smoker. He knows probably better than I know that smoking is going to kill him, but I'll have one more cigarette before I go on the wagon." He spoke of radioactive material that "we're burying . . . everywhere with no thought of what's going to happen"; contemplated the State of Massachusetts becoming "a nuclear wasteland"; and went on to talk of "the poisoning of the earth" as resem-

bling "choking emphysema, . . . slow death," describing how his grandmother died of that disease and "just choked to death . . . the way the
earth is just going to choke to death." By making use of this kind of
imagery, Andy, though seeming to refer to others, conveyed his own bodily involvement in the earth's continuing health and threatened destruction.

Rosalyn K. is, as we know, the opposite of a nature lover and feels
"safer in cities." This does not mean that she feels fully secure in Philadelphia or New York City, as she has read that they are "on a fault line" and
could be susceptible to a destructive earthquake. But she got a sense of
the precariousness of any environment when, in a demonstration against
nuclear weapons at the Nevada test site, she was profoundly struck by the
contradiction between the exquisiteness of the locale and the destructive
activity performed there: "We were standing in just a vast desert—a beautiful, beautiful desert. And this idea that this was a *test* site for nuclear
weapons was just . . . repulsive. You know, you really . . . saw life in danger." Her identification with the planet, that is, transcends her personal
quirks about country and city.

For the "decentralized" protean self, the "unity of consciousness" that
William James once spoke of is a necessary, but never fully attainable,
ideal. Both one's sense of self and one's perception of the world around
one are ever subject to modification or even reversal.

Michael W. was struck by this phenomenon, which can be called the
"open-ended protean surprise," not only in sudden historical shifts but in
behavior he observed in the death encounter of military combat: "A couple of the toughest, oldest, loudest, if not bravest, guys in the ship turned
absolutely to stone or to jelly in a crisis, and a mild little guy from Boston
that was my bunkmate—a very gentle, quiet man—turned out to be an
unbelievable hero. . . . So what the human performance is under stress is
very unpredictable." Andy H. went further in his insistence on the virtues
of protean openness: "The only way you can love one another is without
answers. The only way to help one another is without answers." He
offered a kind of protean credo: "I don't want to manufacture answers
for things that there are not answers to. I want to be able to live my life in
ignorance and in innocence, whatever those words are that say I don't
know, and I can't know, and it's wrong to know." Worse than that: "It's . . .
arrogant to supply answers for other people."

# Chapter 8

## LIFE STORIES

*I tested those waters [because] I was looking for waters.*

—Barbara C.

Pᴿᴏᴛᴇᴀɴ ᴘᴀᴛᴛᴇʀɴꜱ best reveal themselves over the course of entire lives. In this chapter, I examine the life stories of three very different people: a distinguished male lawyer and world leader in human rights, a sensitive young Christian woman in transition; and an elderly, multitalented black male artist. I interviewed the lawyer and the young woman—Arthur M. and Barbara C.—as part of general research on the American self, while the black artist—Gordon Parks—has offered his own compelling narrative in a published autobiography. All three lives are characterized by struggle, search, and achievement; by formidable early trauma that is transformed into insight and vitality; and by accomplishment viewed as part of a journey.

### "I TOLD MYSELF STORIES": JUDGE ARTHUR M.

I knew Arthur M. to be a successful lawyer, a former judge, and a tireless and innovative leader of legal groups advocating human rights. Going to interview him in the comfortable, well-furnished suite of his prominent Boston law firm, I found a heavy-set, energetic man, who seemed younger than his seventy years. He told me that he enjoys the practice of law, but spoke more animatedly of what he described as "my favorite single form of activity" and "main extracurricular activity," his constant pursuit of new approaches to enhance international human rights. But I was not prepared for certain details of his earlier life.

He first referred to his Chicago background as "fairly unpropitious, ... a family that never read books, a strange Jewish family, ... an ugly, lower-depths, empty kind of family." He remembered his father as "a brutal, ... really quite horrible man, ... not certifiable but ... pretty crazy," a man who, constantly and viciously, beat the other three family members—Arthur's mother, his younger sister, and Arthur himself. Though his father earned a reasonable living as a salesman, he spent most of his money on his own pleasures—mainly other women: "We grew up like poor kids, very poor kids." His mother seemed a perpetual victim, inadequate and helpless in the face of her husband's cruelty. When Arthur was ten, his father "physically threw my mother out," and obtained a divorce settlement giving him custody of the children. Arthur and his sister experienced a "quite horrible" separation from their mother and had no contact with her until, six years later, "she screwed up the courage to get a court order to allow her to visit [periodically] with her son and daughter." When Arthur was sixteen, his father gave him a particularly brutal beating, "at the end of which I left" to live with his mother in her small furnished room. He spoke to his father only two times after that: once in person when his father brought Arthur's younger sister, "whom he had quite effectively destroyed," to live with him and his mother; the other time, decades later, by telephone, when his father called him "out of the blue" to request that his son use his influence to help him get into a certain hospital: "I was not displeased to say that I didn't have that kind of influence, and could not." He added, "I'm occasionally embarrassed, though not terribly upset, to realize I don't know when he died."

I listened to this story with some awe. I had no difficulty believing Judge M.'s factual account—his controlled, understated tone was utterly convincing. But I found it hard to reconcile this poised, accomplished, and compassionate man who, in his maturity, seemed at one with his elegant professional setting, with the abused and humiliated child he had described. The compelling question that took shape in my mind was, How had he accomplished this transformation?

When I asked him how he managed to survive during his ugly childhood, he answered, "I told myself stories." He not only imagined alternative worlds but, as one who "always wrote pretty well and was quite verbal," put them down on paper. In junior high school, he began to write "creative adventure stories" as well as "little sketches" and observations. Together with a friend, he wrote an ambitious series for the school paper entitled "Adventures of a Foreign Correspondent," in which, in 1937, "we predicted the downfall of Hitler ... and ... a second world war." Although many details turned out to be inaccurate, "that kind of thing was of great solace to me"—all the more so perhaps because of some unconscious association between Hitler and Arthur's brutal father. And although his family "never read books" ("If I got caught reading a book at home, my father . . . would start beating me"), he began to read widely. The Frank Merriwell adventure stories especially became "a big part" of his life and contributed further to his imaginative transcendence of his immediate environment.

Also, his father's frequent absences provided "periods of relative freedom": "He was off doing his thing, and I doing mine." Arthur's thing included great "pleasure in play"—the "standard street sports" of touch football, softball, and handball, in which he and other boys of his age were passionately involved. Above all, Arthur had extraordinary intellectual ability and was a brilliant student from the beginning, so that "school was a kind of refuge for me," and "here and there a teacher would take some interest in me," providing another "solace." In these various ways, he created an alternative personal narrative almost as absorbing and fulfilling as his family life was painful and humiliating.

Still, the actuality of his life took its toll. Graduating from high school at the age of sixteen while living with a mother he considered incapable of taking care of him, he felt "utterly defeated," without prospects of any kind, was frequently depressed, and at times thought of suicide. Having "always imagined that I would go to college [since] . . . people around me talked as though I would . . . because that was what one did," he made an inquiry to a tuition-free college but was told he was ineligible because he lived just outside the Chicago city limits. He felt "rebuffed" and lacking in "the initiative to [find] some way [to] go to college": "I sort of caved in" and spent an unpleasant year in a government program for jobless young men "feeling sorry for myself"; and after that, "another wretched year" of manual labor, "pushing handtrucks" in a stockroom. After that, however, he experienced a series of what he called "rescue things" that changed his life.

The first took the form of a vague suggestion by a family member who lived near the center of the city: "I don't know what the hell would have happened had there not been this uncle that I never loved very much who said casually, 'Why don't you use my address and apply to the college?'" Entering college at the age of nineteen, "an utterly ignorant smart boy" who "talked exactly like the Dead End Kids," he encountered a dedicated speech teacher ("Bless her memory!") who "said that I needed a lot of work, and she was so right." Then an English teacher "said one of the memorable things of my life," telling Arthur, "You're one of the only two or three people I would ever have advised to try making a career as writers." Although Arthur did not do that, "I spent a lot of time writing for him in his creative writing class [and] for whatever college publications there were." Still another "rescue thing" was the initiative taken by another professor, when Arthur was drafted after three years of college, in making special arrangements for him to gain credits for portions of his military experience and obtain a degree with honors in economics despite his having taken virtually no courses in that discipline. (Arthur had attempted to enlist in the air cadets the day after Pearl Harbor, had his acceptance illegally reversed by an officer angered by his decision to take his final examinations prior to reporting to duty in order not to lose a year of credit, but then served respectably in the army without seeing combat but obtaining valuable life experience.)

In describing these steps, and later ones as well, Judge M. used words like "accidental" and "sheer luck," seeing himself as more or less passively carried along by others. Thus, as he tells it, upon returning from military service, he tried some graduate work, which did not appeal to him, and then encountered a classmate who was signing up for law school; despite having "never given a thought about being a lawyer," Arthur, too, signed up and "sort of flopped into law school." Or, as he summed things up: "I staggered into college and then into the army and then into law school." And even his appointment to the federal court many years later occurred, as he told it, because the attorney general "happened to read an article of mine that he liked."

But further discussion revealed that Arthur excelled at college, "loved the academic world and the people in it," and could "picture myself becoming one of them"; that he was a brilliant law student and graduated first in his class; that he was recognized as an accomplished legal mind when serving in an elite government unit; that he also did outstanding work in subsequent private law practice, and, when given a professorship at his law school, was viewed as an excellent teacher whose writings were greatly respected; and that he was subsequently considered a highly capable and fair-minded federal judge.

Arthur M. recognizes this "discrepancy between my sense of myself and my [actual] self, because I always come out of these situations." He contrasts his experiences with those of his younger sister, who was of no more than average intelligence, "had less equipment" to deal with their father, and became "a more likely product of the way we were brought up," doing relatively menial work and living "in really wretched circumstances." While he stresses the "accidents" that saved him from the same fate, he also concedes something to his own abilities: "I figure if I live another ten or twenty years, I'm going to come around to the view that . . . [my achievements in life] may have something to do with the way I really am."

He sees his life as, again haphazardly, having achieved a certain coherence: "It doesn't feel continuous in the sense that I had a life planned, . . . [but] in retrospect it has had a kind of order. . . . I've written two or three books that I have felt able to write, partly because of the breadth of my experience. I have had several vantage points on the law, but there was no plan. . . . It has been, at a minimum, a set of useful credentials and—beyond that, when you do credit to it all—a set of reinforcing and enriching experiences as it works out. . . . There have been no serious discontinuities." Yet the overall process of achievement and coherence remains to him "mysterious, something rather strange."

Part of that strangeness has to do with his sense of profound vulnerability: "I think of myself now just finishing my seventieth year as a perennially fragile person, always at risk." He stressed the contrast between others' sense of him as "calm and resourceful," in the courtroom "a very well-organized judge always in command"; and his own sense of himself as "frequently . . . on the verge of outbursts, breakdowns, . . . on the verge of a wrong turn or a kind of collapse that never happens." That feared "collapse" is associated in his mind with "falling apart," with a tendency, under pressure, "to want to throw this whole thing over," to say, "Oh, screw it!" Or it could take the form of a particular, subversive act: "I've never spelled it out because I don't want to write the scenarios that tempt myself to follow it. But, you know, I could one day decide that really the stuffiness and the pomposity of judges is more than one ought to bear, and tomorrow I'm going to show up in a court with an earring [in one ear]. I could decide such—I would not do it. Or I could suddenly leap off the bench, throw the robe off, and tell everybody what a goddamn charade this is." He added, "I have never quite come close to doing that," and related the impulse to the fear that when in high places or "at the edge of precipices," he might be tempted to jump off—"a part of my makeup that I've sort of kept at bay, but it's there."

He attributes much of his capacity to hold himself together to his "great second marriage" (his difficult and contentious first marriage ended in divorce) to a university professor, who is a profoundly caring person and able to "take hold and take charge," in contrast to his own "relative incompetence." In an extreme emergency, such as a nuclear holocaust, he imagines her doing just that (see pages 47–48), while he would be "distraught, frantic." Yet he believes that, whatever the destruction, there would be rebuilding and a new start: a conviction he directly associates with "a basic sense of the possibility of rescue, of hope . . . that does play a big part in my life." Moreover, that survival of the entire human "intellectual and artistic enterprise" means a great deal to him because of his "having been privileged to be part of it. Having been a thinking, sentient human being, I . . . contributed microscopically to it, and I have an investment in it in that sense."

"Never very eager for lots of money," as he put it, Judge M. has given up lucrative professional arrangements for activities that engage him intellectually and morally. Favoring a "highly sharing kind of society," and generally peace-minded and inclined toward disarmament, he has found his real ethical métier in his work in human rights. He came to the work through a series of invitations to participate in international legal missions on behalf of people being deprived of their rights. But in this area, more than any other, he can recognize his own strong personal inclinations, acknowledging that were it not for the invitations, "something else would have happened" to bring him into that realm. He spoke with some passion of his moral commitment: "Well, it's a satisfaction that comes from using myself worthily for things that I care about. . . . I'm not a warm person like my wife toward individual people, except a small group of selected friends. But I do care about people who suffer and people who are deprived and exploited. I am against these things. So I've always wanted to work in directions that would oppose those things, . . . and my best friends are people who share these interests."

When I asked Judge M. about his earliest concern with victimization, his answer, by no means surprising, was impressive nonetheless: "This starts basically with me. I think the first serious victim of oppression that evoked my sympathy and concern was me." As he further explained, "I felt all through my childhood and youth a sense of being oppressed and persecuted, mainly by my father but by fate as well." Only later, however, could he begin to envision "the possibility of taking up arms against troubles of other people, and it was like a revelation to learn that if you were smart enough and energetic enough, you actually could imagine yourself acting against these evils, not merely for yourself but for other people." Psychologically speaking, that revelation provided his evolving self with a powerful sense of agency, of extending his reversal of childhood humiliation to a world stage and thereby asserting his own larger human connectedness.

Arthur M.'s achievements depended upon his early capacity to absorb extreme, sustained trauma and parental betrayal without being destroyed or defined by either. His inchoate talent for coping with that environment made possible his later "rescue things" and developed side by side with the sustained abuse. He evolved a personal narrative, a form of proteanism, that relied heavily on prospective imagination (telling stories to himself and others), upon a grasp (at whatever level of awareness) of directions he might take that could contribute to a functional sense of self. His intellectual brilliance contributed greatly to the process, as did his general articulateness and his capacity for play. But he also required considerable psychic numbing, a pattern that had to be itself cultivated and balanced by more active and constructive forms of feeling associated with early acceptance and accomplishment. What is remarkable is not the dissociation as such but the fact that he did not undergo much greater dissociation or splitting (for instance, multiple personality), as is often the case with those abused to this degree. Over time, he developed a capacity to experience selectively, absorb, and make constructive use of death encounters and death equivalents. He told me, for instance, of his "sense of sorrow . . . and some fear and even terror" at the time of the death of "one grandparent . . . I was fond of," and also of his more recent weathering of what he called two "potentially fatal" illnesses. Throughout his life, that is, he has been able to make use of the creative survivor pattern that could take him beyond early threats of disintegration, stasis, and separation, beyond his early experience of a continuous death immersion.

But always precarious has been his equilibrium between dissociation or numbing, on the one hand, and vitality of self, on the other. To maintain that equilibrium he has had to make use of anything positive his environment offered: of whatever nurturing was available from his mother (possibly more than he recalled) and to a lesser extent from his sister, of whatever support he could receive from his extended family (from, for instance, the uncle who provided the address that helped get him into college and the grandparent whose death he mourned), and from a vague but important Jewish subculture with its emphasis upon learning (countering at least partly his father's antagonism to learning); of the array of teachers who did so much to help him and toward whom he must have been more active in his seeking than he describes; of the support of each of his wives, mixed and ambivalent in the case of his first but powerful and sustaining in the case of his second; and, eventually, of broad Western traditions of liberalism, human rights, and professional responsibility, as well as of specifically American mythology (fading but still viable for some people) of the improvished youth making his way, via hard work, to brilliant success (the Horatio Alger myth).

None of this could eliminate the powerful impact of early pain. But his evolving, ever-vulnerable self could gradually achieve a capacity to combine disparate elements, including the original abuse, on behalf of focused goals and steady achievement. His fantasies of radically subverting that achievement (entering the court with an earring or casting off his judicial robes) serve several simultaneous functions. They are, as he knows, an expression of danger, a warning that he is by no means safe from himself, that the possibility of disintegration lurks. But they are also a characteristically protean perception of absurdity, of the self's need to question the authenticity of what it is experiencing and to lubricate with mockery various encounters (especially those that border on the pompous). Though troubling, these fantasies have value to Arthur M., giving expression to a side of himself he also needs: that of raising inner questions concerning the inauthenticity of conventional environments he must inhabit. He can mock both the world and himself while (so long as the fantasy remains just fantasy) holding to existing worldly relationships and accomplishments, all the while constructing the psychological combinations required for his innovative life.

In one sense, the subversive fantasies reflect his disbelief in his personal transformation from helpless victim to assertive advocate of all victims. But in another sense, the transformation itself, as he lives it out suc-

cessfully, requires the absurd underbelly those fantasies provide. What
results is a protean pattern of unplanned achievement and coherence
and a life centered on healing—healing of his own abuse no less than the
world's.

## "IS THAT ALL THERE IS?": BARBARA C.

I interviewed Barbara C. in a small town, just north of New York City,
and encountered a spare, friendly thirty-year-old woman in jeans, who
greeted me with a lively smile. She told me that she had been living in
the area for three years, and that during the last year or so, she had made
a "transition away from [being] a research scientist" and was now supporting herself by tutoring children while also co-teaching a course at a
local community college on nonviolent social change.

Barbara was born in rural Georgia; and when I asked about her ethnic
background, she unhesitatingly replied, with a gently self-mocking
chuckle, "Southern cracker." Her family had lived on that land "for so
many generations we've lost any old-country connections." She described
her mother, whom she spoke of with affection, as often bizarre, she and
her brother having recently agreed that " we were raised by a crazy
woman." Her father was distant from other family members, emotionally
"escaping" by spending endless hours in a small store that provided the
family's livelihood. Barbara had always thought of him as having
"checked out" of the marital relationship, but later gained the impression that he had initially "tried to maintain a marriage" but her mother
"sort of pulled out." In any case, Barbara, although made "something of a
mascot" by her two older brothers, had the frequent feeling that "there
was no marriage" and "I had no parents." In the face of her mother's
inadequacies, Barbara often served as domestic coordinator or family
hostess: "I was the buoy to which the family was moored."

Barbara described the religion in her home as tepid ("generic U.S.—
you know, grace at the table, . . . that's about all"), but there was nonetheless a good deal of Methodist and Southern Baptist influence. And as
long as she can remember, she has been "looking for waters"—that is,
searching for a more authentic religious source than those to which she
had been exposed, as she "slowly wandered down the road to becoming a
Christian." She spoke mockingly of a Methodist kindergarten she
attended ("we did Moses and the Pharaoh"); but her added quip, "Who
knows what sort of things they planted in my little mind?" suggests a
recognition of at least some seeds. She was openly contemptuous of a sec-
ond-grade Baptist summer Bible class with its "ridiculous little crafts,"
including "pasting Jesus' face" on paper. Worse than that: "They took us
in small groups into a room and basically . . . tried to coerce us to

become Christians," an approach that now "horrified" her and seemed "very false even then." Years later, when attending a similar summer camp as a "big sister," she could observe more dispassionately the "psychological terror" being employed and took pride in counseling younger children against succumbing to it. (She seemed pleased to have learned much later that her father had undergone as an adolescent a "very brief experience" with the Southern Baptists but had been sufficiently "terrified" to renounce all organized religion and instead come to live by what he called [invoking his own name], "The Gospel According to Will.")

She believes herself to have been motivated by "a need for completeness, . . . not just in myself but . . . to make sense of what was very slowly and unconsciously developing in me, [the idea that] something's horribly wrong out there . . . [and I needed] a way . . . to make it right." This idea of religion as "a way to justice" has never left her. She spoke contemptuously of the "syrupy white Jesusy" religion with a "feel-good Savior" presented to her in her high school years during her encounter with a Campus Crusade for Christ. She came to resent "the way they limited Christianity and defined it" to include little more than the condemnation of "sex, drugs, and rock 'n roll"; she used the disdainful term "the feltboard set" for those who practiced Christianity in that way, the term referring to a didactic method of telling nice Christian stories by placing representations of characters on feltboard surfaces. Rather than dismiss Christianity itself, however, she continued to examine her own experience with it ("I was willing to say, 'Okay, I'll see how this feels'"). But over her adolescence, she developed a sense that "if this is what Christianity is supposed to be, I have serious problems with God!" For her, "it felt so false, and so wrong" that she found herself constantly invoking the phrase from a Peggy Lee song, "Is that all there is?"

Her quest was influenced by her view of her mother as an unsuccessful seeker who "would have liked to have had a relationship with something she conceived of as God," and who would, under duress, "beseech . . . this God she'd never let herself [approach]." These spiritual limitations seemed to Barbara consistent with her mother's general inadequacy and silent oppression in the family situation: "I was aware of her pain—she was not"; and "I wished . . . that she would just act, make some act to change her life." She saw them reversing roles: "I was my mother's keeper—I became her parent." But this reversal of roles, Barbara later concluded, led her to become more generally the confidante who helps everyone with their problems without ever revealing her own. In this way, she would "maintain distance and be unconnected": "I didn't let myself out . . . [or] even acknowledge to myself that I had something to share."

She was to find a more assertive female model in Harriet Tubman, the escaped slave who became a leader in the Underground Railroad for other fugitive slaves, and then a prominent figure among Abolitionists and a confidante of John Brown in the latter's insurrection in 1859. Barbara could not quite remember where she first heard about Harriet Tubman: in the deep South "they certainly didn't teach it in school." She became "incredibly enamored" of Tubman, sought out whatever information she could, and, with some difficulty, succeeded in convincing an eighth-grade teacher that Tubman was a suitable subject for a report on "a great American." Barbara was deeply moved by her courage ("in hiding runaway slaves and persisting despite injuries sustained in earlier beatings by an overseer") and by "something deeper than that." The added dimension had to do with "a *woman* being that strong," with her "taking a stand" and "challenging the powers that be" no matter what the personal risk, and at the same time articulating all she did "in terms of God and obedience to the Gospel." As she described all this, Barbara said, "I'm fluttering inside," and recalled how "scary for me" it was to discover Harriet Tubman: "There was part of me that knew that [what she did] had to be done" because "that's what our lives should be about." Her discovery of Tubman had been so powerful an experience because the message Barbara C. took from her was that one must live at risk and pursue justice on the basis of a demanding, transformative Christianity. (At about the same time, she read a biography of Jim Thorpe, the early-twentieth-century Native American athlete whose Olympic track medals were stripped from him "for what I thought were pretty bogus reasons," which further fed her evolving concerns about justice for oppressed minorities.)

Upon arriving at college, also in the deep South, Barbara finally found a Christian group that held a deep appeal for her. A campus community there offered a version of the social Gospel stressing "stewardship, justice, and living the Sermon on the Mount . . . [as] a radical manifesto." The stress was on "living in community," and communal events could be relaxed and joyous, with irreverent rock music and lots of mocking and self-mocking humor. At the same time, the group was serious about applying its version of the Gospels to politics, speaking of "the upside-down Kingdom" called for in Christ's image of the the last becoming first; and insisting that "like Christ," we must question the international power structure in which the United States was "living on the backs of the Third World." Barbara was also drawn to the emphatic rejection of the idea of God as a "cosmic bellhop" whose job was to take care of the needs of privileged white people. But, above all, she experienced the group as a call for personal change: "It wasn't something happening out there, . . . [but] it was the power of transformation in my life and, through that transformation, changing the reality in the world."

Along with her religious struggles, Barbara was early attracted to science. She recalled a childhood "sense of wonder and awe" at the miracle of living entities: "It wasn't a sense of power, of wanting to control, but a very simplistic, perhaps naïve kind of wanting to understand, because this is really amazing." She recalled vividly first viewing a single-celled creature under a microscope and being "wowed" by its complexity: "We'll never understand everything that goes on in that paramecium." These feelings combined with triumphant sibling emotions, as science was "what I was good at when my brothers weren't." She became a biology major at college and began work for an advanced degree. She came to feel that her knowledge of science, rather than conflicting with her Christian beliefs, provided evidence for them. She gave as an example her impression from developmental biology that the "odds should be very high against infants being born healthy and within a range of normalcy": the fact that most are healthy "boggles the mind," and, if not a miracle, "it's the closest thing we can come to [one]." When frequently asked by fellow students how she as a scientist could believe in God, her answer would be, "In all honesty, the more . . . I study, it becomes, 'How can I not?'"

For further study, Barbara accepted a position at a prestigious New York research center, but arrived there with some uneasiness about having agreed to begin sooner than she had planned in order to accompany her boyfriend, Ron, who had received an earlier appointment. Over the year at the institute, she began to develop doubts about her career, seeing her "naïve" approach to be "a detriment to my surviving in science," as opposed to the focus she observed in others on control, power, success, and monetary gain. Her Christianity was involved, because a central image for her, "Thy Kingdom come," meant "doing what is right and complete for me," being "called to be perfect just as our Father is perfect," which means "doing what you were meant to do, being . . . what you were meant to be." She could observe that genuine "gift" in a few scientists who were "where [they] should be," but saw herself as "not making the world a wholer place being here"; she felt that a scientific career "would take all that I am" and would therefore be "death dealing as opposed to life giving for me." She also longed for "something more humanitarian and immediate" and was moved and disturbed by a talk given by a Quaker physician about his work in Africa. Insisting that she was not "making [a] . . . judgment on all science" but only on her relationship to it, "I finally let go of the notion that this was my career, my path." She found it painful to surrender a longstanding goal and "image I'd had of what I'd be," but experienced also a great sense of relief.

At the same time, she found herself increasingly unhappy in her relationship with Ron. She experienced it as requiring that she suppress her own inclinations and emotions, especially in the sexual area. In succumbing to his insistence that they live together, despite her strong disinclination to do so, she felt both "violated" and "angry at myself for not standing up for my needs or having my feelings honored" and for "setting myself up as a victim." She resented Ron's insistence that she had "unhealthy attitudes," because she did not wish to have "somebody else's notion of health [imposed] on me." She felt that Ron "wanted a normal, mainstream life," which was incompatible with her religious, political, and personal quests; and that she had been confused by her own ambivalence, by her own partial desire for the same "normalcy." She came to see herself as "becoming dull" in the relationship and ceasing to grow. Although generally considered a "competent, stable, together person"— which, she added, "*was* part of me"—she found herself upset and undergoing "great gnashing of teeth" as she and Ron seemed to be heading toward "destroying" one another. Ending both the relationship and her association with the research institute enabled her to do what she wished to do—continue her search for her own form of self-integration.

For Barbara, that search must be conducted within a religious idiom so intense that it has at times verged on fundamentalism. Indeed, at one point in our interview, she associated the biblical principle of "end time"—of the end of human history and the Second Coming of Jesus— with nuclear holocaust. She spoke of a resulting situation in which human goodness would flourish and our sense of reality would become "something different, . . . more desirable. . . . We'd be in a very different place, . . . where our spiritual reality is given precedence." At that point, she abruptly stopped herself and declared, "This is taking on frightening proportions, . . . the notion of a nuclear bringing-on of the next age"— and added, with her self-mocking humor, "I mean, that's not the way the game should be played." She meant that she had long been opposed to nuclear weapons, had when younger experienced anxiety dreams about nuclear holocaust, and was horrified by her own statement to the effect that nuclear holocaust could bring on an age of deepened spirituality. When I asked her what she thought about the view of some fundamentalists that nuclear war doesn't matter so much because only the subsequent other-worldly events are important, her unhesitating, booming answer was a contemptuous "*Bool*shit!"

She was at that point struggling against her own tendencies toward fundamentalism, in particular against an inclination to accept a certain version of end-time theology that equates nuclear holocaust with biblical realization. But she could look critically at those tendencies and contrast her sustained rejection of fundamentalism with the experience of her older brother in first embracing it and then struggling over years to extricate himself from it. She further clarified her feelings: "What is important in my relationship with God is what I do right now." Ultimately Barbara has rejected what she calls the "bondage" of fundamentalism and the "antichrist" of nuclear weapons—along with the, in her mind, related entities of environmental destruction and racism—in favor of her version of Christian openness.

She continues what she calls her "church shopping" and has recently confirmed her impression of conventional churches as "dead, dead, dead!" She is looking for a spiritual community "based on liberation or transformation," both individual and societal, resembling the one she had known at college. She retains her "obedience to the truth—to what's right for me," to a discipline of looking both inward and outward at the roots of violence and self-destructiveness: "It's not just changing the players, it's changing the game, . . . and doing it out of a call from the words of Christ." She admires the Quakers for "asking important questions," but finds lacking in them what she calls a "Christocentric" emphasis: "For me, I know there is a God and I know that Jesus is my relationship to that God." Yet even here, she qualifies that statement and eschews dogma when she describes seeking "continual and better fellowship . . . with my higher power which I choose to call God"; and when she defines Hell as being "separate from God," so that instead of "a hellfire and brimstone notion of eternal damnation, it could just be nothingness compared to being." She refers to a sense of "infinity," of feeling "connected to and part of something beyond this immediate world," and in her Christianity seeks "to bridge the gap between the finite and the infinite." While believing that religion "ultimately defies reason," she insists on reversing earlier tendencies "to not listen to my feelings" and is now confident about what speaks to her faith and what does not: "When you *know*, you *know!*" In all this she struggles to extend the self in ways that combine vitality and grounding with larger principles of continuity and symbolic immortality. Her perspective, she declares, is associated with "hope—and I guess it keeps me sane."

Barbara's male-female struggles occurred at several levels. She told of a recurrent anxiety dream of nuclear holocaust in which she is protecting victimized children, but is then disturbingly approached by "mutilated lovers trying to draw me to bed," including one situation in which "I . . . was feeling guilty that I was actually repulsed by this person, . . . trying to get away from him, . . . [when] in fact [he was] needing contact with women, needed me in some way." The dream had been influenced by paintings she had seen of Hiroshima and by Hiroshima survivors she had met, as well as by a past relationship with a man with a physical deformity, and by sexual conflicts and fears of physical and psychological "mutilation." She is more clearly unambivalent in her angry condemnation of unfeeling male advocacy of nuclear-weapons use (as occurred, for instance, in a discussion that followed the televised film of nuclear war *The Day After*): "To me there is no greater evil than these men sitting around in a room discussing this stuff calmly, . . . so detached [in contemplating millions of deaths in nuclear holocaust], . . . so completely void of life, . . . totally devoid of connectedness to life. . . . Just sitting here right now, it gives me nausea." And she added, "I remember thinking that . . . Satan doesn't have to lift a finger. Satan can sit by and laugh. We're very capable . . . of just heading right down the path . . . on our own." Walking home after a talk Helen Caldicott, the antinuclear activist, gave at her university on these issues, and thinking about warnings about rape on campus, Barbara experienced rage ("if anyone touched me, I was like a coiled spring"), which she converted into "positive energy" for antinuclear work.

While consolidating her sense of self by connecting strong feelings to feminist concepts, particularly in relation to nuclear threat, she was also coming to terms with her own potential violence. She thus spoke of a "level of anger" toward those who contemplated nuclear war, and of "wanting to kill someone," and thought of a song called "If I Had a Rocket Launcher." She went on to say that she could understand the mentality of people who planned nuclear war, because her own feelings of violence "put me right into it when I think about being at [their] mercy." At the same time, she could also acknowledge softer tendencies, saying that, if confronted with an actual or pending nuclear holocaust, "I would collapse and sob."

Barbara has always been sensitive to the death of creatures of any kind, learning as a small child to accept the life cycle of small sea animals she observed but continuing to struggle in her dreams with images of death, disintegration, and separation. In a series of childhood nightmares, she would be flying but "over time I would lose the ability to fly and I'd lose altitude and eventually crash into the lake we lived on." In another, later dream, she was on an ocean liner where she was fighting with someone, "our struggles taking us over the edge, breaking through the barrier, falling over the edge, and as we fell to the ocean, which I could barely make out below, [we were] falling past these decks and seeing into the portholes of the cabins all those people . . . with their different lives— and [aware] as I'm falling [that] 'I'll never know those people. . . . They don't know I'm out here falling into the ocean. . . . They don't know I exist.'" Her dream imagery and her present associations to it reflect her continuing struggles with sex and with violence, along with her efforts to maintain vitality and larger human connectedness in the face of those struggles, and her fear that her inner aspirations and life experiments could take her "over the edge" into a realm of fragmentation and nonexistence or death.

A more recent "powerful dream," occurring at about the time she broke her engagement, revealed much about the tensions and directions of her self-process. The dream was about "a monster in the closet that everyone told me was very ferocious and vicious and would kill me if it ever got out." She nonetheless decided to let the monster out by freeing it of layers of chains and locks until, reaching its "large sarcophagus sort of box, I could reach in and touch the monster." And "with each layer I peeled, the monster was getting smaller, until finally . . . he was sort of a Muppet-type monster, kind of big and fuzzy, . . . ferocious but no longer vicious. I knew it could kill me if it wanted to, but I knew it wasn't going to." Finally, it "evolved down to a man." She understood the dream to portray the "monstrous" rage inside herself and her new ability to "embrace" her anger in charting her own path. But she associated it as well to "me and my anger [when] thinking about the nuclear monster." Also involved was her sense of now feeling able to bring "out of the closet" her deepest fears, whether about death (sarcophagus) or about her own "abnormality" (possibly involving inclinations toward a change in sexual orientation) or "viciousness" (her seething anger in response to certain situations and certain men), and about her risky life choices in general. In her further discussion of sex, Barbara spoke of it as "something very powerful that I have seen destroy a lot of people," but also "very spiritual and emotional" and "an incredibly beautiful thing." The dream seemed to be saying that what is most fearful and threatening in her life could be confronted, "tamed," and rendered humanly malleable.

Barbara C. could not be more earnest about what she seeks, but she constantly injects subversive humor crucial to her struggles and outlook. For instance, when discussing some form of spiritual continuity that might follow upon a nuclear holocaust, she commented (in connection with the gates of heaven), "It'd be a real bottleneck," and then, mimicking either God or Saint Peter, "We're backed up for days!" And when stressing one of her central principles, "What is important in my relationship with God is what I do right now," she paraphrased Jesus in a way that was both sympathetic and rendered him something close to a carnival barker: "You know, folks, it's . . . today, . . . it's not yesterday, it's not tomorrow, it's right now! And don't hang around and wait to bury your dead! You've gotta deal with what's going on right now!" On another occasion, when mentioning her "nausea" at contemplating total nuclear destruction, she added, "Well, it's [at least] egalitarian"—reminding one of the line in a Tom Lehrer song, "We'll all go together when we go." Barbara's sense of humor permits her to experiment with doubt, conflict, and contradiction, while at the same time to assert her most profound beliefs. This form of lubrication thus contributes to both the fluidity and the coherence of her self-process.

Barbara knows that her tutoring work is temporary but is by no means sure of a next step. She has considered going to medical school in order to be able to provide medical care to people at risk in poor countries, a way of combining her involvement in science with her religious principles of compassion and service. In her moral and political efforts, she seeks to avoid the tendency of some activists "to beat up on themselves" out of the feeling that what they do is "never enough": "I will never be able to change everything, . . . but I can do what I can do." Yet the struggle with self can become wearying, so much so that, when contemplating nuclear holocaust, despite her horror, "the word that . . . [comes] to me is *relief*," by which she means "not having to struggle any more against the acute planetary diseases of humanity." She also sometimes finds herself "wishing I could arrive sometime, . . . could get to a place where you [don't] have to [keep searching] any more, . . . and knowing that that's not gonna happen." She stresses that, whatever course she takes, she will be guided by that "little voice inside," and that the "spiritual principle is the bottom line."

Barbara's proteanism began with her reversal of roles with her parents and evolved in virtually every area of her life—her career switches, her geographical and social arrangements, her intimate relationships, and, above all, her spiritual quest. Yet she retains a powerful grounding in her version of Christian belief and practice. Her intent is not endless experimentation but rather to achieve, in her terms, coherence and meaning. The "perfection" of which she speaks has to do with personal authenticity, with a sense of psychological and moral integration. But she makes it clear that her search for inner and outer arrangements that might provide such authenticity is lifelong. Along the way, she is vulnerable to a variety of confusions and a tendency toward purism that could turn her theme song, "Is That All There Is?" into a rejection of virtually every available involvement. Yet she shows impressive resilience in pursuing her quest, a sensitive capacity for self-examination, and an unusual combination of openness and grounding.

## SLIPPING THROUGH THE NETS: GORDON PARKS

Gordon Parks, the black photographer and also novelist, musician, painter, and film director, tells a life story made up of extraordinary protean forays. In his autobiography, written in his late seventies, Parks describes himself as "a wayfarer on an alien planet," as having "lived in so many different skins it is impossible for one skin to claim me." He further explains: "I became an actor and gave myself the name of 'I.' . . . Not only did I play myself; it was also necessary to take on the roles of others who were shrewder than I, and masters of their own plots." He sees his blackness as integral to his proteanism: "Maybe my small black finger expanded into a greater consciousness that helps presage the right or wrong of things headed my way." He sums up his life as "a complex, transitory, bittersweet existence that keeps shifting with time."

Parks begins with the words, "At times I find myself surprised at just being here; somewhat astonished to have made it this far"; and the theme of the survivor dominates the entire book. His life, too, began on that theme, at least according to family mythology, when the doctor delivering him pronounced him dead (and "was wrapping me for disposal") until his assistant (Dr. Gordon, after whom Parks is named) insisted upon attempting to resuscitate the baby. As a black child growing up in Fort Scott, Kansas, constantly "close to death and violence," he was almost drowned when thrown into a river at the age of eleven by three white boys who knew he could not swim; and he presents a litany of young black friends "all dead by the gun": "I consider myself lucky to be alive. . . . I also consider myself lucky that I didn't kill someone."

His family, however he may idealize it in retrospect, was clearly a sustaining force in his precarious proteanism. In conditions of impoverishment, his mother exemplified to him Christian principles of generosity and at the same time had enough strength and presence to disarm on several occasions a drunk and violent family member. He saw his father as possessing similar traits, on one occasion quietly entering the hospital to offer extensive skin from his back, arms, and legs to graft onto a little black girl who had been severely burned the night before. Parks refers to his parents as "my just heroes" and tells of a later incident when, under desperate circumstances, he came close to robbing a trolley conductor at knife point but held back when his "father's black face . . . replaced . . . [the conductor's] white one." He undoubtedly derived from his parents certain principles of order; and from an invalid brother (Parks was one of fourteen siblings) who died young, Parks was given a permanent mantra: "Fight with your brain. It's got a lot more power than your fists."

As an adolescent and young adult, against a backdrop of depression, poverty, and black victimization, Parks embarked on several highly perilous but always instructive travels. They included, at the age of fifteen in 1927, his being literally thrown out of his sister's Minneapolis house by her violent husband (the boy's belongings strewn about in the snow reflecting the psychological fragmentation threatening him at the time); a ghastly freight-car trip from St. Paul to Chicago with a severely frostbitten acquaintance and a thieving hobo; and a "job" in a flophouse among "pickpockets, alcoholics, bums, addicts, perverts, panhandlers, and thugs . . . of the lowest order [who] . . . spoke with an intolerable vulgarity that was catching." Degradation always inspired Parks to rise from it, as he attempted to do in subsequent disparate adventures: having a song he wrote stolen from him, getting a job with a musical group that was abandoned by its leader, being beaten up by white men and then thrust into jail, making illegal drug deliveries, spending time in the Civilian Conservation Corps, and becoming a member of the semiprofessional House of David basketball team. His unerring capacity for advantageous shapeshifting was exemplified by his arrangements in an early job where he played piano "for tips" in a brothel: the pimp in charge "blessed me with my first suit, . . . one of his old pinstripe numbers," and "I slicked down my hair with a heavy grease to get that Rudolf Valentino look, and then I was ready for the evening." In the same spirit, when working as a porter or a waiter on a train, he was able closely to observe the rich in their "customs, mannerisms, expensive clothes, luggage, and first-class conversations," to all of which he himself aspired.

During an age of railroads and magazines, he took full advantage of his access to both. He devoured the many magazines people left on the trains on which he worked, and found unforgettable the photographs of impoverished, dispossessed migrant workers taken by such people as Carl Mydans, Walker Evans, Ben Shahn, and Dorothea Lange, all of whom were then employed by a New Deal government agency, the Farm Security Administration. He began to educate himself, reading photographic essays by Margaret Bourke-White and books by John Steinbeck and Erskine Caldwell; during layovers in Chicago, he would visit the Art Institute where he was fascinated by the impressionist paintings. He was partly inspired to become a photographer by the hero's celebration Norman Alley received after photographing Japanese planes bombing the United States gunboat *Panay*. In acquiring his first camera from a pawn shop, Parks obtained "what was to become my weapon against poverty [including certainly his own] and racism." He tried photographing everything in sight—gravitating, for reasons both of career and social conscience, to the depressed scenes of the Chicago Black Belt. He had also studied the fashion photography in *Vogue* magazine and obtained his first paid work as a photographer by boldly walking into an elegant woman's store in St. Paul and convincing the wife of the owner that he could do their fashion photography—which was to lead to extensive work in that area.

A basic step in his evolution as a photographer was a grant for a fellowship in 1942 in Washington, D.C., with the Farm Security Administration, where he met many of the famous photographers "whose work had beckoned to me" from the magazines he had found on trains. He experienced painful racism in wartime Washington but also encountered Roy Stryker, a white man who encouraged him to record black experience, and was to become an important sponsor-mentor over the years. Parks now began to look at black history and its burdens, while producing some memorable photographs and emerging as a documentary journalist. Among other valued sponsors were the grade-school teacher who awakened his interest in literature, the woman who gave him his first fashion assignment at her husband's clothing store, and the *Vogue* editor who offered him fashion work for that magazine. As he tells us, "The memory of [the latter two] prevents my looking at all white faces with the same set of eyes."

Parks's main realization as a professional photographer came in his longstanding association with *Life* magazine. There, too, his fast-talking helped him acquire "a prestigious base for me to work from": for his

interviewer he "hurriedly . . . concocted" a specific project he claimed to
have in mind, but then actually embarked on it. He was calling forth, in
his self-promotion, a potential moral sensibility that had not yet been
coordinated into his professional work. *Life* was an ideal protean vehicle
for him, with "[t]he fierce energy of the New York bureau [as a]
. . . nerve center": "A mother gave birth to quintuplets in Canada. Indians rioted in Calcutta; civil strife flared in Spain. A plane went down over
Iceland—within a short time a *Life* team [frequently including Parks] was
on its way." His fashion work for the magazine in Paris on "the French
collections" was "a golden time," when he luxuriated in the comforts of
the boat trip on the *Queen Mary* ("a far cry from the leaky little fishing
skiff I paddled about on Marmaton River back in Fort Scott") and in the
"splendor of the Hotel Crillon" (which he contrasted with the brothels,
freight cars, and flophouses of his past); and although he had initially
found it "difficult to pronounce" the names of the fashion houses, he was
soon referring to them "so casually one would have thought I was
brought up in their showrooms." He was sent to the Italian island of
Stromboli to cover the notorious affair between Ingrid Bergman and
Roberto Rossellini, obtained extensive photographs of the actress and
the Italian director, and was flattered when Bergman asked if he would
like to stay on and assist Rossellini in the filming (though the arrangement never materialized).

Assigned to Paris for a year, Parks thrived on its culture, especially its
art, "reacting against the intellectual voids of my own childhood" and
"moving through centuries of history . . . not unaware of the possibility of
its help in shaping my future." From there he was assigned to photograph a variety of monarchs and dictators in exile or at watering spots; he
enjoyed the gossip about their behavior, and at one point was ordered by
King Farouk of Egypt to hit tennis balls with him, the session ending
rather quickly because of the king's difficulty in moving his three-hun-
dred-pound body around the court. Parks took pride in photographing
Dwight Eisenhower while engaging him in friendly conversation about
Kansas; and in being invited by Winston Churchill, whom he met on an
ocean liner, into his cabin for "a brandy and a good cigar," although
Parks had to leave rather quickly when the British prime minister,
answering the phone, addressed his caller: "Good morning to you, Mr.
President."

Despite Parks's cosmopolitan name dropping and pursuit of luxury,
he is always aware of his blackness, which enters into much professional
work. He has photographed endless numbers of ghetto people and black
celebrities, becoming intensely involved with some of them in ways not
entirely comfortable for him. He received early recognition for a photograph, *Ella Watson, American Gothic,* taken in Washington, D.C., while he
was under Stryker's influence: in the photograph, against the backdrop

of an American flag, an elderly cleaning lady holds up a broom and a mop. In carrying out the study of Harlem's gang wars he had talked himself into as his first assignment for *Life*, Parks came to feel great affection for Red Jackson, the sixteen-year-old "crown prince" of a leading gang, and even invited him and other gang members to his home and, in turn, permitted his own son to spend a week with them (with a "no rumbles" promise) in Harlem. In Paris, he took Richard Wright to an elegant lunch and talked with him about his work and about the experience of blacks living abroad. Parks spent time with the great boxing champion Sugar Ray Robinson and more or less took care of him when he was ignominiously defeated in a London fight. In working on a photographic essay on crime in America, in which he encountered many black criminals, Parks concluded, "Perhaps the only slightly redeemable thing about my assignment through the world of crime was the realization that I had managed to escape it. . . . Without my upbringing I might have been behind those prison walls."

It was in connection with black-power movements of the 1960s and 1970s that Parks had his most intense and uneasy encounters. He was aware that as *Life*'s only black photographer he was regarded "with dubious eyes" by black militants, and that he himself "would be walking a tightrope—on the one side a raging fire, on the other a conservative white publication," so that he sometimes felt "like a black man in white man's clothing." Ambivalence was the theme of each relationship he formed. He had reservations about the "separatism" of the black Muslims, but felt "stirred" by the words of Malcolm X and drawn to him as a person. When Malcolm was murdered by the Muslims, Parks was given bodyguards because, having written sympathetically about him, his own life was considered to be in danger. Although he tried to hold to his objectivity as a journalist, "[a]t times I found myself not really knowing where I belonged—a social oddity in one world, while emerging a stranger to another." He became fond of Muhammad Ali, the great heavyweight boxer, but seemed constantly concerned with trying to get him to behave better in order to be more widely accepted as a champion, and even took him to Saville Row to help him acquire a "gentleman's" wardrobe. With the murder of Martin Luther King, Jr., in 1968, however, Parks let loose some of his own anger: speaking to his white readers, he said, "This has just about eliminated the last symbol of peace between us. . . . We have grave doubts about your promises." He became aware that "[m]y anguish had swept me dangerously close to hatred." When covering the Black Panthers, he was struck by the contrast between their humble living arrangements and the plush hotel where he was staying; he felt momentarily "out of place, disloyal, even traitorous," though he had no difficulty refusing an offer to become the Black Panther party's minister of information.

But he remained adamant in asserting his personal opposition to racism. When he was publicly honored as Kansan of the Year in 1985 and his poem "Kansas Land" read by the master of ceremonies, he experienced "governable fury" (an accurate general term for his strong but contained emotions) at the omission of the poem's last two lines; and, in his acceptance, he recited them himself: "Yes, all this I would miss— along with the fear, hatred and violence / we blacks had suffered upon this beautiful land." Parks extended his involvement to other oppressed groups, notably in the slums, or *favela,* of Rio de Janiero where he befriended a tubercular little boy, Flavio. Asserting, "I have, for a long time, worked under the premise that everyone is worth something; that every life is valuable to our own existence," he referred to "my camera's responsibility to shed light on any condition that hinders human growth or warps the spirit of those trapped in the ruinous evils of poverty." Parks spent hours and days with Flavio and his family, arranged for the boy to be treated in the United States, and eventually—when Flavio had grown up and become a father—visited him, but still he felt helpless and guilty before the young man's unfulfillable hopes of returning to make his life in America.

Parks's multiple talents loom large in his proteanism. To "[t]he question frequently asked of me [as to] why I have undertaken so many professions," his answer centers on survival: "At first I wasn't sure that I had the talent for any of them, but I did know I had an intense fear of failure, and that fear compelled me to fight off anything that might abet it—bigotry, hatred, discrimination, poverty, or hunger." An element of searing anxiety emerges in his nightmares, and he is always aware of "calculation" about succeeding, whatever the obstacles: "Sometimes I play the piano with my eyes firmly shut—considering the small possibility of blindness. Under such a handicap, I would learn to photograph an object or person by the feel of the light. If I lost my legs I could still write. And if I should loose both arms I'm sure I would try painting with my toes."

Parks's musical creations include, as a very young man, several popular songs and, in the early 1950s, a piano concerto. He identified himself with modern Russian composers of concerti (Prokofiev and Rachmaninoff) and overcame gaps in his technical knowledge by devising his own mathematical system for notes and harmonic structures. He was offered generous musical guidance by a black conductor, Dean Dickson, who also performed the concerto, providing Parks with inchoate joy as well as pride in being listed on concert posters together with such composers as Elgar, Britten, and Gershwin. His career as a novelist was also initiated with the help of a mentor—the great photographer Carl Mydans, who, after hearing Parks reminisce about his Kansas childhood, declared, "I think you have a novel inside you." Parks took the title of his first novel from a phrase used by his mother. In reply to her young son's asking whether they had to stay in Fort Scott forever, she told him: "I don't really know, son, but you're to let this place be your learning tree." *The Learning Tree* (1964) was followed by several other novels, with the help of still another mentor, the editor Genevieve Young, with whom he also fell in love.

When offered the opportunity to direct a film of *The Learning Tree* and to compose its score, he felt, "Now after thirty-odd years, my photography, words and music were about to come together." More still came together in the process, as he relived his experience when, at the age of fifteen, he spent the night next to his mother's coffin, and hoped, "Perhaps she would lift that terrible fear of death from my insides forever and take it with her." While he by no means fully overcame that fear, Parks did learn to transmute it into various creative efforts, each of which he achieved in relation to death anxiety (or death equivalents) in an unending but highly productive struggle he always perceived as one of survival. Part of his proteanism is attributable to his need for new risks to tap the death anxiety and new forms to contain it.

In any case, Parks took pride in seeing himself as the first black Hollywood director—he would direct several additional films—the medium serving his continuous efforts to pull together his many-sided talents. In his film work, he advocated that black producers and directors move beyond black themes and "channel their efforts into pictures that are universally acceptable": "It isn't enough to talk, read, write, and sing blackness to a smattering of black people." One can view this attitude either as containing a certain avoidance of blackness or as seeking universal human standards: in Parks, it represents both. He tells us that he has learned "take human beings as they are . . . [and] not to expect any more, or less, from a black stranger than I would a white one. It all depends upon the stranger." Then he speaks of his own "admixture of kinships": "Of three mothers-in-laws I have acquired at different times, one has been Swedish, one black, and another Chinese. In turn I have been father-in-law to a Frenchman, a Jew, a Britisher, and a Yugoslavian—and you might add my father's Cherokee heritage to this very grand mix." His friends, too, "represent such a pastiche of hues, I no longer assign to them colors. . . . [T]he closest of them could hardly be called homogeneous—a black, a Chinese, a Frenchman, a German, a Jew, an Irishman, and a white Southerner from Louisiana. Altogether they are like one big sheltering tree with different colored leaves." His response to the racism of "my tormentors" is to "glance back at them and manage a smile, knowing they remain puzzled for letting me slip through their nets." Indeed, slipping through nets is how he sees much of his life, and it requires having access to everything offered by the larger world beyond.

Most elusive in Gordon Parks's life—the area in which he has perhaps been least successful—is a capacity for achieving and sustaining intimate relationships. His autobiography does not evoke with clarity or depth any of the three women to whom he has been married. He speaks of "many good hours . . . and the beauty of those hours" with each, points to his inability to live up to their expectations, and adds that "ambition carved my image out of stone." What stands out is his inability to give himself, or hold, to a love relationship—neither in his marriages nor in his infidelities. And for close human bonds he has tended to substitute immersion in high society—or the bestowal of dramatic gifts. In a painful scene in the book, he tries to celebrate Genevieve Young's appointment as vice president of a publishing firm by picking out "a lovely gown" in a Park Avenue store and arranging for her to meet him there, only for her to be appalled by the exorbitant price and insist, "It would be vulgar." He had attempted something similar in surprising his first wife, Sally, when their relationship was strained, with a flamboyant new fur coat (much cheaper than the gown for Genevieve Young but a grand gesture at the time); and sadly observed, "It pains me that neither Gene's coat [which they settled for instead of the gown], nor Sally's, solved the problems of the man who bought them." Those problems had to do with his exaggerated need for unceasing fluidity and his self-absorbed preoccupation with survival via creativity.

Parks expresses considerable love for his children, and was grief-stricken when his oldest son was killed in an airplane accident. He was left with the children when his first marriage broke up, and he refers to them frequently and affectionately. But he also admits to having been an erratic father. With it all, however, his elaborate network of family, beginning with his own parents, means a great deal to him. And he was elated by the appearance in his life of an adult granddaughter, whom his son David had unknowingly fathered, and of her child as well. He concluded, "Life is a strange circle where sometimes things move inexplicably behind—yet ahead of one another." He is intent always on his place on the human "tree"—on the great chain of being.

A key element in Parks's mutability is his capacity to make use of negative self-judgments as stimuli to transformation and achievement. The image of his title *Voices in the Mirror* comes from such an inner dialogue. He tells of actually staring into the mirror and raising "some rather bothersome questions," which he himself answered unsparingly and which included: "You squander too much time on trivial things, always hurrying to nowhere, and in a rush to get there. [*Take your time, man. Think things out first, then go.*] You avoid questions about yourself that you find hard to answer. [*Figure things out. You just don't have the right answers. So admit to it*]." Parks tells us that nothing came easy, but "I was just born with a need to explore every tool shop of my mind." And most important:

*I became devoted to my restlessness;* to chasing down poetry in the best of what I found; to opening doors that allowed me entrance into their universe, no matter how small. If I found nothing, I tried another door. Today my imagination refuses to be confined to boredom. It stays hungry and I feed it with things that surround me.

He became devoted to his fierce proteanism, always expressed in a context of perceived threat. That threat is both personal ("incalculable forces lying in wait to do me in . . . to burn me up like firewood and scatter my ashes when nothing is left") and planetary ("Since Hiroshima the entire world goes to bed with murder on its mind; morning finds it thankful to be in one piece. What I give here is meant to show how I tried to drum up courage to keep going"). He speaks of the possibility that his blackness has contributed to a "greater consciousness," to the breadth of his proteanism, and to his unusually sensitive antennae.

He ends with an admission of confusion: "I've yet to figure out what life is really about, and I doubt that I will ever come up with the answer." The protean affirmation that follows applies as much to Arthur M. and Barbara C. as to Gordon Parks: "I do find a certain fascination with the unpredictable. The transitory years we wade through are what they are— what we make of them. I'm still happy to be here, and I'm clever enough to know that my date of departure remains time's secret. I trust time. It has been my friend for a long while, and we have been through a lot together."

Chapter 9

_____

# THE FUNDAMENTALIST
# SELF

_____

*We will unmake the veil of history and when it is unraveled, we
will see Paradise standing there, in all its glory and light.*
　　　—Salman Rushdie (depicting a fundamentalist disciple)

THE SELF CAN respond to historical pressures not only by opening out
but also by closing down. The same historical forces that evoke proteanism—dislocation, the mass media revolution, and the threat of
extinction—evoke antiprotean reactions as well. These include various
forms of constriction of the self, the most powerful of which can be
grouped under the terms fundamentalism and fundamentalist self.
More than imposing restraints on the self, fundamentalism mounts—in
the service of an agenda of its own—an all-out attack on various manifestations of proteanism.

Indeed, fundamentalism is largely a reaction *to* proteanism, an alternative mode of being which draws primarily upon a sacred past. Thus, as
faltering expressions of protean openness appear in various parts of the
world, so do expressions of fundamentalism that claim unfaltering certainty. But although an antagonistic negation of proteanism, fundamentalism tends to be intertwined with proteanism; they may even require
one another. Personal narratives reveal the fundamentalist self to contain much of what it opposes. In any case, proteanism cannot be adequately understood without some exploration of its formidable adversary from without and within.

# Fundamentalists Everywhere

## REVOLT AGAINST HISTORY

The early-twentieth-century Protestant religious movement that provided the term *fundamentalism* was directed against "modernism in theology and the cultural changes that modernism endorsed"—that is, against emerging protean tendencies in liberal theology that took it beyond literal, traditional dogma. The actual term did not appear until 1920, when fundamentalists were described as those ready "to do battle royal for the Fundamentals." The Fundamentals in question had been the subject of a series of twelve volumes published under that general title between 1910 and 1915, and included such basic principles as the inerrancy and divine origin of Biblical scripture, the virgin birth, the miracles of Christ, and His substitutionary atonement and bodily resurrection. Also included "gently" in these volumes were the more controversial doctrines of premillennialism, which sees human history violently ending to usher in the millennium of Christ's rule on earth, followed by the ultimate achievement of a "new heaven and new earth"; and of dispensationalism, the doctrine of God's provision (or dispensations) of specific sequences of events bringing about this violent end and new beginning. Fundamentalism drew upon the long American tradition of Bible-centeredness, going back to the Puritans and spurred by the great waves of revivalism during the nineteenth and twentieth centuries. In response to the fear that "liberal or secular American culture had led to moral disintegration," fundamentalism could become a quest for reintegration, for a firm sense of order.

Parallel psychological and historical patterns have occurred elsewhere, in both theological and political realms, so that the term *fundamentalist* may broadly include any movement that embraces a fierce defense of its sacred, literalized text in a purification process aimed at alleged contaminants—all in the name of a past of perfect harmony that never was, and of an equally visionary future created by a violent "end" to impure, profane history. Fundamentalism can occur, then, in relation to various forms of *religious* practice that are Hindu, Jewish, and Islamic, as well as Christian; and of *political* practice that are revolutionary or nationalistic or both, including many Nazi, neo-Nazi, and Communist forms. Fundamentalism can create the most extreme expressions of totalism, of the self's immersion in all-or-none ideological systems and behavior patterns. Salman Rushdie evokes that mentality of absolute unity when he speaks of the Prophet's "terrifying singularity," his message of "one, one, one." The verses of the title of his book are deemed "satanic" precisely because they advocate a more protean acceptance of elements of Hindu polytheism in the form of three local, patron goddesses. Late in the book, Rushdie portrays a contemporary prophet as proclaiming "a revolution, . . . a revolt . . . against history," a return to a "faith of Submission," in which "no aspect of human existence was to be left unregulated, free."

Fundamentalism is accurately seen as a form of militant antimodernism: in its embrace of supernatural rather than natural truth, and in its vehement condemnation of virtually every form of pluralism (whether intellectual, social, or religious) as degenerate "secular humanism." Yet there are very modern aspects to that antimodernism. In practical terms, fundamentalist movements have been in the vanguard of available technology (automated mailings and elaborate television hookups in the United States, and audiocassettes in Iran). More important, these movements reflect, if in caricature, certain forms of logic basic to modernism. Their literalism, for instance, is partly a product of the tendency of the scientific revolution of the eighteenth century "to weight the balance in favor of fact, even within the church," so that millennarian advocates "staked their entire conception of Christianity upon a particular view of the Bible based ultimately upon 18th-century standards of rationality." Here, as in many other ways, fundamentalism is attracted to what it opposes. In pursuing this "modern antimodernism," fundamentalism seeks to replace history with doctrine, to view all of experience "through the lens of Scripture." Its own dynamic is not devoid of change since, like proteanism, it must be viewed as a contemporary struggle to "find and assert symbols"—to construct or recover meaning.

## THE FUNDAMENTALIST REACH

Generally speaking, fundamentalist movements, particularly those focused on end time, are called forth by a perception that sacred dimensions of self and community are dying or being "killed"; they are, therefore, an extreme expression of the human psychological repertoire. In its global spread, such expression has a continuum from relatively nonviolent dogmatism at one end to totalistic violence on the other. A notable example of the latter is the American blending of neo-Nazi white supremacism, anti-Semitism, antiblack racism, and violent nuclear survivalism, all "subsumed within a religious framework." This shared theological position, sometimes known as "Christian Identity," is advocated or approximated by such radical right-wing groups as the Aryan Nations, the Order, Posse Comitatus, the Covenant, Sword, Arm of the Lord, and Klan groups. Their version of end time is an Armageddon-like racial struggle, involving nuclear weapons, between virtuous Aryans and evil blacks and Jews. In embracing a nuclearized fundamentalist Armageddon in the service of violent antiprotean racial and ethnic purification, these groups take on what has been called "Messianic sanctions for terror." Such "holy terror" is exercised in the United States by bombers of abortion clinics and of the World Trade Center building in New York City (in 1993), and by groups elsewhere—in Israel and throughout the Middle East, and in India and Pakistan—that promote violence toward people and temples in the name of their own purification procedures decreed or prophesized in sacred documents. Holy terror, as linked to messianism, has important historical models in the Islamic Assassins of the eleventh to thirteenth centuries, the Jewish zealots of the first century, and the Christian crusades of the eleventh to thirteenth centuries. All were attacking individuals and groups considered threatening to the attackers' own immortality system and therefore impure. Contemporary successors to such holy terror have a broader field of imagined impurity, a vast sea of proteanism to drain and destroy.

Also included in this fundamentalist panoply are a legion of cults or "new religions" which have sprung up in recent decades throughout the world, and usually embrace some form of endism. Prominent American examples include the Unification Church or "Moonies" (a worldwide enterprise), the People's Temple, the Scientologists, and the Branch Davidians; these and groups similar to them have appeared in just about all American geographical and professional areas.

Nationalism has always lent itself to fundamentalism, all the more so in the case of revolutionary nationalism. Nazism, for instance, was not only fundamentalist but millennarial as well, as reflected in its central self-designation as the "Thousand Year Reich." Much else in the movement suggested violent millennialism, the extermination of the Jews being a kind of Armageddon, as was Hitler's impulse toward a *Götterdammerung*—a "twilight of the gods," or massive self-destruction of his own people—explicit at the end but perhaps implicit throughout. There is also a strong millennial tone in the Chinese communist slogan "May the Revolutionary Regime stay Red for ten thousand generations." In a poem Mao wrote in 1963, a time he considered himself and his revolution to be under considerable duress, he declared: "Time presses,/Ten thousand years is too long,/We must seize the day." And the poem concludes with an Armageddon-like image: "The five continents tremble, wind and thunder are unleashed,/We must sweep away all the harmful insects/ Until not a single enemy remains." More recently, following the breakup first of the Soviet empire and then of the Soviet Union itself, there have been intense, frequently violent expressions of ethnic nationalism throughout Central and Eastern Europe. Immediate antagonisms (as in, for instance, the Serbs' attack on Bosnian Muslims) have become totalized and genocidal in their visions of purification, or "ethnic cleansing."

The United States has manifested a consistently spiritualized nationalism, originating in our vision of ourselves as a "redeemer nation," and expressed in such historical images and policies as the doctrine of Manifest Destiny and the post–Second World War commitment to military predominance and to the "American Century." The American obsession with the flag—and the frequent attempts at legislation that would criminalize artistic and other expressions of disrespect for it—are in keeping with our sense of ourselves as a sacred if not messianic national community. This sense is embraced and played upon by groups that seek to combine narrow nationalism with fundamentalist religious fervor—such as the Moral Majority during the 1980s and its remnants and reincarnations in right-wing religious or pseudoreligious entities. This broad American impulse toward combinations of fundamentalism and nationalism may well be, in large part, a reaction to the pervasive proteanism that has characterized our history.

## PITFALLS TO PURITY

Fundamentalists distrust intellectual or spiritual suppleness. Above all, they feel impelled to obliterate the subversive effects of humor, as Rushdie comments: "The general fear of Mahound [his Mohammed figure] had destroyed the market for insults and wit." They can be equally intolerant of people who take on cultural complexity: Islamic fundamentalists refer derisively to professionals and intellectuals exposed to Western influence as *chameleons*, thereby equating them with lizards who constantly change color. In contrast is the Khomeini-like figure described by Rushdie as "ignorant, and therefore unsullied, unaltered, pure." Yet highly educated intellectuals and professionals who pride themselves on open-mindedness can also take on totalistic, and sometimes fundamentalist, thought patterns. I have found this to be true, for instance, of certain educators who conduct tightly controlled graduate teaching programs or psychological training procedures. Much more egregious, however, are those intellectuals who provide fundamentalist rationales for terror or even (like the leaders of the Cambodian Khmer Rouge) genocide. In remaking themselves and their society, such ideologists can seek to annihilate every glimmer of proteanism by insisting on (in DeLillo's words) "total politics, total authority, total being."

Yet fundamentalists cannot, as inhabitants of our multifaceted world, be immune from its protean influences. And, however they may envision forms of static purity at "the end," along the way their movement tends to be active and transformative, always at odds with the status quo and always demanding that one change one's life. Moreover, as the fundamentalist movements expand to near-mainstream status, they must cater to varied interests, become "more compromising, more assimilable," and are "hard-pressed to say how divine providence interacts with human choice and decision-making in the process." They can readily "transform . . . a biblical conception of hope into a right-wing political hype and . . . change . . . the role of prophet into that of promoter." These tendencies extend to the emergence of fundamentalism as big business: billions of dollars changing hands in response to the appeals of television evangelists and to their aggressively entrepreneurial publishing projects; endless Bibles and end-time tracts, as well as personal testimonies, novels, and how-to books providing spiritual and psychological advice on marriage, childrearing, and dealing with grief and loss. These vast enterprises, even as they disseminate fundamentalist principles, require elaborate technical, commercial, and intellectual interaction with the protean currents of the larger society.

The process also creates celebrities with clay feet—capable of worldly hunger, corruption, deception, hypocrisy, and rivalry. Consider this sequence of events:

> Jim Bakker, with his wife, Tammy, created the most widely watched Evangelical telecast, with an audience of millions, by apparently modeling it on Johnny Carson's "Tonight" show. Bakker was revealed to have had an extensive sexual affair with a beautiful church worker named Jessica Hahn and to have bought her silence for $265,000 taken from people's religious donations, leading to humorous plays on the initials of the PTL clubs that formed the Bakker empire, said to stand for both "Praise the Lord" and "People That Love," but subsequently referred to as meaning "Pass the Loot" and "Pay the Lady." Jimmy Swaggart, an equally successful televangelist who combined extraordinary emotional exhortation with "pummel[ing] a piano, bouncing his right leg to his band's pounding Nashville beat, and belting out hymns that often make him cry," denounced Bakker, his fellow minister in the Assembly of God church, as a "cancer that needed to be excised from the body of Christ," and was then himself revealed to have had sexual relations with a prostitute in a Louisiana motel. Marvin Gorman, another defrocked Assembly of God minister, mounted a defamation suit against Swaggart for having spread stories in church circles that Gorman had been guilty of "hundreds" of sexual indiscretions with various women, "knowing at the time that [he] made them that there only was one woman."

Of course, Satan was blamed: one member of the Swaggart Ministries spoke of the "powers of light and the powers of darkness exchanging blows," with "so much potential for discrediting Christianity here that the Devil has to have a hand in it." But Satan, it seems, consisted of none other than human foibles and contradictions having to do with opportunities in the larger world.

Perhaps the most extreme fundamentalist conflict between ideological purity and actual worldly experiment was the plan for televising the Second Coming. Devised by Pat Robertson, founder of the Christian Broadcasting Network, presidential candidate, and influential Republican, the plan (as revealed by a former associate) was known as GSP or "God's Secret Project":

> The greatest show on earth was in our hands. I wondered where we would put the cameras. Jerusalem was the obvious place. We even discussed how Jesus' radiance might be too bright for the cameras and how we would have to make adjustments for that problem. Can you imagine telling Jesus, "Hey, Lord, please tone down your luminosity; we're having a problem with contrast. You're causing the picture to flare."

At a prosaic, everyday level, American fundamentalists struggle with personal and family problems of every kind. In marriage, there can be considerable suffering because couples can be miserable together, but "divorce is never legitimate just because they cannot get along." And while most fundamentalists see a "biblical mandate" for female submission to male authority, this mandate can be strongly "at odds with the norms in the larger society." The same can be true of authoritarian standards imposed on children; the relative latitude of the larger society, however condemned, is always available to subvert the tightly controlled fundamentalist family. The fundamentalist "explanations" for experienced pain and disarray may cease to be convincing; and when that happens, "only the church and the Bible stand between the believer and total uncertainty."

For these reasons, it is difficult to sustain the fundamentalist worldview over generations. Surveys suggest that about half the people who grow up in a fundamentalist community fail to maintain their allegiance to it. Hence, "[a]lthough fundamentalism may continue to exist as an institution as long as there is modernity against which to define itself, individual commitment to fundamentalism is often impermanent, unable to survive throughout lifetimes and across generations." Those glimmers of proteanism ever beckon.

## The Fundamentalist Self

> *[I] . . . practice the profession of penitent to be able to end up as a judge: . . . the more I accuse myself, the more I have a right to judge you.*
>
> —Albert Camus

### GUIDELINES

The fundamentalists interviewed at our center were evangelical Christians who believe in Biblical inerrancy, consider themselves reborn, may

speak in tongues, and tend to feel that the end of history—or end time as described in the Book of Revelation—is imminent. But the dispensation-alist element of their belief means that only God can decide the moment, and thereby enables them to avoid the bizarre "Biblical arithmetic" of exact prediction that has embarrassed millenarial groups in the past. This "endist" focus is psychologically at the heart of their fundamental-ism and is, moreover, associated with nuclear weapons—with what has been called "the 'nuclearization' of the Bible"—though in highly varied forms. That is, these fundamentalists have been exposed to versions of end-time ideology in which nuclear holocaust becomes the contempo-rary Armageddon, the vehicle for the Second Coming. This belief system is made into a form of survivalism by the additional doctrine of the "Rap-ture": of true believers escaping death prior to (or, in some belief sys-tems, during or after) the "Tribulation," or time of persecution and death, by being suddenly transported "to meet the Lord in the air."

This juxtaposition of nuclear threat with already-existing end-time doctrine has undoubtedly contributed to the extraordinary spread of fundamentalism in American life and throughout the world during the last decades of the twentieth century, to its shift from a marginal form of religious extremism to the American religious and political mainstream. By the late 1980s, some fifty million Americans had come to believe that these are the last days; and Hal Lindsey's *The Late Great Planet Earth,* a declaration of this end-time faith, first published in 1970, had sold more than eighteen million copies, making him "the most widely-read writer on prophetic themes in history." Yet, as I shall discuss, fundamentalists are confused and ambivalent concerning nuclear holocaust, and this ambivalence reflects stirrings of their own proteanism.

During interviews, fundamentalists frequently made determined efforts to convert the interviewer. In doing so, they were "witnessing," sharing their Christian message with the goal of winning over another person to it. Indeed, for fundamentalists, as for many different evangeli-cal groups, "their world is a mission field"; an important reason for their cooperation with us was their sense that our interviews provided an opportunity to explore and influence the "spiritual journey" of the inter-viewer. Crucial to witnessing is the closely related convention of giving "personal testimony"—describing, usually with great intensity, one's jour-ney from pre-Christian sinful confusion to the embrace of Jesus and divine truth. Although witnessing and personal testimony are ritual con-ventions and can, therefore, contain much "canned" Biblical language and stereotypical assumptions of cause and effect (both of which were present in our interviews), they are of enormous psychological impor-tance. Personal testimony enables one to construct, reconstruct, and finally establish one's Christian life narrative and sense of self. The very repetition in the process helps achieve fixity. Personal testimony and witness, then, become means of sealing oneself off against renewed protean incursion.

There thus takes shape what can be called a "fundamentalist self." That self is paradoxical: embracing a sense of safe haven under the protection of an ultimate power, yet maintaining a highly suspicious vigilance in the face of ever-threatening evil and danger. The safe haven includes the fundamentalists' "simple antitheses," their polarization of all experience "into the realm of God and the realm of Satan"—into that which is not only right but absolutely necessary for the self, and that which is not only wrong but absolutely incumbent upon the self to reject and condemn. In that way the boundaries of the self become sharply defined according to "what is good and evil, godly and un-godly, and who are the redeemed and the condemned." There is a potential for childlike simplicity in this arrangement: Mary N. tells us, "I'm doing today what I did when I was three, four, or five years old. I was a very pure little child. Loved Bible stories, loved singing, playing the piano, doing plays. I do today."

Guidelines for the fundamentalist self extend into every corner of existence. These derive from "the Scriptures"—in effect, the prevailing fundamentalist interpretation of Biblical principles—and provide a "well-marked roadmap for living the Christian life ... in the midst of an uncharted, chaotic, modern wilderness." Fundamentalists are told "how to have a Christian marriage, what to teach Christian children, what is permissible in Christian socializing"; they are offered "a sheltering canopy" against the chaos they perceive not only without but "sometimes ... within their own souls." The fundamentalist ideology protects the self with the insistence that "God has life under control" and the flexibility to interpret even troubling experiences as "just part of God's strategy" for strengthening faith and bringing about necessary surrender to Him. However the self may seem to be falling apart, "fundamentalism provides explanations that put everything back together again." The self becomes increasingly totalized, ensconced in an all-embracing ideological structure.

But fundamentalists remain haunted by the specter of evil. Satan is as real and necessary a construct as is Jesus or God. Indeed, there is the belief that "those who are most faithful to God are singled out by Satan for his worst attacks." Hence, when one encounters decency and kindness, one must be vigilant lest these be manifestations of Satan or of his agent in the end-time drama, the Antichrist. Guilt and sin, the constant objects of fundamentalist purification, become synonymous with protean exploration. Stifling any such exploration is begun early with the child-rearing principle, frequently in fundamentalist literature, of "breaking the will" of the very young, usually by a combination of corporal punishment and the early instilling of painful and pervasive guilt. These lifelong struggles against evil forces, especially those within, help define and maintain the fundamentalist self, but allow it no rest.


## END TIME: THE IMMORTALITY FELLOWSHIP

This self-surrender provides an additional reward of profound importance—the experience of transcendence, of "high states" that are timeless and deathless. That experience is made available by expressive forms of worship—through prayer, music, and various forms of church service that involve manifestations of faith and contemplation of Jesus or of end time. High states can themselves become conventionalized, as in the ritual expression of *glossolalia,* or "speaking in tongues"—"where the believer, in a state of spiritual ecstasy, babbles in an unfamiliar language, just as the early Christians did on the original day of Pentecost." This sense of being "Spirit-filled" can provide an everyday form of ecstasy, particularly for pentecostal fundamentalists who give great emphasis to "tongues" and related forms of transcendence during religious worship. The self can experience an immediate sense of exaltation or bliss, of profound pleasure and vitality in "losing itself" to a larger, encompassing force; and at the same time affirm its place in the fundamentalist immortality system. Mary N. thus relates her practice of glossolalia to "the prayer language that God gave to me baptizing me with the Holy Spirit," speaks of it as "a miraculous type of experience" which can "buttress someone in some foreign land who just lost a child" or "intercede [so that] a great tragedy will be averted."

Over time, the guilt-ridden fundamentalist self is offered a certain amount of leeway: through an opportunity for continuous confession of one's personal sins, and through being able to see these sins as having been perpetrated by an outsider, Satan. Even the fundamentalist vision of end time has its own leeway, a double dimension that includes not only literal events but elements of a "sacred drama" on the order of a medieval morality play or a Balinese dance depicting the struggle between good and evil. Participants in such sacred dramas can experience an uncompromising, polarized struggle while at the same time being aware of an aspect of performance, of being part of a project that includes pretense and expanded imagination. (Hence Pastor Charles's sense of a "fairy tale" [epigraph, page 177]; and also a reference by Mary N. to Hal Lindsey's apocalyptic *The Late Great Planet Earth* as a "fun account.") The difficulty is that where humor and irony are usually permitted performers in a sacred drama, fundamentalism is always ready to stifle any such lubrication and reassert a literal inner version of the sacred event.

The promise of end time is the psychological fulcrum that holds together the fundamentalist self, and provides its controlling image. End time, as the historian Charles Strozier points out, is an inclusive symbol of desired *event,* spiritual *process,* and mystical *vision.* In literalizing the Book of Revelation's account of the end of human history and Jesus' thousand-year reign on earth, the self also literalizes, and fixes in place, that version of immortality. End time is the realization of the self's fundamentalist narrative, for which everything else is mere preparation. Since that narrative includes the battle of Armageddon with its destruction of most of humankind, it is a narrative that "fits" the nuclear age. Subsuming nuclear-weapons–related imagery of extinction to the Book of Revelation provides the fundamentalist self with an important psychological means of coping with nuclear fear and futurelessness. What would otherwise be wanton and absurd devastation becomes imbued with profound meaning and immortalizing purpose. Fundamentalists are, as I shall discuss, varied and contradictory in their relationship to the nuclear connection; but that connection, when held firmly, can cause some to view opposition to nuclear war as "a hostile rejection of God's already-announced intentions."

Whatever the relationship to nuclear holocaust, one must press for end time as a source of blissful fixity. Thus Mary N. tells us, "Literally, I believe it literally," and is not alone in adding, "We look forward to the end." In preparing for that end, she, like others, insists, "You need to get right with God." The heaven in which eternal life is to take place is not given the usual amorphous representation but rendered as something close or immediate, virtually at hand. Mary says, "We are already heaven-minded. We already have conversations that are in heaven." And she speaks of that realm as "not a place with clouds, harps, . . . and angels [as depicted by] big paintings," but "a city [Jerusalem] for those redeemed people of God where the whole light of the place is the light of Jesus Christ." Monroe L. is even more concrete in telling us that, during the millennium, "Christ rules with an iron hand," and "there is a hierarchy, . . . rulers of mighty cities, rulers of lesser cities." That literalized imagery of iron enclosure could not contrast more with protean imagery of open, watery (as in the case of Carol C.) flow.

Fundamentalism announces to the self that its restless protean search for larger meanings and, above all, for immortality systems is over. The answer has been found in end time and, in being rendered absolute and immutable, conquers both death and proteanism. Alternative paths to immortality are wrong; equally wrong is the search itself unless it leads conclusively to end time. Again Mary N.: "My hope [in end time] is the only hope. The hope that I have today is the hope I will have at the end and throughout eternity." Fundamentalists create a fellowship of the *only* immortals. Within that fellowship, the two related messages for the individual self are: *Genuine* immortality is yours! and, Proteanism stops here!

## THE FIGHT AGAINST CHAOS: CONVERSION

Fundamentalists are obsessed with chaos and loss of control, and there is all too much in the world today to evoke such feelings. Charles V., a black pastor, spoke to our black interviewer in a tone of passionate helplessness about the violence in Harlem, about general social and economic breakdown, and the "death of this country": "On all fronts, Willie, it looks dark," "We're out of control now," and "Man does not seem to have the power to bring it under control." "The only answer," for Pastor Charles V., "is for Christ to come and bring about an end": that is, the broad fundamentalist requirement for "concerted supernatural intervention" to end the perceived chaos. Fundamentalists require a "high measure of control" because proteanism means chaos, and chaos is evil. Mary N. had that evil chaos in mind when referring to the moral decline of the twentieth century from "existentialism on downward." And Pastor Lester M. spoke of our "warped society," in which "people are egotist and selfish and proud, . . . [and] it's gonna get worse, worse, worse, worse, . . . until one day when Judgment takes place." He went on to say that the chaos threatens him personally: "If I didn't have Jesus Christ, if I didn't know the Bible, if I didn't have peace right now, . . . I would be very confused, and it would be a very depressing world for me."

That fundamentalist impulse in response to a sense that things are out of control can occur in people with otherwise protean tendencies—as it has with both Pastor Charles V. (pages 181–83) and with George R., the successful executive with radically innovative talents. The latter's impulses toward violent purification in relation to the drug problem emerged, as we have seen, from his anxious perception of threat—to his own family and to his national faith that Americans in high places can manage things. His impulse to annihilate all members of a foreign drug cartel became a means of regaining control, of returning both family and country to a pre-drug utopia of decency and harmony. Another senior industrialist, impressively protean in setting up a profit-making business that contributed to overcoming environmental pollution, also expressed fiercely fundamentalist attitudes toward drugs and toward the AIDS epidemic. His son's expulsion from prep school because of a one-time use of pot evoked the fatherly response: "Thank God he was caught!" And, strongly troubled by the permissiveness of our society, he declared, "The Lord put AIDS on the planet to slow all this down a bit."

Conversion delivers one from chaos. This powerful personal moment is also a shared ritual for crossing the threshold into the fundamentalist Christian realm. As Mary N. explained (using a phrase undoubtedly of wider currency), "God has no grandchildren. He has to revive each generation." In our research, we found that conversion usually followed upon a sense of severe life crisis, often involving a subjective experience or threat of falling apart, of disintegration or fragmentation of the self. That sequence—from the collapse or death of the self to illumination and rebirth—then takes its place at the center of one's life narrative and one's identity as a Christian. Pastor Charles V. put the matter most strongly, after referring to the violent deaths of many of the people he grew up with: "I know my survival depended only on Christ coming into my life, my receiving Him."

The following vignettes reveal ways in which personal perceptions of chaos, along with anxiety over one's own elements of proteanism, can lead directly to fundamentalist conversion.

Pastor Martin Y.'s narrative was one of renouncing proteanism. Growing up in a religious family, he had experienced a conversion at the age of eleven or twelve, but "fell away" partly because of his great attraction to the youth culture of that time. He described it as "the drug era and the rock era" of the early 1970s, a "sort of . . . rebellious, independent time, . . . [when] everything was called into question, . . . the cold war, nuclear war. . . . The Vietnam thing was raging, and Columbia was being taken over by students, and . . . right down the line, flags were being burned in the street." He admits, with a bit of nostalgia, that "it became rebellion on my part," and "the music was my music"; and that he underwent "a period of searching and questioning and trying on different roles." But the search turned into chaos. He began to see the "fallacies of this 'love, joy, peace thing,'" as personal friendships "dissolved" and people he knew would "half kill themselves on drugs" and become violent and get into trouble with the law. The destructive chaos came to be epitomized by a single image of a friend, after an all-night graduation party, "wak[ing] . . . up . . . in [a] ditch . . . destroyed on drugs and [with] frost in his eyebrows." Martin became increasingly confused and upset and had thoughts of suicide (in relation to which he now expresses the Biblical warning, "The wages of sin is death").

He was then given a "small magazine," whose very title, *Jesus Christ, Solid Rock,* suggested a way to overcome the chaos. The magazine contained articles by well-known fundamentalist writers (including Hal Lindsey, Pat Boone, and David Wilkerson) which conveyed the "end-time message" in relation to various examples of degeneration in different parts of the culture. Martin felt there was so much evidence that the evils predicted by the Bible "were happening all around" that "you couldn't argue with it," and "those things . . . *did* leave me with that sense—the phrase of the time was 'Wow!'—with a sense of awe." He experienced, at eighteen, "the power of God plus His presence" in a way he had at age twelve: "I went forward, . . . and I haven't ever looked back." He saw himself as "having come out of total confusion" and returned to "something I could rely on." As for "my whole existence during those four or five or six

years"—his prior protean experimentation and experience of chaos—
"[I] totally dismissed it."

As a rock musician, Pastor Lester M. had indulged considerably in drugs.
He and his wife were "hippies together" at the age of sixteen and then
"found Jesus together." He used to play his guitar and sing at peace rallies
and now does the same at services he leads. He described having been so
stoned when reading the Bible that he thought he was Jesus, and how at a
religious camp he thought that the person trying to convert him was the
devil. But he came soon to feel (perhaps still identifying with Jesus),
"God, if this is what you want, take my life." He had come to realize that
"people are trying to satisfy their desires the wrong way, through drugs or
alcohol or . . . sex"; that this behavior, the Bible teaches us, is "associated
with witchcraft and sorcery, . . . a whole spiritual world of evil forces that
come into a person's life"; and that "the Gospel is so exciting because we
find an identity in knowing that there is inner peace and there is eternal
fulfillment in knowing God."

Monroe L.'s conversion experience in his mid-forties—retrospectively
colored, as were Martin Y.'s and Lester M.'s to create a particular life narrative—radically interrupted a complex life sequence. He had joined the
military to try to realize his childhood ambition of becoming a general,
but, after seven years, came to feel that he lacked the necessary motivation and focus. He did, however, serve briefly in Vietnam, and it left him
with an indelible image of grotesque killing. He had been one of a few
American officers responsible for looking after six captured Vietcong soldiers whose hands were tied behind their backs; while he turned around
briefly, the prisoners were shot by Vietnamese allies, and Monroe was
immediately told by an American superior, "Don't say anything or we'll
be dead." He was shocked, guilty, and "awful disgusted by it, . . . because
they were murdered." He subsequently turned to making money,
another childhood ambition, and built a multimillion-dollar business
enterprise employing about thirty people. He acquired a mansion, an
elegant Mercedes Benz, took increasingly long vacations, and wondered
about the meaning of it all. He seemed to experience both a sense of stasis ("I just did not want to spend seventy, eighty, ninety years . . . of life on
this earth" without making it "any better or any worse than when I
came") and pointless flux ("[I learned that] every ten years the rules [of
business] change, and I would say, '[There's] nothing lasting. There's
nothing permanent'"). His impaired larger connectedness ("How can I
leave anything lasting behind?") was exacerbated by his two failed marriages, both women having left him with great resulting confusion in his
mind about what had happened and about intimate relationships in general. He then "dated a lot of people" and "always had too many things to

go to": "It was exciting, [but] there was an emptiness." He began to experience "that gnawing, . . . numbing thing, something wasn't right," and began to ask himself frequently and self-critically, "Why am I here?"

Then several Christian friends took Monroe to a "witnessing" breakfast, where they confronted him with several questions, of which the most powerful was, "What would happen to you if you died?" The question stunned him, and he could not answer it. He was also strongly affected by a Biblical passage his friends quoted to him, of Jesus' words: "I am the way, the truth and the life; no man cometh unto the Father, but by me." He became "convinced at that point the only way I was going to get to heaven was when I placed my trust in Jesus Christ." Monroe went on to make dramatic changes in his life, selling his business, attending a theological seminary, and then working full-time at converting others. By "taking God at His word," as he put it, Monroe was able to step out of his various life experiments and anchor his sense of self in a fixed life mission.

Nigel T., interviewed at the age of twenty-eight in a plush private club, had undergone his conversion experience about six years earlier: "All of a sudden there are a lot of things that you don't have to worry about. . . . You don't have to wake up in the middle of the night and wonder whether or not you're gonna be able to pay the bills next week, or worry about how you're gonna deal with tragedy in your life or other things. . . . In putting your life in God's hands, He takes care of those things and He provides for you." Nigel could also look forward to an immortal future that would bring relief from anxieties having to do with lust and other pleasures: "One of the big things I look forward to in going to heaven is the end of that struggle against the flesh. All of a sudden you're not gonna have those temptations and you're not gonna have to worry about dropping the ball [failing God's tests] if you know what I mean. That's where that ends." Nigel thus depicted a two-step sequence in the self's negation of proteanism and chaos: the first achieved via the fixity provided by conversion; the second imagined in terms of heaven's unchanging perfection and absolute psychological quietude.

## END-TIME CONTRADICTIONS

But the central fundamentalist tenet of end time—and especially the relationship between nuclear holocaust and the Second Coming of Jesus—is a constant source of confusion, allowing for the intrusion of protean currents. Not only does a wide array of groups embrace end-time ideology (various denominations of evangelicals and Pentecostals, who may or may not be fundamentalist in my terms), but there is an equally divergent approach to the details of end-time theology. That is, fundamentalists embrace end time as a profoundly transformative event involving vast destruction (the Biblical Armageddon) prior to their being united forever with Jesus, but they are unclear and endlessly contradictory concerning how all that will come about, most of all concerning the role played by nuclear holocaust. Fundamentalists are exposed repeatedly to end-time theological assertions of nuclear holocaust as inevitable, and even desirable, as a means of bringing about the Second Coming. But the people we interviewed are uneasy with that theology, to the point of circumventing or denying it.

Ian X., an organist in a fundamentalist church, has centered his life on the return of Jesus and thinks that nuclear holocaust will somehow play an important role in millennial events; but when asked what he thought about nuclear war, he answered simply and emphatically, "I'm against it!" And Darlene N. said, "No, I don't look forward to the end. I want to live, don't you?"—then added, in a way that legitimated this desire theologically, "I love life. I always thank God for life." Indeed, she believes that Jesus will return to *prevent* nuclear destruction: "He sees everything. . . . He can see the danger. . . . I think that's why He will come back." Her concern is that it will be too late: "I think we're going to destroy ourselves if God doesn't escalate the time when He's coming back." Although she uses a nuclear-weapons verb in respect to God's redemptive power, she insists, "Anything that is of a destructive nature is not of God."

Similar contradictions were expressed by Otto T., who is both an ordinary parishioner in one church and the leader of a tiny congregation in another. He first blandly calculated the mathematics of the Apocalypse (concluding that half the earth's population would be killed) and said he was "concerned, I guess, in a way" about all that, but not too much because Scripture makes clear that "it will be a judgment that is just." Yet he seemed to recoil from the idea of nuclear holocaust and gave an odd reason for doing so: "I really don't think man's going to blow this world up because the Scriptures speak of God judging it, and I feel there has to be something for God to judge." He laughed a bit here, as though slightly mocking his own literalism, but then added that God is so powerful that He does not require the weapons: "He didn't need a nuclear bomb to pour out fire and brimstone on Sodom and Gomorrah." Such responses indicate both how, by dissociation, fundamentalists protect themselves from psychologically experiencing—from actually *feeling*—the bloody consequences of their vision; and the extent to which their very literalism (so needed to fend off protean alternatives) can undermine their belief system by creating a vicious circle of more literalism, and more need to improvise in order to deal with contradictions and unanswerable questions.

Significantly, not one among the fundamentalists we interviewed, despite their depth of longing for end-time merging with Jesus, directly advocated nuclear war. Rather, their humane sentiments were sufficiently strong to take precedence over the abstract theology of nuclearized Armageddon. But their responses varied greatly concerning whether nuclear war would occur, how one should feel about its occurrence, who would be responsible for it, and how that possibility should affect one's own life. Darlene N., for instance, attributes the danger of nuclear holocaust only to human evil: "It gets to a certain point where God just withdraws himself from it, and there's nothing but destruction left." God must not be held responsible, that is, for human evil; but at the same time, one must find some explanation—and, of course, these explanations greatly diverge—for why God, who controls everything, might let it happen. The uncertainties and contradictions result from the need to combine fundamentalist literalism with contemporary scientific, logical, and moral influences, from which fundamentalists cannot be completely removed.

Fundamentalists must deal with the extraordinary dimensions of violence that their ideology calls forth. "Violence washes over everything" in a fierce expression of God's anger but also a surgical action that is just and necessary to the millennial scenario of redemption. Wilma M. could state calmly, "Burning will cleanse the earth." Again, personal inclinations toward decency and life enhancement can contest these fierce ideological requirements, but they can be negated in turn by suspicion of an Antichrist in peacemaker's clothing. Thus, Thelma M. said, "The Bible warns us that when men cry peace, then sudden destruction [comes], . . . so I'm not interested in world peace because I know it's not what God says will be." Some fundamentalists echo Otto T.'s claim that God doesn't need nuclear weapons. "If He wanted to destroy this earth, He could do it in a second," Nigel T. said. And Pastor Allen E. reflected the views of many: "God's plan is going to be perfected regardless of what weaponry men may have." Much in these attitudes derives from traditional Biblical imagery—from both Testaments and the Book of Revelation; but nuclear weapons and related environmental threats constitute a new ingredient in the imagery of destruction. Biblical imagery must be reimagined to absorb this new ingredient and, however difficult, render it part of the process of renewal.

Of course, end time is a nonrational vision which can, at least to a degree, transcend logic and absorb contradictions. But with the psychological and intellectual demands of the vision so extreme and so antithetical to common sense, the contradictions and inner questions can never be fully overcome. This profound source of personal identity—this image at the heart of the fundamentalist project—thus becomes an agitated constellation of mystical yearning, dread, and nagging uncertainty. One way fundamentalists handle this demanding psychological situation is to move in and out of the end-time self. The dissociative process comes close to that of "doubling" (see chapter 10), where the end-time self and the everyday self exist relatively independently, the former in relation to end-time worship and expectation, the latter to going about such ordinary matters as working, paying bills, and planning for one's children. One of the problems with this psychological arrangement is that, within the doubling, nuclear threat is now perceived by one self, now by the other; is sometimes a vehicle for the much-sought millennium, sometimes a grotesque view of mass killing and human suffering. Nuclear-weapons–related visions of end time, then, are urgent and ultimate, a source of anxious questions and improvisations.

## Protean Fundamentalists

> *Listen, let me sum it up like this. When you and I get to the end, get to the grave . . . you'll find the Bible is . . . truth. If [it turns out] there is no heaven, there is no hell, all this was just a mirage, an illusion. . . . If it's a fairytale, it's a fairytale in which I find hope. I found joy. At least in this fairytale, a man is a man, a husband, a father. . . . It's helped, . . . it's dealt with a lot of belief or disbelief. I've benefitted by embracing it. [It's] given me a fulfillment, a direction for my life, . . . so it is that kind of thing that keeps me going.*

> —Pastor Charles V.

### "DON'T QUOTE ME ON THE EXACT SPECIFICS": NIGEL T.

Individual struggles with end-time imagery can reveal more general protean tendencies at the heart of the fundamentalist self. Nigel T., whose conversion was bound up with end-time beliefs, is nonetheless vague about those beliefs. He hews to Biblical imagery in saying that Christ "is gonna come like a thief in the night when we least expect it," but he is hesitant and uncertain concerning the end-time sequence: "In the Old Testament, there is a Tribulation period and then there is a millennium period where maybe people are given a second opportunity or something. I'm not exactly sure on that. . . . Don't quote me on the exact specifics." As to being close to the end: "I believe that there is a strong possibility that we could be, [but] . . . I'm a little reluctant to say that, since we had five earthquakes or four famines or droughts or whatever, that we are in the end time." In a personal sense, he is clear: "You go to heaven, you don't go to purgatory"; but concerning the state one will be in, he, after a brief confident burst, again became hesitant: "Revelation talks about that, and what it says is that we'll be given a new body, a body made of incorruptible seed, . . . a body that doesn't perish, you know, . . . a perfect body, a beautiful body. . . . Uh, I don't know exactly what that will be, and that's sort of one of the question marks that Christ leaves open."

He even seems to slip out of fundamentalist literalism into a more or less historical and metaphorical interpretation: "There are a lot of things about the Bible that you can sort of read between the lines about"; and, "You have to sort of put yourself in the shoes of somebody that lived at that time to really understand fully what they were going through." He quickly heads off these tendencies in himself, however, by reverting to a cautious literalism: "But when you consider things in Revelation or things that you don't have an answer to, you really don't want to speculate too much. You wanna leave God's work to speak for itself and just believe what it says."

In his life in general, Nigel T. experiences parallel pulls and conflicts. He looks for leeway by stressing Christ's forgiveness toward sins ("He doesn't bring it up, and there is no reason why I should either"); and then comments further, with some uneasiness, about what such a principle of forgiveness means: "In going through life, we sort of have a license to sin, but that's not the way we should look at it." In connection with his conversion, he said that the "good person" he has in a sense become is "not me but Christ living in my heart," and added, "I'm just a different person and it's not me"—all of which suggests questions and confusions concerning the authenticity of his conversion and the inner reality of his overall fundamentalist identity. In relation to divine influence, he struggles with "knowing that it's gonna happen eventually," and at the same time being "motivated [to] . . . affect [events]." But then, in highly unfundamentalist terms, he said that all this raises "the old question about, was this God's will or did we create His will, or He willed it for us to do this in the beginning anyhow?" In saying that, he was flirting with something close to a naturalistic philosophy in which God becomes merely a projection of the human imagination. But he brought himself firmly back into the fundamentalist orbit by invoking as a personal model the life of a man who did much to create the structures for converting wealthy businessmen: "Here is a gentleman who . . . had attained wealth to such a degree that . . . he was riding every day in the back of a limousine. But he would literally be on his knees in . . . the limousine praying for people, . . . like a thousand people a day." The same man, while actively pursuing business goals, would start every conversation with the question, "How is your relationship with Christ, what's gonna happen to you when you die?" Nigel T.'s model, combining unabashed pursuit of worldly goals with equally unabashed insistence upon fundamentalist

proselytizing, provides him with a heroic ideal for his own similar struggle. In his intense effort to convert the interviewer, he was attempting to
live up to that standard and, at the same time, to ward off as much as possible of his own troublesome proteanism.

### "THOSE FEELINGS . . . COME RUSHING BACK IN": PASTOR MARTIN Y.

Pastor Martin Y., whose embrace of end-time imagery helped stem his
1960s rebellion, expressed the view that such imagery has been neglected
in recent years; that he would "like to see it reemphasized . . . so that we
don't forget, . . . don't let these things slip, because that is our heritage."
Yet when questioned about his own views on end time, he was extremely
vague, could recall only a few images, and those not from the Scriptures
but from Hal Lindsey's book. He admitted that his interest in such things
"has certainly fallen off," perhaps because "I've been just so caught up in
things that are happening presently." He also spoke of end time as "a two-
edged sword": it is supposed to serve as a warning, "but . . . only to spur
us on to those things we should do anyway." And when he went on to
Christ's injunction to "work while it is yet day, for the night comes and no
man can work," and to say that this "outweighs it all," he was, in effect,
saying that the millennium is less important than what we do now. He was
very tentative indeed when asked whether he and his family were preparing for end time ("Yes, I think so, . . . yes, I think they are"), and pre-
ferred to change the subject.

In telling a little "in" joke ("God forbid what would happen [if] Christ
comes to Jimmy Swaggert at that motel [where he was having illicit
sex]"), Pastor Y. may well have been expressing a bit of protean mockery
not just at Swaggert's hypocrisy but at end-time dogma in general. For
that demanding dogma defies much of the contemporary sensibility both
intellectually (in its far-out scenario) and morally (in its acceptance of
massive human death and suffering). Thus, for Pastor Y., nuclear
weapons are less agents for the Second Coming than a menace to the
human future (commenting on the television film *The Day After,* he spoke
of "a generation of young people that . . . don't think they'll live through
high school"). A man of many interests, he is still nostalgic for the 1960s
and 1970s experiences he had ostensibly renounced with his conversion.
He spoke of the "sense of hope" at the time that "we were going to make
a better world." And he defends, or half-defends, the spirit that prevailed
against inclinations toward fundamentalist condemnation ("I don't think
it was an evil spirit necessarily, . . . just a feeling that permeated society"),
adding that when he hears an old Simon and Garfunkel or Crosby, Stills
and Nash song (snapping his fingers as he talks), he can "go right back to
that and identify with all those feelings—they come rushing back in."

Residual protean sentiments, though not unique to Pastor Y., are particularly strong in him, and he was unusually candid about them. They are part of a balance he maintains in his life as a fundamentalist preacher, a balance that requires him to be ever vigilant about his own openness.

## "ALMOST LIKE A CREDIT CARD": PASTOR LESTER M.

Pastor Lester M., the rock musician who sees Jesus as a buttress against confusion and depression, is particularly focused on the science and technology of end time. Stating as Biblical prophecy, "The elements will melt with intense heat," he added, "We are talking about hydrogen bombs; we are talking about atomic bombs, nuclear warheads." Yet end time is desirable (and here he is traditionally Biblical) to bring about "new heavens and a new earth in which righteousness dwells," and inevitable: "It's the nature of human nature to go astray, . . . the nature of the world to get worse, . . . like the laws of thermodynamics. Everything is . . . burning up, and spiritually that's true, too." He maintains this Biblical/technological combination for identifying the saved: amidst the release of everything "from hailstones to demons," believers will be afforded "a proper numerical sign, . . . invisible or not, on their hands or on their forehead, almost like a credit card. . . . Instead of carrying a plastic card, you'll go to some place and you'll get a number on your forehead that can be read by some machine." Those who have not converted "are not gonna have these numbers, and they will be persecuted and . . . hounded, and they will be judged . . . through this . . . Tribulation period." As for his own expectation of Rapture: "Yeah, we won't be around here, we are out of here."

He went on to speak of the experience in glowing terms: "It will be almost like a honeymoon. Jesus, the bridegroom, comes for the church, the bride; this is the beautiful symbolism. I'm looking forward to some exciting stuff." Then he pulled back and said that end time "doesn't dominate my thinking," that he did not preach it: "You know, most people don't need to be told [here he used 1960s-style mockery], 'Man, judgment is coming!' People don't need to hear that." What people do need to hear is, he believes, "the explanation of the Epistles on how to walk and live in kindness and love and joy and be filled with God's spirit": and one way he conveys this message is through his music, his contemporary renderings via guitar and voice of hymns and spiritual affirmations. He, too, requires a variety of protean expressions in blending his versions of music and of science and technology, at times a bit uneasily, with his fundamentalist dogma.

## "YES, WELL, YES, NO": PASTOR ALLEN E.

Pastor Allen E. wavered still more on the subject. He also was reluctant to preach end time: "Although it might work to some degree, you can't frighten people into the Kingdom of God." Moreover, he felt that nuclear war could be avoided: among decision makers, "someone who is God-conscious is checked in his concepts [and behavior]," while "the other person will go the limit." Furthermore, "I don't think the planet's going to be annihilated because God, it's His, He made it, and He'll take care of it." But then Pastor E. hedged, saying that the weapons could possibly "be used with God's permission if . . . that's the only authority that can withstand satanic power upon the world." He then said that the "solidarity" of believers was "keeping this thing from disintegrating right now"; when asked whether such solidarity might delay the Second Coming, his answer was pained, contradictory, and confused: "Yes, well, yes, no. I haven't said delay it, no. Nothing is delayed. The Lord will not delay His coming, it's His timeclock. Now that's what we don't know. We say 'delay,' but we don't know what the time is." Everything will "disintegrate" only when God is ready to say, "All right, old world, you've had it." And Pastor E., too, went on to make clear that he was in no hurry for end time, and that it might in fact be a "dissatisfaction" for him in the sense that before such an event occurs, "I want to see many, many more come to the Lord." Even as disciplined a fundamentalist as Pastor Allen has a continuously ambivalent struggle with the extreme requirements of end-time belief and their relation to this-worldly commitments.

## THE "END-TIME HARVEST": PASTOR CHARLES V.

The black pastor, Charles V., perhaps the most protean fundamentalist encountered in our work, was at the same time extraordinarily intense about end time and equally extraordinarily conflicted. He considered the signs of deterioration all around—"this scourge of drug addiction," which he sometimes suspected (as do many blacks) of being "a planned genocide [of] . . . the black community"; the ubiquitous violence ("I mean folks cutting people up in little pieces, stuffing them in plastic bags"); the AIDS epidemic; the vast technology of destruction ("they can . . . almost put [a nuclear missile] in my backyard")—and spoke of an "end-time plague": "I look around me, I read the papers and read my news weekly, check out the television, and, man!, this is the Last Days stuff." In referring to Christ's return as "the only answer," he was articulating the collective longing institutionalized in his own "end-time church."

His response, however, is not one of mere preparation for the event but rather an energetic address to human problems. "This is the time to get *involved*," he declared, and has done so with a sense of being pressured by the nearness of the end: "I feel that whatever I must do, . . . do it quickly, do it with all my might, . . . bend my energies in whatever way I can, spiritually, to change, to help, maybe build this community." He even referred to this vitality as an "end-time harvest." He has managed to renovate a large, old building to make it into a place of worship, classrooms, meetings, and athletic events. While he referred to some of these services as "the net we use to catch them [people for his end-time teachings]," he always combines those teachings with extensive outreach programs, such as a counseling center for alcoholics and addicts and a project for preparing people for jobs. Emphasizing his concern with people's immediate lives, he declared, "We're not just a Sunday church, this is a community church." So his people go out into the area with coffee and sandwiches and "meet [people] at the point of their need," offering "a room upstairs with all sorts of good new and used clothing." He insists that the church be "relevant" to desperate problems: "So many homeless men, our fathers and our husbands in jail [or] out in the streets, and we've got to try to salvage some of them." His approach is to demonstrate Christian love in action: "We can't go out there with just the fact that Christ is the answer, 'Pardon me, sir, but Jesus loves you.' We've got to show forth that love. . . . I try to embed in our people a reaching out for one another, a caring for one another. I don't always succeed . . . to the extent that I want to, but I will never stop striving."

Pastor Charles thus draws power from his other-worldliness to apply in this world at this time an impressive and compassionate array of protean talents and concerns. A sustaining model for him is that of transformation. A survivor of the ghetto, he feels he has been miraculously salvaged by God, and his survivor mission is to continue to salvage others by genuinely changing their lives. As he explained, "It's not enough to get a man off drugs . . . if he still has on his old sneakers"; what is required is "a renewing of the entire mind and of all that person is." "This," he proudly said to our interviewer, "is really black power." But everything, including the church's financial dealings, is done in the shadow of the end time: a policy of short-term, interest-free loans because "God doesn't get much glory out of 7 percent [or] out of the 5 percent [interest]."

Throughout, the Reverend Charles maintains a tense but effective balance between end-time expectation and urgent worldly responsibility: "[Jesus] could come next week, next month, but I'm gonna plan for two or three years." He actually plans for a longer period—investments for his children's education—while at the same time "keeping my eyes on not getting overly attached . . . because . . . I have this end-time feeling . . . that propels me."

He also draws constantly upon his own transformative past, his experience of moving "over and above and beyond where your original roots might have been, and going around and [here sounding like Barbara C.] testing a lot of waters." This principle enabled him to emerge from a youth in which he had little educational opportunity, worked at every variety of manual labor, and "was the least likely to succeed, not because I didn't have the brain matter but I was prone to get in mischief and trouble." Rebellious and fiercely sensitive to racism and economic deprivation, he had been in many situations in which his life was threatened, and came close several times to being "trapped" by destructive forces that could have led to his own violence. He remarked at one point that, had he not become a minister, "I would have been a revolutionary."

Later, as a noncommissioned officer in the military in charge of training men for combat, he discovered in himself a talent for changing people: "I had to transform them from a civilian to a soldier in twelve weeks. . . . I lived with them, and I pushed them and forced them, and I forced myself and stayed on them . . . so the fat got skinny, the skinnys got husky, you know, the weak got strong, and the strong got discipline." He came to view that experience as "preparation for, and as part of, my vision and goals even now, taking sinners, with the help of God, and bringing them into spiritual maturity, molding and making them disciples." He also struggled with his own inner transformations, above all with the question, "Where is my place?"—until sometime later "a calling gripped me," and he made his way toward his present life. He feels that over the course of that life he has touched every kind of person and situation: "I've been with saved and unsaved, believers and unbelievers, and dealt with death in so many areas." He remains torn between a longing for end time as the only salvation for the world and himself, and his desperate salvational struggles *against* the timing of the end.

But at one point during the interviews, he paused to tell about a revealing conversation with a man who challenged his beliefs, especially about end time. His answer (the epigraph to this section)—even if a fairytale, it is one of hope—is remarkable for his admission of inner doubt or, at least, of his difficulty in maintaining full belief in the end-time vision; and at the same time for his affirmation of the fragile tightrope on which he walks to bring together the protean revolutionary in himself and the fundamentalist builder of the "quality Christian academy" he aspires to create.

## LASERS, DOLBY SCREENS, AND "TECHNICAL QUESTIONS"

For some fundamentalists, high technology becomes an integral part of the end-time process. Otto T. had studied engineering and sees himself as always adhering to a basic principle he was taught: "Never just accept something because someone tells it to you. Prove it." In his vision of end time, he combines the principle of "the mark of the beast" (which the Book of Revelation says will be stamped on unbelievers) with computer technology (which he closely studies) to distinguishing sinners from saved ("I'm told they could put a little computer chip on the back of your hand, and you just put it under a scanner or . . . it could be a laser-type tattoo or something"). But he worries lest the Antichrist get hold of the technology "to work out a system of pressing on people [who are actually saved] the mark of the beast," and that such deception is made all the more possible by brilliant recent advances in "this miniaturization [radically smaller computer equipment] which boggles my mind." His technocratic approach is bound up with other worldly interests, as reflected in his comment about Jimmy Swaggert's sexual misbehavior: "There's times I've felt like, if I see him on TV crying one more time, you know, 'I have sinned,' . . . that I feel like smashing the TV. But that'd be stupid, because then I couldn't watch the Mets ball games."

Otto's complexity of belief and doubt were revealed in his associating from Swaggert to the story of a brilliant teenage preacher who had an uncanny ability to convince and convert people until, at age twenty, "he just chucked the whole thing," declared that "he was acting the whole time," and from then on followed the career of a professional actor. Otto's comment that, even when a fallible "messenger" claims, "I didn't mean what I was saying, I didn't really believe it," the power of God's word is such that "He can still work through that messenger." The concept is ingenious, but I wondered how much of Otto was in the fallible, doubting messenger, especially when he admitted that his demanding fundamentalist activities (as leader of a small congregation and active worshiper in a larger one) could be wearing: "If I wasn't called, I would have quit long ago because it's a no fun life, . . . no picnic, so to speak." What is especially "no picnic" to Otto—what constantly strains his ingenuity—is the difficult integration of his technological and Biblical visions.

## "A NO-MAN'S LAND OF UNDERSTANDING": FRANK K.

Frank K., interviewed in his early thirties, is a Jew who overcame formidable barriers to undergo a fierce conversion to Protestant fundamentalism. His view of God's judgment during end time is not only technological but filmic: "I picture God taking us individually and showing us our lives in review in seventy-millimeter Dolby [a wide-screen motion picture technology]. We are going to see every time . . . we've cheated, . . . see it all in seventy-millimeter Dolby, right there." And there will be "an added dimension: our thoughts are heard, our very thoughts are as loud for us to hear as anything else." Frank was unusual in lubricating his vision with a little humor as he and the interviewer laughed over its resemblance to a scene in a Woody Allen film.

Before committing himself to "faith in Jesus as the Messiah," Frank had rejected the "everything in moderation" principle of his liberal, middle-class Jewish parents, explored various forms of Eastern philosophy and mysticism as well as some of the experiential psychological ideas of Abraham Maslow, held a lucrative business position, and unsuccessfully sought pleasure "with other singles, . . . dancing a lot and hang[ing] out in rock-'n-roll clubs and stuff like that." He combined a self-mocking Jewish style with fundamentalist fervor in talking about "my schtick," touring campuses with a musical group affiliated with the Jews for Jesus movement and called "The Liberated Wailing Wall"; and about how God "uses little *nebishes* ["poor unfortunates" or "nothings"] like me . . . [in] invisible work that He does in people's hearts [which is] far more miraculous than the parting of the Red Sea." In all this work, Frank claimed he sought to "deepen [his] appreciation" of his Jewishness.

Frank extends his technological absorptions to what he called "a morbid preoccupation with nuclear weaponry," and admits being "fascinated" with "the sheer power of it" and the "fear and awe" of it. While he believes that "there can be nothing good about building nuclear weapons," and that our "increased wickedness" makes us use the technology "for evil," he feels that "the power itself is what draws people, . . . speaks to people"—and revealed the extent of his own attraction to this power when, in the middle of this discussion, he made a loud noise to represent an enormous explosion. He considers an association of nuclear annihilation with the millennium to be "natural in our day and age." He thinks of a potential nuclear holocaust as "the very, very end times," as representing a decision by God, having been rejected by non-believers, to "remove His influence . . . [and] let man go the way he wants to go." Frank's pained ambivalence toward nuclear technology is deepened by his reverential gratitude toward it in connection with the successful diagnosis and treatment of a serious medical condition some time after his conversion. That ambivalence was evident in his answer to the question whether he looked forward to nuclear end time. In an unconvincing tone, he said, "Yeah, definitely," but added, "I'm not living there now. I'm here now and dealing with right here and now."

Frank tends to be "all over the place" in his views and tones. He can be highly intellectualized in speaking of his "inductive study" of Biblical phenomena using "principles of hermeneutics" (he had studied some theology following his conversion) and admitted that end time with the Rapture is for "some people . . . as though they were reading *Peter Pan*." He added, "It's hard in our natural understanding to picture God coming down out of the sky. . . . Some people would laugh at that"; and he acknowledged that a great deal in the Scriptures is "poetry" and "figures of speech" which it would be "ridiculous" to take literally. But he quickly reversed himself: "Much of the Bible is narrative and . . . could be taken very literally," and, "I don't believe in relative truth when it comes to God." Not surprisingly, Frank ends up viewing all people "as a jigsaw puzzle in a sense, many pieces, many aspects of our lives, . . . a composite." He insists that the jigsaw puzzle always needs God as the missing piece. But then he describes himself as "a citizen of no land here on earth, . . . at odds with the majority of the Jewish community, . . . and . . . never going to be really understood . . . by a large majority of the church, . . . never going to be a gentile." His characterization of his situation as a "no-man's land of understanding" surely includes not only the conflicts surrounding his conversion, but extends also to his technocratic, strikingly multifaceted, precariously ordered sense of self and to the ingeniously fragile approach to reality reflected in his seventy-millimeter Dolby rendition of end time.

## "DOUBLE-ENTRY BOOKKEEPING": MONROE L.

Monroe L., the converted businessman, echoed Frank's sense of the absurd elements in the end-time scenario: "If I were you, I'd say, 'How can you believe that?'"; he added, "Some of [it] is real preposterous, outlandish," and even more significantly, "I . . . have a little bit of that [sense of] . . . science fiction." His contradictions arise not from a relationship to technology as such but from a need to pursue what he calls "technical questions" concerning the literal details of postmillennial arrangements. Not surprisingly, such questions reflect immediate conflicts and losses. Convinced that the millennium will create an "industrial order" that is "productive" with tight hierarchical arrangements ("We're not all the same in eternity"), he is concerned about achieving the best possible "quality of life" in those arrangements. In that spirit, he asked his teachers at the seminary he attended, "What kind of body am I gonna have?" Other "technical questions" that trouble him include: which of his two divorced wives will he be reunited with in heaven, and who during the millennium will be able to have children—only converts (his current understanding) or "Resurrected Saints" (original Christians) as well? He remains troublingly uncertain about "how that all works out" and about "how I'd sort it out emotionally."

Monroe L. is unusually reluctant to discuss nuclearized end time for turns out an unusual reason. Should he take a clear position about the nature and timing of the great event, that would be "put[ting] all your eggs over there"; and if things do not turn out that way, he will be left wondering about everything ("You say, 'Well, gee whiz!'"). What concerns him is not the morality of nuclear weapons or the like but the possibility that, should he turn out to be wrong, his faith could be threatened! He, too, resists the idea of the millennium coming very soon because he has so much more to accomplish before that moment, but he is contrite about that attitude: "I don't want Him to come today but, I mean, that's wrong."

When exploring details of the millennium, Monroe L. invariably expressed confusion—at one point interrupting himself by saying, "Let me just stop there!," then quickly declaring, "I really believe Christ is going to return like he said." Monroe was trying to stop the protean flow, which, however, always reasserts itself. He was described by his interviewer as struggling with "something seriously wrong underneath his Christian demeanor," as warding off fragmentation of the self by means of a "desperate and intense belief system." Monroe himself at one point related some of his difficulties to "a midlife crisis," and at another time revealed a sense of sad confusion in saying, "I don't know how He slips away from me so badly." And in speaking of "a double-entry bookkeeping system," his immediate reference was to God's basis for ultimate judgment on people, but the term applies equally to his own back-and-forth protean-antiprotean self-process. No wonder Monroe mused, "We . . . live in a dream world."

## The Protean-Antiprotean Dance

The dynamic between fundamentalism and proteanism has to do with how one copes with threat, confusion, and the psychological danger of fragmentation—and the degree of control one seeks to impose on historical forces. Yet much that I have said suggests something close to an organic relationship between proteanism and fundamentalism, between transformationism and restorationism, between the self historically opened and the effort to close it down: in every fundamentalist assertion, there may well be some kind of protean underside, some potential for alternative imagery and symbolization. Correspondingly, every protean exploration may require some protective structuring or even partial closing down of experience. Hence, proteanism is never absolute, and fundamentalism can never succeed in its agenda of complete purification. There is always an interweaving of tendencies, so that fundamentalist and protean selves each end up with compromises that are both necessary and fragile.

That organic relationship has existed within the historical "self" of the

American nation: simultaneous protean forays and fundamentalist-like religious (revivalist) and political (nativist or antiforeign) outbreaks, both tendencies always important to existing popular culture. But fundamentalism, in its essence a reactive force, takes on the impossible task of fully controlling the symbolizing process and eliminating its spontaneity and unpredictability. Hence, the fundamentalist self feels unable to live up to what is demanded of it, feels that there is—as one fundamentalist is quoted as saying—a "war all day long."

Collective fundamentalist energies can expand that metaphor and, indeed, convert it into literal behavior, as in the case of three recent expressions of violence: the bloody confrontation between the Branch Davidian cult and the Federal Bureau of Investigation in Waco, Texas (1993), resulting in the deaths of four FBI agents from gunfire and over seventy cult members, many of them infants and small children, from a conflagration of uncertain origin and from gunshot wounds thought to be largely self-inflicted; the bombing of the World Trade Center building in New York City (1993); and the genocide carried out by Serbian forces in Bosnia (1992–93). While differing radically in their dimensions and in the affiliations of the perpetrators, all three events are products of fiercely fundamentalist ideological visions. The Branch Davidian cult, under the fanatical leadership of David Koresh, collected and used weapons of heavy firepower and endlessly viewed films of the Vietnam War, all in preparation for a battle (provided by the FBI) that would be part of the larger end-time Armageddon. The group responsible for the bombing of the World Trade Center was affiliated with Islamic fundamentalism, whose tenets include "holy war" against evil enemies or those considered to be associated with such enemies. And the Serb forces in Bosnia have carried out their slaughter of Muslims in the service of a totalistic nationalism and a near-mystical Greater Serbia. Each of the ideological visions rewards violence with purification and a variety of immortality—whether in Christian or Islamic heaven or nationalistic glory.

These violent expressions of fundamentalism can be understood as more general societal conflicts writ large. They transform the protean-antiprotean dance into a death march. Even without the violence, however, the fundamentalist part of the dance can be immersed in painful dualities: for instance, the intense communal ties with fellow believers along with profound alienation from everyone else. Another duality holds for the fundamentalist immortality system: it can help one to cope with death, but can also in many cases do the reverse. One may find oneself (as was true of a number of those we interviewed) on a treadmill of being confronted with death, seeking and finding some relief in the end-time immortality system, and then experiencing newly intensified death anxiety as that immortality system fails to be completely believable and, in fact, generates unresolvable protean questions. One may be left, like

Otto T., with a sense of overall fatigue and inner deadness. Or, more commonly, a pattern of dissociation enables one to move in and out of one's end time and ordinary selves.

The process can be adaptive, with the two selves held together by compassionate elements of Christian belief. But the doubling can itself become unstable—and in some cases, a mechanism for violence—under the constant pressure of the protean-antiprotean dance. The fundamentalist self can then resemble Albert Camus's "judge-penitent" (epigraph, page 166) who, because he accuses himself of everything, arrogates the right to judge—and, I would add, to condemn and destroy—all offending others. When that happens, the organic tie to proteanism means little, except as one to be radically severed at any cost.

# Chapter 10

---

# THE DARK SIDE

---

*There is somebody who's living my life. And I know nothing about him.*

—Luigi Pirandello

*We are trapped in the terrible jaws of something shaking the life out of us, something . . . deep-down bad.*

—John Edgar Wideman

PROTEANISM CAN GO WRONG in many different ways. There is the ever-present danger of diffusion, to a point of rendering the self incoherent and immobile: a "chaos of possibilities." The protean hunger for meaning can be fierce and ever unsatisfied. Endless forays into possibility can become endlessly superficial, leaving the self with a sense of diminished, rather than enhanced, meaning. (The pattern lends itself to burlesque: "The Post-Impulsives are here. Or were just a second ago. The Post-Impulsives. They can't even remember what an attention span is. The Post-Impulsives. They haven't got time for instant gratification.") And even with less extreme fluidity, the failure of a series of protean forays can contribute to a cumulative sense of loss, leaving one vulnerable to withdrawal, apathy, and depression. One's commitment to proteanism, moreover, may cause one to respond to the self's disarray by accelerating one's shifts, while clinging to an illusion of salvation via perpetual transformation. In the process, lacking even minimal psychological continuity, one can slip readily from fluidity to fragmentation, and from there to violence.

Negative proteanism, which I will explore throughout this chapter, is fluidity so lacking in moral content and sustainable inner form that it is likely to result in fragmentation (or near fragmentation) of the self, harm to others, or both. One can engage in amoral reversals, as, say, Jerry Rubin's journey from 1960s Yippie to 1990s Yuppie—from the young man who declared, "Don't trust anyone over thirty!" and "Capitalism killed my father!" to the fiftyish businessman engaged in "multi-level marketing" of powders and potions that consumer groups have called "hype" and "horsefeathers." Rubin is hardly alone: increasingly, American political candidates at all levels have tended to shifts in opinion, in positions on issues, in approaches to audiences, even in self-definitions— a pattern that can teeter between political savvy and protean formlessness. There have been parallels in postcommunist Europe: the once-feared Czech communist turned unscrupulous capitalist "shamelessly and unequivocally laughing in the face of the same worker whose interests he once claimed to defend"; and most sinister of all, Serbian former communists shifting to a combination of fanatical nationalism and mendacious self-aggrandizement in pursuing a genocidal project.

A shadowy version of American negative proteanism was made painfully visible in the assassination of John F. Kennedy by Lee Harvey Oswald. Oswald seemed to have floated through endless social and ideological spheres—as confused child, soldier, defector to the Soviet Union, husband and father, and social activist—in ways that still leave us confused as to what, if anything, he wished to represent or accomplish. He is the prototype of the American "drifter," who "seems scripted out of doctored photos, tourist cards, change-of-address cards, mail-order forms, visa applications, altered signatures, pseudonyms": the quintessential fragmented American, created and re-created by his environment or his manipulators, so that, rather than being able to act, "actions find him." Oswald becomes the ultimate expression of negative proteanism, of world-destroying violence in the service of a private quest—or several private quests—for meaning. The gates are opened to protean demagogy, protean fascism, protean murder.

Negative proteanism is furthered by the threat of actual world destruction, a meaningless nuclear or environmental "end." At issue is not only the twentieth century's "astonishing new offer: death for everybody, . . . by hemlock or hardware," but the disturbing reverberations of a pointless apocalypse (we recall Martin Amis's words in chapter 2: "If, at any moment, nothing might matter, then who said that nothing didn't matter already?"). That pointless apocalypse could be seen by activists like Carol C. as part of "ongoing destruction" which includes radical environmental damage, worldwide poverty and depression, and general irresponsibility in relation to the AIDS epidemic—leading her to experience a "gut feeling . . . of injustice" and "a hell of a powerlessness," feelings she has had since childhood. And for groups at the bottom rung of our society, there can be a still more encompassing, and psychologically damaging, blending of accumulated traumas. For Jessica C. (the young black woman who associated nuclear annihilation with various forms of environmental destruction and with AIDS, declaring: "They're just killing everything" [see chapter 3]), AIDS in particular creates a community of death: "That's the worst, . . . a sexual disease that can kill you. . . . You sleep with someone—it's terrible. . . . I don't know who he slept with before. . . . If I'm sleeping with him, I'm sleeping with everybody he slept with, and everybody they slept with, and everybody they slept with." Equating nature with people, Jessica implies that both are "slowly dying" because of the destructiveness and radical hypocrisy of our own leaders: "All the people that are supposed to be . . . good people, . . . reverends and priests, they're the ones that are . . . stealing, . . . people in the Senate, . . . our presidents and military people. They're the ones that are sleeping with everybody, . . . dealing drugs, . . . or alcoholic, . . . or [else] they're not capable of doing good." For Jessica, as for many other poor blacks, hypocrisy, evil, and disease render living deadly and place the self constantly at extreme risk. A life pattern of trauma and degradation can result in degrees of fragmentation consistent with what have been called the "battered identities" of certain blacks. It is also what the black novelist John Edgar Wideman meant (chapter epigraph) in speaking of being "trapped in the terrible jaws of something shaking the life out of us."

But the potential for the fragmentation of negative proteanism is more general. Poor whites in rural America can experience society as both suffocating and anarchic and "turn . . . their ordinary lives into early disasters and never know why, [which] can make a man crazy." Russell Banks's novel *Affliction* depicts the transmission of violence from father to son, including sustained physical abuse, in those who feel left out of society, uncared for, put upon, and unable to emerge from poverty or make sense of their lives. William Faulkner earlier evoked a more primitive Southern white subculture, whose violence is associated with profound ignorance and isolation and with every form of incest and early abuse: people he describes as forever "cursed" and "doomed."

We can speak, then, of a *fragmented self* that appears in many places and guises. I shall discuss how fundamentalism and other forms of totalism, embraced to overcome fragmentation, can intensify that fragmentation in turn; and how much the same can be said of the *static self*. The latter, in its relation to technology and to the modern "neutralization and disappearance of symbols" can proceed to a "zero point" of immobilization. Any such negative proteanism succumbs to a formlessness that is inseparable from dissociation, whose extreme expression is the bizarre phenomenon of multiple personality. Dissociative patterns can occur readily in groups with painful historical legacies, resulting in a rootless or *deracinated* self. Important to this kind of historical sequence is the dark side of the American settler and frontier experience, including (as revealed by a recent study) depression with suicidal inclinations and self-destructive behavior. Given such legacies, along with recent obstacles to self-definition, it is no wonder that some observers are inclined to jettison the entire concept of self—an inclination we do well to resist.

## "Battered Identities": The Black Poor

*It's over. It's over. It's just a matter of time.*

—James E.

Among the black poor interviewed, the high degree of individual fragmentation was inseparable from equally fragmented communities— parental authority giving way to that of ghetto youths, of drug users and dealers, and of criminal groups and prison inmates. Such fragmented communities can offer erratic and precarious support and recognition, but demand in return fierce battles with rivals, violent lawlessness, and constant deception and self-deception. By requiring the identity of the "bad dude" (or "badass") as the only workable one, such a community combats constructive inclinations in its members and becomes itself a trap. That has certainly been the case with Cliff F. and James E., whose narratives follow. Black women in these environments can be victimized still more, often in the form of physical and sexual abuse from men, as is true of Arlene L.

W. E. B. Du Bois, the early-twentieth-century black activist and social theorist, saw African-Americans, as, from the beginning, denied "true self-consciousness," as requiring instead a "double-consciousness" or "sense of always looking at one's self through the eyes of others." While the resulting "double voice" could be a source of resilience and creativity (see chapter 3), under the conditions of the ghetto it can contribute to confusion and inner division. At issue, as Cornel West tells us, is the brutal absurdity imposed on the entire history of blacks in America—as slaves, postslavery victims, and people alienated from their own dissolving communities; the result is an overwhelming "collapse of meaning." Subjected to extensive white manipulation, blacks retain a pervasive sense, also evident in our interviews, of being made into social guinea pigs: "Put a handful of niggers in this test tube and shook it up and watched it bubble," is the way Wideman describes it, so that people are "walking round like ghosts of they own goddamned selves." That feeling extended to attitudes we encountered toward nuclear weapons as just one more example of malignant white experimentation, together with unusual vividness in imagining nuclear destruction on the basis of the vast inner and outer destruction already experienced. In general, work with the black poor revealed that when dislocation and social breakdown are extreme and brutally absurd, functional proteanism is likely to give way to fragmentation.


## A "ZERO"—A "SOMEBODY": CLIFF F.

That is very much evident with Cliff F., the thirty-five-year-old black prisoner. Cliff grew up in a violent ghetto neighborhood, has no memory of his father ever staying with the family, and does not know exactly when his parents separated and divorced. His father had held a steady job as a security guard, but "didn't really care too much about his kids," taking the attitude (as Cliff now sees it) of "You can keep 'em." Over his childhood and adult life, Cliff has seen his father infrequently; and in recent years, when Cliff has become a criminal and a crack addict, his father has refused to let him in his house lest his son rob or harm him, a fear partly shared by Cliff himself. Cliff retains feelings of deep resentment as well as affectionate longing for his father.

His mother "did it all" in bringing him up but in a rather strange way. He described her as "a con woman," who "could sell the devil a glass of ice water," always "fast [and] running around," drinking, and especially gambling, heavily. Although highly intelligent, she was always on welfare and never held a job, encouraged her children to steal small amounts of money to help with her gambling, and took that gambling so seriously that, when winning at cards from Cliff and his brothers, she would "actually keep our money." Within those extreme limitations, she did make erratic efforts to care for her seven sons (Cliff was the fifth), prohibiting any curse words in the house (although the boys would "do everything else") and whipping her sons "with an iron cord" when they misbehaved. She settled down a bit when she got older, so that for a while Cliff and his brothers "became her best friends," and he can now say, "I love my mother." But he also spoke bitterly of her rejection "when we needed her," and his unmanageable ambivalence toward her was expressed by his failure to visit her in the hospital when she was seriously ill. Upon hearing of her death, he was "hurt, crushed, pissed," and almost immediately afterward took part in a robbery and a bit later threatened a man with a pistol and was arrested. Cliff identifies many of his own traits with those of his mother (in whom he believed there was "something . . . missing"): his unusual "gift of gab," while "know[ing] in my heart I'm bullshittin', I'm a zero, it's just a con."

Rather than making for protean adaptability, Cliff's fatherlessness was literal and hurtful, especially in combination with the maternal chaos, which contributed to his guilt-ridden attachment to her and a negative model of self. His criminal acts (neither his first nor his last) at the time of his mother's death were triggered by unresolved grief and loss, a pattern common in people who are vulnerable to impulsive, violent, and self-destructive behavior. Over time, Cliff's very proteanness became identified in his own eyes with a con game as he assumed a series of identities: a streetwise "bad dude" or "badass" with a façade of macho toughness; a self-styled "punk" or "zero"; a confused, erratic, and guilty son, husband (his wife left him after a brief marriage), and boyfriend (to a series of women); a criminal and prison inmate increasingly involved in violence; a sometimes wise self-critic with a wry sense of humor; an articulate and angry opponent of mass violence and racial injustice, longing sometimes for harmony and sometimes for vengeance. He would go from failure (beginning with the fourth grade), to momentary success (through a combination of "conning" and ability) in an occasional friendship or job (in the Marine Corps, he performed well but made his way by faking a college degree), to crushing failure along with public exposure and self-humiliation. Because his external and internal impediments have not permitted him to integrate much of his experience, his proteanism has become dissociation and fragmentation.

Contributing greatly to this negative proteanism was Cliff's rage at his heritage in America, at the images of slavery he carries actively within him ("the beatings, the hangings, the lynching, the raping of women"), images he connects to present-day treatment of blacks. When he characterizes white attitudes as "they niggers, they animals," these are attitudes he has himself partly internalized. For these reasons, he could not stand watching the television production of *Roots*. Cliff's experience with bizarre parenting and family breakup, his subsequent heavy drug use, and the perpetual ghetto violence he has witnessed and been part of have all contributed to a lifelong survivor mentality, but with limited capacity for survivor insight or illumination.

Important to the "conning" or inauthentic aspect of Cliff's proteanism is his relationship to the gun and to drug use. Cliff told a representative ghetto story when he described how his acquisition at the age of sixteen (from money hard earned at a job) of "a nice .25 automatic" could transform him from being "a punk [who] . . . didn't fit in" to "a bad dude" who was now a threat to others ("If I have a gun, *you* fear . . . getting shot"). Rather than being a "zero," "I felt that when I had the gun, I am somebody." Heavy drug use, especially crack, gave him, in a somewhat parallel way, the false sense that "you have control of the substance controlling you." His reversion to drugs, after a commitment to staying off them, destroyed an attempt at reconciliation with his ex-wife, who perceived it as a deception; and Cliff repeated that pattern with a subsequent girlfriend to whom he had "sold . . . a dream" of a loving life together based on his promised personal reform, return to school, and steady work. Drugs and violence have contributed to compensatory feelings of omnipotence (at one point in his Bible readings, he identified himself with Moses), which alternate with his sense of being a worthless "nobody." Nor has he been able to mobilize and sustain more authentic protean elements that could enable him to move beyond that static vacillation: "Ya know, after you bin in the streets and runnin' so long and bullshittin' your way through life, you just can't . . . decipher what's right and what's wrong sometimes. Because you've been bullshittin' and sugarcoatin' wrong for so long, it looks right."

Cliff attributed much of his confusion to the deceptions of white society. Concerning nuclear weapons, for instance, he recalled with some bitterness the school air-raid drills when the children were told to duck under desks: "What kind of game was they playing with us when we was little?" After undergoing Marine Corps training in nuclear, biological, and chemical warfare, he could conclude: "Damn, this shit's crazy!" But to the possibility of actual nuclear attack, he brought a fantasy that turned out to be frequent among blacks we interviewed. There would be selective survival in which whites would be "dead, most of them" while "we [blacks] still alive." And there would be a general black revitalization, in which Jesse Jackson would become president; black churches would be a source of strength enabling people "to see God"; and blacks in control, recalling slavery, will "treat you [whites] all in terms of that way. . . . Hate to say that, but it's true." On the general issue of world destruction, he pointed out, "A lot of black people just don't give a fuck, . . . why should I bother to protest? The bomb will kill . . . all you fuckin' white people." The Russians destroyed would be "mostly white," and in any case, "You white people's the one pushin' the buttons anyway."

At times Cliff could transcend, even renounce, such attitudes, address his own inauthenticity (recognizing, for instance, that taking drugs was "easier than tryin' to bust my ass workin"), and seemed to be groping toward a more constructive form of proteanism. During such moments, he overcame his vengeful feelings toward whites to mock *all* racial stereotypes: "Some people think all Puerto Ricans carry knives, . . . all black people are savages, . . . all black guys got big dicks, . . . and Jews got little dicks and shit. That's stereotyping, man. . . . [You are] no different than me except the pigmentation of the skin, and you could help me and I can help you." In one interview, he recalled enthusiastically how in the past "blacks and whites was pullin' together" to end the Vietnam War, referred warmly to the role of Christianity and the church in that process, and then repeated, sadly but reverentially, Martin Luther King's words "Let freedom ring." Cliff spoke with eloquence and compassion of

Hiroshima and the Holocaust and the overall horrors of the twentieth century: "That's wrong, man, . . . to kill so many innocent people. . . . Why does millions of people have to die, I don't know. . . . There got to be a better way." And he reflected on his life, asking, "Where did I go wrong? . . . And how can I change that?"

What Cliff has found virtually impossible to do, however, is to maintain these constructive patterns as part of a functional everyday self. His underlying sense of always being close to "falling apart" has contributed to uncontrollable emotions and behavior, including rage and violence. Those are most likely to occur when he is overwhelmed by guilt and loss (as following his mother's death) or when an imagined possibility in his life ("*That's* what I'm reaching for") is frustrated, and he perceives as forced upon him the message "Your growth . . . will stop." The violence itself can, at least temporarily, replace feelings of disintegration with a form of personal transcendence. Cliff told of a situation in which, when surprised by a man and a woman whose home he was robbing while "cracked out" and "scared shit," he rushed the man and emitted a fierce scream—sounds and behavior he learned from Marine training. In the melee, he savagely bit each of them and cut them brutally with glass from a broken bottle; only when the woman began to plead that he not kill her and her babies was Cliff "brought . . . back to reality": "I felt like, 'What the fuck am I doin'? I'm fuckin' crazy.'" Then he stopped fighting and ran away. The explosiveness and ferocity of Cliff's free-floating emotions make it almost impossible for him to connect them even imperfectly with integrative combinations of the self. Instead, for him as for so many ghetto blacks, rage and violence form a psychological constellation of their own whose consequences contribute to further fragmentation in the vicious behavioral circle mentioned earlier.

Cliff explained this psychological and social entrapment in relation to his antinuclear feelings. Observing protestors on television, "You say, 'Yeah, I believe that . . . because they doin' the right thing,'" but for Cliff himself to join them would be "going against the image," and "the badass doesn't really want to [violate that image]": "Once you cut the TV off, . . . that's out of your mind. And [it's] 'Let me look at this bag of dope, . . . this cocaine and shit, gonna do my thing.'" While there can be lots of activity, the life cycle of the badass becomes essentially static: "There is no progress. . . . I see old guys [like that], . . . guys in their forties." Cliff explained that during one's early twenties, "you're constantly changing, changing jobs, . . . tryin' to find what's comfortable for you"; then at twenty-five "you're supposed to know exactly which way you're headin'"; and at thirty-five, Cliff's age, "You're supposed to be there. . . . You're supposed to have your course plotted." In that vision of a life of steady growth and direction, so far from anything Cliff has known, he expresses his sad awareness of the underlying stasis in his self-defeating negative proteanism.

His sense of the life cycle is further distorted by the many deaths he has witnessed of young people, mostly through drugs or violence. More than that, he internalizes a death taint that can be imposed on the designated victims of any society, in this case on blacks in a white society: "I'm some kind of piece of shit, or I'm a walking germ, and he's [a white guy] going to get contaminated 'cause I look like this." Cliff has a sense (like the Wideman character quoted earlier) of being not just a victim but a guinea pig as well, one who is crassly experimented upon by the dominant society. He offered as one example his Marine Corps experience, in which white society was ostensibly testing him to discover, "Am I going to save myself enough so I can keep going on fighting the war for them?" And as other examples, he cited experimental government use of gases for riot control during the 1960s and in present-day treatment of people in prison, "the ideal place to run experiments—all you have to do is put it in the food, in the drinks." (His general suspiciousness extends to doubting that we have ever really put a man on the moon and wondering whether "they were out in the California desert somewhere, fakin' all of it.") Here again Cliff is locked into his negations: he wishes to cast off his death taint as a guinea-pig victim, but feels prevented from doing so not only by the formidable barriers of a white society but by his own inner sense of himself as a con man, as a "fake, big fake, big zero." Hence, Cliff, in looking ahead, sees only more of the same: "If I keep goin' the way I'm goin', I ain't gonna have a future. I know what my future is. Death, institutions, jail."

## "I WANNA BE THIS, I WANNA BE THAT": JAMES E.

James E., a twenty-year-old black interviewed at a youth center, felt tainted by his neighborhood ("South Bronx—oh, negative. He's negative. There's nobody positive from the South Bronx . . . drugs, violence, graffiti . . . that's basically it") and inundated by immediate horrors around him. Immersed in such violence and soon participating in it, James developed an early psychological pattern of dissociation, and would muse on the idea that "messages come from the brain . . . [and] tell . . . your hand to stab somebody. . . . Is it the mind that . . . kills people or is it the hand?" His early goal was what he called "power," meaning "gold, money, women, cars"; and he felt, "I was just like . . . a tool," his body in particular being "just a tool." He was what he called "a bad kid," and emphasized his lack of feeling in relation to his shooting another young man in an argument over a girl, saying it was only "physical," that the "mental . . . wasn't there at all. Just astral, you know." He was talking about a numbed physicality, about himself not being "there" in the violence.

Another violent episode involved his being "sliced" (cut badly) on the thigh by a girlfriend while they were making love because she was enraged at him for having just had intercourse with her twin sister (whom he had mistaken for the girlfriend). He was also shot in the leg as part of the same conflict, possibly by one of the sisters. When the interviewer expressed horror at these events, James replied, "It was funny if you ask me." That response was part of his detachment and, above all, of his numbed omnipotence, the feelings he has had that "I'm not gonna get killed. Nobody's gonna kill me," at a time when (referring to his relatively diminutive size and gentle manner) "I was like a little giant." He associated those attitudes—and his overall sequence of repeated school suspensions, drug taking and drug dealing, extensive stealing, and escalating involvement in violence culminating in the use of guns ("everything, you know")—with his having been a superficially protean nonperson, living out an "image struggle": "My whole person . . . was KOed, you know, taken over by someone else, some other image. It was like, 'I wanna be this, I wanna be that.' . . . I wanted to be like everybody. One day I'm like Johnny over here because I like the way he talks. So I'll try and talk like him. This guy walks pretty cool, I'll walk like this guy. The day was like a puzzle. I didn't even know which—you know, Who am I?"

The seeds of this empty self were planted early for James. He was very young when his father left the family, but not too young to witness the man's brutal beatings of James's mother. In her turn, his mother, whom he loves, beat him regularly for misbehavior, and he has increasingly rebelled from her as she has moved toward religious fundamentalism. His resentment, along with considerable guilt, is also related to the special attention she has always given a younger brother who had become brain-damaged through an accident in which James himself was indirectly involved. James still has extensive fantasies of violence, of "destroying the world" or harming or killing individual people: "I love to fuck with people's heads, mental, physical, whatever." He has also had suicidal ideas, described himself as at times attracted to "death, death, death!" and talked of having had the experience of "feeling death" at the time he was shot.

In counseling sessions at the youth center, James was critical of his own past behavior and insisted that he had "more self-control now" and could "take responsibility" for what he does. But his negative proteanism was still evident in his continuous preoccupation with what he called "sex, money, power, destruction," though his self-critical awareness of that preoccupation is a step toward modifying the pattern. James clearly remains vulnerable to longstanding fragmentation, dissociation, and violence. To overcome these patterns, he must, as Vietnam veterans liked to put it, "learn to feel." But that, too, has its risks. He told how, when recently viewing a picture of a truckload of bodies in a Nazi death camp, "It really did hurt." Through most of his life James has sought to manage his world by fending off precisely such painful compassion. And given the degree of his fragmentation, his resources for sustaining such compassion and transforming his violent impulses are at best uncertain.

## "I HAVE NO BOUNDARIES": ARLENE L.

An extreme form of fragmentation in women is demonstrated by Arlene L., who was interviewed in prison. Although only thirty-one, she has already experienced painful dislocation (in leaving her native Jamaica as a child), years of periodic prostitution (beginning at the age of fourteen), two marriages (one to a violent pimp and another to an elderly Jewish businessman), severe alcoholism and equally severe crack addiction, violent victimization and sexual abuse, extensive time in prison for involvement in a robbery of her second husband's (that is, her own) home, violent behavior and several suicide attempts, and recently a conversion to a humane form of fundamentalism that has provided her with renewed energy and hope. Arlene, who is bright and articulate and has had some psychotherapy, speaks of her own "battered personality."

Arlene is also physically battered, as evidenced by a deep scar on her left arm from a knife wound and a distortion of her left jawbone caused by a severe fracture, both injuries resulting from beatings at the hands of her most recent boyfriend. Contributing to her overall psychological and physical battering were an alcoholic father, who abused her mother and "wasn't there" (but was also "magical" and adored by Arlene), and a moralistic, distant mother toward whom Arlene felt added resentment for failing to protect her from her stepfather (who sexually molested her regularly) and for having moved the family from Jamaica to the confusions of Brooklyn. Arlene made two unsuccessful suicide attempts during her early teens, and at the age of fourteen was willingly recruited for prostitution in various cities in the United States and Canada. She entered impulsively into her first marriage at the age of sixteen to a pimp, who was controlling and unstable; even after she left the marriage, he beat and raped her. Arlene had from that marriage a daughter, whom she turned over to her mother to raise.

Her second marriage was to a rich, white widower, thirty years older than she, whom she met while working as a prostitute. The interracial tie caused her to be largely rejected by both families and by blacks and whites in general, and could not protect Arlene from further traumas (including the death of two brothers victimized in a robbery), from her own fragmentation (her increasing use of cocaine developing into severe crack addiction), or from heavy drinking (in which her husband joined her). She finally collaborated in, or at least acceded to, a bizarre robbery of their home by a black woman friend who, Arlene claimed, took much more than they had originally agreed upon, leaving Arlene regretful but "numbed out." Convicted of the crime, Arlene found the resulting jail term a combination of a more or less welcome "rest" and painful contact with "the lowest [human] spectrum." Released after several years of imprisonment, she divorced her husband and jumped parole by running off with a new boyfriend into a downward spiral of crack addiction, heavy alcoholism, prostitution, and various forms of violence as both victim and victimizer, and finally a terrible series of fights with the boyfriend, which culminated in her pouring a can of gasoline over him and almost lighting it until she stopped herself and asked for help by calling the police.

Returned to prison, she plunged deep into a relatively flexible version of fundamentalist Christianity and began to condemn much of her own past behavior and to embark on a struggle to achieve new moral standards. While she finds difficulty living up to them, her Christianity has increasing power for her; she has an image of God as an old black woman, since black women are, she says, the "nurturers of the earth," and has been so effective in organizing Christian programs in prison that she has been told she was "called to be an evangelist." She has a more immediate plan of studying to become a nurse; has righted her relationship with her mother, whom she now deeply admires; and insists, to a much greater extent than most poor blacks we interviewed, "I do have a tomorrow."

A large question, of course, is whether she can sufficiently draw upon this new spiritual tie, and upon her intelligence and capacity for introspection, to build functional elements of self that can counter the formidable trauma and psychological fragmentation that have dominated her life. She acknowledges the deficiencies of her proteanism to date in declaring, "I have no boundaries," and insists that she and others of her background have been deprived of necessary "rules" ("I love rules. I love order"), and that a major "psychological drawback" for her has been that "there is no middle ground, . . . no levelness, . . . just . . . one big high or one big low." That elusive "levelness" would require a renewal of her protean capacities in directions of coherence and form.

# The Fragmented Self

*The confusion is not my invention. . . . It is all around us and our*
*only chance is to let it in . . . to open our eyes and see the mess. . . .*
*There will be new form, and . . . this form will be of such a type that it*
*admits the chaos and does not try to say that it is really something else.*

—Samuel Beckett

Fragmentation can be associated with different kinds of self-process, all of them precarious: with contradictory fundamentalism, with defensive self-constriction, and with various forms of negative or caricatured proteanism. The fragmented self is radically bereft of coherence and continuity, an extreme expression of dissociation.

## FRAGMENTATION AND FUNDAMENTALISM

One embraces fundamentalism in order to overcome the sense of despair and individual futurelessness associated with fragmentation and nonfunctional proteanism. That new relationship to fundamentalism can help sustain the self, at least for a while; but it may also lead to further fragmentation. Always totalistic in spirit, it presses toward a purity that must be attained but is unattainable, toward a clear and literal immortality that may come to seem (as it partly did to Pastor Charles V.) a "fairy-tale." Fundamentalist groups and institutions can constitute a "terrorist society," where "terror is diffuse . . . exerted on all sides on its members [so that] each member betrays and chastises himself." Fundamentalism is, moreover, always on the edge of violence because it ever mobilizes for an absolute confrontation with designated evil, thereby justifying any actions taken to eliminate that evil. Fundamentalism thus creates a thwarted self, never free of actual or potential fragmentation.

In the case of poor blacks who embrace fundamentalism in order to replace formlessness and unmanageable despair with absolute "rules" (as Arlene seeks to do), prior fragmentation may render that fundamentalism jumbled, loose, and uncertain. In addition, poor blacks tend to differ from other end-time fundamentalists in making much less distinction between saved believers and doomed nonbelievers. Some, as we have seen, equate survival only with blackness, while at least partially aware that they are engaging in a fantasy of reversal and revenge. But the more general feeling among poor blacks is that everyone is to be annihilated. One of them put it: "I don't think the Lord is going to take us up. We're going to destroy ourselves. It's as simple as that." And Jessica C. (not a fundamentalist, though she embraces certain fundamentalist images) conveys a similar vision, as summed up by one of our interviewers: "All things go together: drugs, homelessness, AIDS, sex, sky, nuclear bombs, everything burning, the air, the rainforest, ourselves, black and white. What she sees, hurts." Thus, the fragmented self puts its stamp on the image of the end.

There are global parallels to this process: for example, the ethnic conflicts that erupted after the demise of communism in what was previously the Soviet Union and in Eastern and Central Europe. These have involved many groups, including Czechs and Slovaks, Serbs and Croats and Slovenes and Bosnians, and Russians, Ukrainians, Georgians, Armenians, Azerbaijanis, Lithuanians, and Estonians; and religious divergences including Russian Orthodox, Roman Catholic, Protestant, and Islamic subcultures and belief systems. Profound confusion following upon longstanding communist suppression contributed to widespread feelings of fragmentation; these in turn led to tense ethnic reassertion that could veer toward fundamentalism, religious or political, and toward expressions of violence that could result in further fragmentation.

China provides a different but equally relevant example. Prior to the Democracy Movement of 1989, Chairman Deng Xiaoping had shown notable protean tendencies in emerging from the fundamentalist political impulses of Maoism: encouraging the development of technology, where Mao had sought to replace it with human will; liberalizing political controls, where Mao had stressed constant emphasis upon political purity and "thought reform"; and encouraging international trade and the development of modern economic institutions, in contrast to Mao's emphasis on China's going it alone. But during that crisis of 1989, when hundreds of thousands of students and workers marched on behalf of democracy, Deng reverted to military control, resulting in the notorious killings at Tiananmen Square; and then imposed cruel penalties and prison sentences on participants in the protest movement while reinstituting national efforts at thought reform. He had reverted to elements of Maoist fundamentalism and surely carried within him some Maoist nostalgia for revolutionary purity.* Deng subsequently continued with economic liberalization while maintaining political suppression (which in turn may be gradually diminishing). The overall sequence suggested here is that of, first, the revolutionary regime's overcoming Chinese tendencies toward fragmentation by means of its fundamentalist political reintegration; then itself bringing about new expressions of general fragmentation (the corruption and political suppression that led to the

---

*Deng is the last Chinese leader to have accompanied Mao on the heroic Long March (from 1934–36), the great mythic event of the revolution which is frequently invoked as a model for achievement and purity.

Democracy Movement); and finally, when threatened with its own fragmentation (with loss of Communist authority and revolutionary hegemony), the reassertion of political fundamentalism by a leader who had committed himself to seemingly opposite tendencies and policies.

Still another grim example, one closer to home, has to do with the partial breakdown of what I have called "nuclear fundamentalism"—that is the American (and international) pseudoreligion of nuclearism. Nuclearism entails an exaggerated dependency upon the weapons—to provide "security," to keep the peace, to keep the world going. Over the decades from the late 1940s through the mid-1980s, nuclear weapons became objects of deification, of salvation, in a form of worship of the ultimate technology and ultimate power they represent. But in the late 1980s and after, nuclearism has been increasingly undermined by the disappearance of the Soviets as the enemy superpower against whom the ideology was directed. As a result, in 1992, the most ardent nuclearists (led by Edward Teller, the patron saint of nuclearism) met at the Los Alamos laboratory, where the original atomic bomb was built in the 1940s, in order to issue what has been termed "a call to arms." That included advocacy of both "a fleet of 1,200 powerful new missiles to be made ready and armed with the world's entire arsenal of nuclear warheads," and "a new superbomb—10,000 times more powerful than any bomb ever built, a bomb so powerful it could never be detonated on earth"—all for the purpose of combatting giant asteroids that might in some remote future ("millenniums—or thousands of millenniums") threaten us with cosmic disaster. The most revealing utterance of this "revival meeting" was made by Lowell Wood, Teller's protégé at the Lawrence Livermore National Laboratory, who shouted from the back of the auditorium, "Nukes Forever!" While there might have been some self-mockery in that utterance, observers thought it heartfelt; it clearly represented the most fundamentalist reassertion of a declining nuclearistic ideology, together with a degree of fragmentation of self and thought so extreme as to resemble—were it not so deadly—a comic opera or the wildly humorous imagination of a Robin Williams.

Equally bizarre is the totalistic behavior of a cult called the Church of the Realized Fantasy in New York City's East Village. One of a number of devil-worshiping cults that have sprung up in the past decade or so,* this "church" distinguished itself by murdering a ballerina, offering her as a sacrifice, and dissecting the corpse. The leader of the cult, Daniel Rakowitz, known as "the butcher of Tompkins Square Park," was said to go about the Village quoting Adolf Hitler and carrying a live rooster. Rakowitz is also thought to have supervised three cult members as they

---

*Although such devil-worshiping cults exist, a great deal of fantasy is connected with them.

cooked the flesh of the victim as a satanic offering and served it to the homeless. The grotesque narrative reflects an extreme fragmentation against a backdrop of some basic problems of contemporary American society.

## THE STATIC SELF

There is a quality of self that is less antiprotean than fundamentalism, but perhaps less protean as well. This static self seeks by closure and numbing to block out much of the imagery and information available to it, to build a protective wall against all that questions or threatens its structure and content. In our time, the static self is especially likely to find meaning in technology and technique. The vision of the purely technical, of what the philosopher William Barrett calls "the illusion of technique," can come to dominate virtually any area of thought, the study of English literature as much as engineering or physics. Such embrace of technology renders it something of a mystical body, an ultimate source of goodness and truth. Technicized in this way, the static self can doubly endanger the human future: by endorsing draconian weaponry and by undermining more humane cultural and ethical standards. The static self, like the protean self, is less an absolute entity than a matter of tendencies. A number of civic leaders embodied such tendencies; yet they were often able to combine a technocratic mindset with a certain flexibility in self-process (George R., for instance). Their need to control and manage their world could be at odds with their own protean inclinations.

The other three groups in our study also struggle with stasis, if in different fashion. Fundamentalists seek fixity and even a kind of static paradise, but feel ever driven by its requirements. Poor blacks (such as Cliff F.) can alternate between a sense of overall personal stasis and of unmanageable, fragmented fluidity, while struggling, often against considerable odds, to bring some integration to their proteanism. Social activists view stasis as a profound threat to both society and self; yet because they are personally no more immune from it than the larger society, they are engaged in a never-ending struggle against it. Static patterns of the self seem to be always available, in any category of person, as a resting place to move in and out of, depending upon what one is experiencing, what one can take in, and what one needs to keep out. That resting place can become a form of inner deadness or a pained battleground. The dangers of the static self in our protean time are not so much its one-dimensionality (it almost never stays that way) as its potential for extreme and destructive actions on behalf of overcoming that inner deadness and claiming some form of revitalization.

## DISSOCIATION AND FORMLESSNESS

All varieties of fragmentation of the self involve dissociation and form-lessness. The fragmentation stems from severe trauma, which—if it occurs early in life—can shape, or misshape, the self and deny it adequate form virtually from its beginnings. What can be strikingly impaired is the sense of *I*: one's active awareness of having, or being, a self, or of (in Erik H. Erikson's words) "being a sensory and thinking creature endowed with language." Erikson goes on to associate *I* with "a sense of being *centered* and *active, whole* and *aware*," as contrasted with "a feeling of being peripheral or inactivated, fragmented and obscured." The thwarting of the self associated with violence is, above all, a thwarting of *I*, of one's capacity for vitality and personal agency. The loss of a viable *I* can make one susceptible to death imagery. One may experience the self as dead, the world as dead, everything as dead or dying, along with intense feelings of separation, stasis, and disintegration—the death equivalents. One may destroy or kill in what is psychologically and, in a sense, literally "self-defense"—that is, defense of the honor or existence of *I* (as suggested in the experiences of both Cliff and James). In thus defending one's *I* (whether from a stance of chaotic proteanism or one of absolutized fundamentalism), one can kill with a sense of "a righteous passion, . . . a last stand in defense of respectability," and perform "righteously enraged slaughter."

As the self fragments, its capacity for empathy is lost. At best (as the psychoanalyst Michael Basch points out), empathy as a process tends to be selective and, in some measure, situational: I can think and feel into one person's experience and not that of another, and do so more at certain times and places. Still, individuals vary in that capacity, depending upon the experience and development of the self. So absorbed in its own struggle to hold together, the fragmenting self is unable to be concerned with others, and tends to be unable to mobilize the cohesiveness to perform the empathic act. For that act, one needs to be capable of *decentering*, of stepping back from one's own involvements sufficiently to enter into the mind of another. And for that decentering, one requires prior *centering*, a prior capacity for ordering of experience along various dimensions—temporal (past, present, and future), spatial (proximate and ultimate experience), and emotional (allocating or "valencing" of the intensity of feelings and actions). The fragmented self is neither centered nor decentered, but *uncentered*, in the sense of lacking precisely these forms of self-ordering. Instead of empathy, one may experience a series of temporary identifications in which one may "lose oneself" for a time, but with little compassion or coherence (as was the case with James E.). Or one's limited empathy for particular persons or groups may be quickly overwhelmed by destructive emotions in response to fragmentation, forcing one to withdraw that empathy in favor of rage and violence.

Some years ago, when applying a paradigm of life continuity (or the symbolization of life and death) to the major psychiatric syndromes, I evaluated each by looking at it in terms of three themes: psychic numbing and related impairment to symbolization; threatening imagery having to do with death and its equivalents; and impediments to meaning. These same three themes turn out to bear on the endangered self in situations where one would not speak of psychiatric illness as such. I have observed how combinations of early trauma and a violent, death-saturated environment contribute to strong patterns of numbing and to disturbances in meaning that lead to bizarre, destructive behavior. This is consistent with Cornel West's stress on black nihilism as growing out of a combination of "psychological depression, personal worthlessness, and social despair." That despair is a manifestation of a sense of futurelessness, a breakdown of connection to groups or principles larger than the self; and there can be a back-and-forth process involving shattered meaning structures on the one hand and impoverishment and fragmentation of the self on the other. Also at issue here is the loss of adequate grounding, of a sense of being connected to one's own history and biology. As a result, experience takes on a floating quality; actions and associations, whether protean or static, become isolated from one's own prior experience as well as from others around one, and nothing seems psychologically trustworthy.

With deficient centering and grounding, one also becomes vulnerable to the excesses of one's own symbolizing process. A group ethos evolved under similar duress can contribute to those excesses. Symbolization can then go wild in its destructiveness—as occurs in the life and thought of the "bad dude" (or "badass") in the ghetto; and among poor whites who evolve their own violent requirements for male and female toughness, which may include scapegoating of blacks or attacks on homosexuals. Killing can become good and decency a form of weakness; or in an aberrant protean mode, holding still long enough to become *anything* may be seen as static and deadly. Group ideologies, spoken or unspoken, can mobilize these self-destructive patterns of symbolization, including the elaborate forms that surround gang warfare in young people throughout American inner cities. Not only do these forms of symbolization become antithetical to reasonable adaptation, but they undermine the very sense of self that seeks vitality from that adaptation. The decline in autonomy is accompanied by a loss of genuine *agency*, of the self's capacity to mobilize inner power, act effectively, and initiate constructive behavior.

In all this, I am talking about *dissociation*, about the separation of a portion of the mind from the whole, so that each part may act in some degree separately from the other. The concept was originally developed in the late nineteenth century by the French physician and psychologist Pierre Janet, and embraced by Freud, who came to prefer the word *splitting* for the same phenomenon. There can also take place what I call a "dissociative field," an environment within which a collective pattern of dissociation is rendered not only "normal" but expectable, even required. Such a dissociative field is maintained by *psychic numbing* and by what I call *doubling.* Psychic numbing, simply defined, means diminished capacity or inclination to feel. Symbolization is impaired, often with a marked separation of thought from feeling: one is able to receive information cognitively while ceasing to experience its impact. In extreme versions of psychic numbing, one can become anesthetized to the cognitive dimension as well. What I consider a quintessential form of numbing occurred among Hiroshima survivors who told me that, able to see what was going on around them at the time of the bomb, they could grasp that large numbers of people were dying and that much of their city had been destroyed, but that very quickly they simply ceased to feel. Psychic numbing is thus invoked, usually unconsciously, to prevent the self from being overwhelmed and perhaps destroyed by the images and events around it. In being inactivated, the self undergoes a temporary death in the service of preventing a permanent one. But where the self is under continuous trauma, it may remain "dead"; the numbing itself becomes a permanent feature that can color all experience. With its feeling level increasingly diminished, the self becomes ever more detached and disaffiliated from the outside world.

Doubling, also a form of dissociation, entails the formation of a functional second self that is, psychologically and morally, at odds with the prior self. One's *I,* or active expression of the self, goes either way—that is, both ways. Doubling enables an ordinary or even generally decent person to become actively involved in a murderous project (as I have tried to demonstrate not only in Nazi doctors but in American nuclear weapons designers and strategists). Among certain whites and blacks growing up in deprived settings—members, say, of terrorist and criminal organizations—doubling can mean living simultaneously as an ordinary person and as a brutally violent one.

## MULTIPLE PERSONALITY—PROTEAN CARICATURE

Multiple personality goes far beyond numbing and doubling in producing selves with distinct separateness from each other. Multiple personality develops as an extreme solution to the still more extreme threat of self-disintegration, a threat brought about by severe and repeated childhood trauma, almost always parental physical and sexual abuse. As a result, "[s]ome means of denial to blot out the pain of the intolerable reality becomes necessary, . . . [a] new self or selves, a new being which can escape the overwhelming pain of the cruel reality," pain that includes the most extreme confusions between parental protection and danger. The severe patterns of dissociation, the blotting out of most of the original trauma and the separating off of the emerging selves from each other, can be viewed as compromise fragmentations. What is striking is the extent to which the separate selves become structured, achieve sufficient form as to be disconcertingly autonomous. They can also be numerous: in 1988, it was estimated that the average number of selves in a multiple personality patient was eleven.

There are typically a dominant or "host" personality and various "alters," each tending to express, in exaggerated ways, particular inclinations such as anger, childishness, sexiness, and nurturing, which permits a "division of emotional labor" or "self-replacement therapy." The different selves can vary to a remarkable degree in dress, posture, age, and even in gender and physiology (different heart rates, allergic tendencies, and so on). It is as if the overall self (which, in my view, still exists in multiple personality) has, under duress, surrendered its integrative function to the separate subselves. In that sense, the protean process has been literalized to the point of caricature, more or less stopped in time. While individual subselves may continue a certain protean flow, that flow is radically undermined by their defensive function and by the all-pervasive dissociation. As in schizophrenia, in which there is still more extreme fragmentation of the self, multiple personality can produce moments of illumination and tendencies toward charisma (raising the question whether certain charismatic historical figures—Joan of Arc, for instance —might have been "multiples").

But the more fundamental feature of the condition is its pathological and dysfunctional quality. Operating here is the "double bind" of the abuse: coming from a father or mother, it takes on "the bizarre quality of combining intense and longed-for attention from a parent with pain and humiliation"; this renders "the sense of personal fragmentation . . . more profound," and victims are "made helpless to control both their own body and their own internal state." As a result of this "uncontrolled dissociation," "[a]ny one self in an MPD patient is by definition incomplete, unacceptable, and out of control, never knowing when some other personality will emerge and take charge." Rather than flexible protean experiments, there take place chaotic, dissociative maneuvers, sometimes impressive in their ingenuity, but never free of fragmentation.

By demonstrating the capacity of the self for extreme divisions and for literal multiplicity, the disorder has much to teach us about the far reaches of self-process. But the multiple personality syndrome does not, as some claim, suggest that any degree of unity or integration of the ordinary self is a mirage. Indeed, the bizarre arrangements of the subselves can be interpreted as a desperate effort to maintain at least a modicum of order. And we can interpret the syndrome as evidence for the *requirement* of minimal integration and unity for adequate function of the self. The historical record is important here. Only a handful of cases of multiple personality were reported in North America during the nineteenth and most of the twentieth century; by 1983, a leading researcher knew of one thousand in all; by 1985, of five thousand; and reported an increased incidence of "more than tenfold" during the decade between 1975 and 1985. Much of the increase may have to do with the fact that clinicians, rendered more sensitive to the condition today, are more likely to diagnose it. There is also suspicion of an iatrogenic factor: that the condition, in at least some cases, may be produced by influences exerted on patients by overzealous, multiple personality-minded hypnotists, therapists, and diagnosticians. But there is also a real possibility that the actual number of cases has radically increased. If so, that actual increase could be related to the historical forces responsible for contemporary proteanism. Multiple personality may well be part of a pathological edge of our historical confusions, a histrionic rendition of the plight of the endangered self.

## THE DERACINATED SELF

Negative historical legacies can, especially among groups of poor blacks and poor whites, interact with contemporary social trauma to endanger the self. A sense of worthlessness, or taint, can be transmitted over the generations, along with various dissociative mechanisms of survival. And these mechanisms can be maintained and intensified: in blacks, by ghetto pressures; and in whites, by related forms of economic and social duress. Also transmitted historically are attitudes toward technology, weapons technology in particular, that promote dissociative patterns and add to other threats to connectedness and coherence. So subject are people today to dissociative patterns that ours is, in fact, an age of numbing—and close to an age of doubling and splitting as well. A clinical manifestation here is the widespread diagnosis during recent decades of "borderline states" (or "borderline personality disorder"). That syndrome, named to suggest a state between neurosis and psychosis, includes severe disturbances and "splits" in self, ego, or identity, highly impulsive and self-damaging behavior, instability and lack of intimacy in personal relationships, and severe mood swings with frequent depression and suicidal ideation or actions. There is now thought to be considerable overlap between borderline states and multiple personality disorder, with as many as 70 percent of the latter fitting the criteria of the former.

Historical forces may also be contributing to a dissociative constellation that includes: multiple personality and borderline states as clinical syndromes; a general increase in child abuse, especially sexual, and particularly by parents and other relatives; and a very different social manifestation, the dramatic expansion of the UFO (unidentified flying object) phenomenon in the form of sightings and descriptions of "missing time" attributed to "abductions" by extraterrestrial creatures. There is at least the possibility that these three elements are interrelated. Nicholas Humphrey and Daniel Dennett raise the possibility that much of the UFO experience, particularly its component of medical or surgical procedures ostensibly performed on abductees by humanoid creatures, could be a "mythic version" of actual child abuse. There is some evidence of increased incidence of child abuse in people reporting such abductions; but even if this correlation is uncertain, all of these states and our ways of talking about them could be greatly influenced by the vast dissociative trend in our time. Also related to the dissociative constellation could be the massive expansion of cult formation and of contemporary fundamentalism; and the increasing evidence of a "false memory syndrome," in which accusations of early parental abuse are made by adult children on the basis of claimed recovery of memories that had ostensibly been repressed for decades, the memories sometimes including satanic rituals—the entire sequence considerably influenced by therapists and support groups focused on such repressed memories.

At their most destructive, these historical forces can help create what can be called a "deracinated self," a self so rootless as to be rendered hollow, a condition aptly described by a Salman Rushdie character: "I could see the centre of you, that question so frightful that you had to protect it with all that posturing certainty. That empty space." Every form of behavioral mask, including violence, can be mustered in behalf of denying or filling that void. In the process, one may experience a euphoric state associated with what feels like happy proteanism. (A Frederick Barthelme character describes feeling "splendidly safe and happy" in a "place I could stay forever" when driving along a maze of freeways, just before a gruesome accident.) Euphoria can be inseparable from dissociation and thereby precede, and contribute to, disaster. And once the self-destructive process gets under way, it can be extremely difficult to interrupt. As an artist and commentator puts the matter in another context: "It is innocent to hope that this process of disintegration will stop at the time and in the place where we want it to."

## THE ENDANGERED CONCEPT OF SELF

Maintaining a concept of self is crucial for grasping contemporary duress, as well as for recording possibilities beyond it. Such a concept is our only means of examining struggles with structure, coherence, and fragmentation. Here we are well served by Samuel Beckett, the poet of the endangered self: by imaginatively reducing the self—the person—to virtual nonexistence ("Finished, it's finished, nearly finished, it must be nearly finished"), Beckett takes us to the very edge of our very own precariousness. The vision of a computer self does the opposite. Brilliant electronic simulations of cognitive functions are put forward as a model to encompass complex human feelings and attachments; the model deprives us of a sensitive approach to questions of motivation and meaning, including the kinds of destructive motivation discussed in this chapter. In contrast, a biological or neurophysiological model of consciousness and of selfhood, based on complex "mappings" of brain cells, can contribute to our grasp of motivation and meaning, to "a more complete notion of the free individual." But it would be a grave misuse of these biological developments to relegate the self, as some are inclined to do, to a secondary physiological excrescence; or to declare its demise as a useful concept.

The self-concept can also be endangered by certain psychological and cultural approaches. More or less fundamentalist expressions of classical psychoanalysis can seek to undermine a focus on self because it is seen as a threat to the idea of instinct as the motor of human behavior. Or those who do theorize about the self can so dogmatize and isolate the concept as to negate the possibility of ebb and flow, especially in relation to larger historical forces. Others may, while putting forward a theory of mind, be impressed by the material absence of the self to the point of declaring its nonexistence—as in the claim that "There need be no psychic self as a subjective centre of consciousness over and above sets of experiences: just as there is no such thing as a hole in the ground over and above the sides and the base"; the argument misses the point that it is not the self but its absence or radical fragmentation that constitutes the void. And finally, there is the inclination among certain postmodernists to view the very idea of self as a remnant of discredited modernism (though I believe that most would join me in stressing the self's multiplicity as opposed to its nonexistence). These negations of a concept of self from within psychology and cultural theory are potentially more harmful than the biologized or computerized self. For they subvert, so to speak, from within what may be our last best hope to grasp the nature of our pain—and, above all, our potential for renewal—as we close out the twentieth century.

# Chapter 11

---

# THE PROTEAN PATH

---

*For the real question is whether the "brighter future" is really always so distant. What if, on the contrary, it has been here for a long time already, and only our own blindness and weakness has prevented us from seeing it around us and within us, and kept us from developing it?*

—Václav Havel

*What looks like a human potentiality that ought to be actualized in some distant future is often only a cornered cultural strain waiting to be renewed or rediscovered.*

—Ashis Nandy

IN A TIME of fragmentation and trauma, proteanism can awaken our species belonging, our species self. We can assert our organic relationship to each other and to nature. That assertion, for symbolizers like ourselves, is a matter of the psyche, of the imagination. We can come to *feel* what we (according to our best scientific categories) *are:* members of a common species. We can experience, amidst our cultural diversity, that common humanity. The diversity is integral to the process, as: "We are multiple from the start."

Rather than sameness or even close similarity, I am proposing a principle of *commonality:* that of the characteristics we share as a species, and, even more, the life experiences we share as well.

# The Common Language We Speak Today

*The common language we speak today is not the language of the West, now adopted by the East. It is an intrinsically universal language which belongs to nobody in particular and to everybody. It is the language of an open society.*

—Ralf Dahrendorff

In 1992, the frozen corpse of a late Neolithic man was discovered in an Alpine region on the border between Italy and Austria. In discussing the find, an American writer noted the skillful stitching of the "long-lost hunter's" deerskin clothing and his "unfinished" bow (had he been making a replacement for one stolen from him?), wondered whether he had lost his way and then frozen to death, and concluded, "It was impossible to think of him without imagining the dread of his family he never came home to." This effort to imagine the experience of a man and his family—fellow human beings who lived five thousand years ago in ways that could not be more different from our own—expresses the full reach of the principle of commonality. For members of all human cultures, at any historical moment, bring their bodies and minds to lovemaking and to childbirth, to pain and to sickness. We all must deal with the nurturing of the young, with family and sexual relationships, with adult responsibility, and the reality of death. It is this commonality the antinuclear activist Helen Caldicott so often evoked in the 1970s and 1980s with her simple declaration: "A baby is a baby is a baby!"

## EMPATHY AND COMMONALITY

We assert our commonality through our capacity for empathy, for thinking and feeling our way into the minds of others. In allowing us to "resonate" with other people, "experiencing their experience," empathy is a key to species awareness, and to a protean path to that awareness. Empathy is to be distinguished from *sympathy* (in that one may not necessarily admire what one experiences of the other) and from *identification* (one need not "become" the other). What empathy does require is that one include the other's humanity in one's own imagination.

There is, according to the British psychologist Nicholas Humphrey, an evolution of a "natural psychology" which provides "every member of the human species both the power and the inclination *to use a privileged picture of his own self as a model for what it is like to be another person.*" Empathy is believed to begin with imitation: infants only thirty-six hours old have been observed to imitate the facial expressions of those around them; and one researcher claims that the capacity for empathy is present "in some precursor form" at birth, to be "elaborated by cognitive maturation and . . . subsequent experiences in the social milieu." To be sure, much can happen, over the lives of individuals and groups, that suppresses and interferes with empathy of various kinds and toward various people; and individuals or groups intent upon harming or killing others must withdraw even minimal empathy. It is always collectively withdrawn by those committing mass murder or genocide: Nazis withheld and blocked empathy for Jews, as did members of the Khmer Rouge for Cambodian compatriot-victims.* But the capacity cannot be absolutely or permanently eliminated: it is part of the human equipment; and as human beings we are always capable of reasserting it.

Proteanism keeps open the possibility of that reassertion. One's empathic understanding of a person or a group is transient rather than permanent. Protean flexibility enables one to move toward empathy or to return to it after a lapse. Failed empathy is, like empathy itself, subject to reversal. Contributing to the empathic directon can be what one feminist scholar calls "female connectivity," the inclination of women to form webs of relationships with relatively "fluid ego boundaries," as contrasted with a male focus on relatively rigid separateness. That "female sense of connection with the world" is consistent with true individuation and part of the broad human potential for empathy. Proteanism enables men and women alike to call forth that potential for weblike connectedness and empathic sensitivity generally associated, for whatever combination of cultural and psychobiological reasons, with women.

## TRAUMA AND TRANSFORMATION

Crucial to the development of species awareness is empathy for trauma and suffering. Trauma these days is everywhere, and posttraumatic reactions are worldwide. Whether in relation to the malignant confusions of postcommunist Europe, to struggles for survival in the Third World, to universal military and nuclear and ecological threats, to specifically American fears of social disintegration—nowhere are people exempt from feeling assaulted by forces that seem out of control. Accompanying this experience of trauma is a growing sense, also widely shared, that fundamental changes are both needed and inevitable in some form.

---

*One can make use of empathy, as I did in my interviews with Nazi doctors, to probe the psychology of evil. Victimizers can also utilize empathy to exploit others' vulnerabilities.

The vision of a "new world order" has too often been merely rhetorical or worse, but the idea that such a vision is needed stems from precisely this widespread trauma, and from the equally widespread yearning for its transformation into a genuine version of a new world order.

For such transformation to occur, one must remain aware not only of one's own trauma but of others': only then can one integrate the pain into a larger understanding, into a worldview or set of humane policies and actions. Doing so can be difficult for a number of reasons. One is the simple human tendency toward numbing in the face of pain, all the more when the people experiencing the pain are geographically and ethnically far removed from oneself. Or, when suffering is close to home, particularly when it involves a family member or a person one loves, there is an inclination to respond exclusively to that immediate pain and to block out any of its larger significance. When I learned, a few years ago, that my son had developed advanced kidney disease, my preoccupation with his specific condition and how I could help him took precedence over any larger principles I was struggling with in my work or in my life in general. Only later, when his condition had been greatly improved, first by dialysis and then by kidney transplant, could I begin to place his suffering in a larger context. Only then could I reflect on the general problems of kidney disease in various parts of the world and imagine how things would be for a person so afflicted in other countries, or how a Chinese or Nigerian or Palestinian father might feel and act in that situation. Only then could I begin to probe the species dimension of my son's and my own pain. But such probing of trauma can be greatly enhanced by an evolving species self, which can in turn be strengthened by its inclination to transform new traumas in a species direction—all this taking the form, not of a vicious circle of the closing of empathy, but of what I call an "empathic circle" of protean expression and expanding humanity.

In the volatile, dangerous, and open-ended world of the late twentieth century, that trauma is always susceptible to transformation. Artists are, according to the *New York Times*, experiencing greater leeway in "putting the unimaginable to imaginative use"—specifically the Holocaust. They reach for ever bolder fantasy (Hitler waltzing with Stalin while candy falls from the ceiling and children pick it up, in Agnieszka Holland's film *Europa, Europa*); or the literal reversal of time and of the life cycle (as in Martin Amis's novel *Time's Arrow* about the life of a Nazi doctor lived backward); or the use of animal characters in a comic-book format (as in Art Spiegelman's *Maus: A Survivor's Tale*); or searingly satirical self-involvement (as in the German painter Anselm Kiefer's photographs of himself giving the Nazi salute). In all these experimental efforts to revisit the suffering while at the same time struggling "to reinvent the Holocaust and its legacy, stretching . . . imaginations to the breaking point," artists bring protean fluidity and multiplicity seriously to bear on extending the Holocaust experience and universalizing it.

At issue here is the capacity to absorb suffering and learn from it. Suffering should never be romanticized; one can only strive to interrupt it. But, as the Indian psychological and social theorist Ashis Nandy tells us (referring to colonialism's subjugation of the Third World), suffering can be "a great teacher": "Those who maintain, or try to maintain, their humanity in the face of such experience perhaps develop the skill to give special meaning to the fundamental contradictions and schisms in the human condition"; and, "Human consciousness has used the experience of oppression to sharpen its sensitivities and see meanings which are otherwise lost in the limbo of over-socialized thinking." That capacity to create from suffering was epitomized by Gandhi, whose tough-minded protean transformations began with himself as he made himself into "a nonplayer for the existing system—one who plays another game, refusing to be either a player or a counter-player."

Suffering in Latin America has been the source of a convergence of religious and political currents in the species-oriented proteanism of "liberation theology." Jesus' mission is viewed as "an injunction to achieve justice and freedom in the present" and to bring about an "earthly incarnation of the Kingdom of God." The movement has been innovative in its "response to the perceived inadequacies of both developmentalism and leftist revolutionary doctrines." Early Christianity has been combined with humanistic Marxism, the principle of "feeling and living as Christ" now made available in "exploited and alienated man." This "catacomb culture," as it came to be called, also embraced elements of feminism and environmentalism "with a vision that was antihierarchical, communitarian, and libertarian." (This openness to diverse, life-enhancing elements contrasts sharply with the closed, totalistic violence of other protest groups, such as the Peruvian Marxist guerrilla organization known as the Shining Path.) Consistent with a species mentality is liberation theology's focus on "a rebirth of radical democratic politics," a reexamination of the "just society," and a combination of the visionary and the pragmatic: "prayer united with political sagacity, . . . mystical theology articulated with a critical analysis of society."

This focus seeks to counteract the modern tendency to ignore suffering, to reject not only religion but politics as well, to render virtually all issues as "technical in character, matters of allocating resources for purposes of efficient use, leaving decisions in the hands (or heads) of technical experts, or better, computerized procedures." Thus, as the international legal and political theorist Richard Falk has observed, in various parts of the world (Latin America, Eastern Europe, and Third World countries), religion and politics are working together: "Religion provides the materials out of which to . . . recast politics. . . . A religious grounding deepens and extends struggle" and brings "seriousness about suffering as central to its undertaking. Since this approach includes environmentalism, as it "endows all of nature with a sacred, privileged status," it gives rise to a species-oriented "political sensibility that is animated by ... a kind of religious politics or political religion, but not growing out of the mainstream of established world religions," an orientation "ecological at its foundation, finding spiritual coherence in the processes of nature itself."

## TRAUMA AND THE ECOLOGICAL SELF

A terrifying rumor swept Hiroshima, soon after the bomb fell on 6 August 1945, that trees, grass, and flowers would never again grow there; that the city would be unable to sustain vegetation of any kind—that nature was drying up altogether, and life had been extinguished at its source. I understood the rumor to suggest an ultimate desolation, a state that not only encompassed human death but went beyond it. That foreboding of ultimate trauma had much to do with the emergence of environmental movements, first during the 1960s and 1970s and then, more powerfully, during the 1980s and 1990s. Early environmentalists, such as Rachel Carson and Barry Commoner, saw nuclear threat as the original source of their concern. More generally, the movement's "basic themes—dismay with technological authorities and systems that seemed about to doom the entire world—had first been thrust upon the public by hydrogen bombs." In the individual relationship to that sequence of trauma and illumination, there emerged an "ecological self," in which "[p]ersonal and global pain are not separate spheres; they are intimately related": that is, the self becomes vitally anchored in the mode of symbolic immortality that has to do with our natural world. We can extend Helen Caldicott's universalization of babies to "A river is a river is a river," or "An ocean is an ocean is an ocean"—the commonality of existential state in relation to our earthly environment. The passion of that commonality was brought to a climax on Earth Day (22 April) of 1990, when, according to the New York Times, "two hundred million people in one hundred forty nations ... [took] part in the largest grass-roots demonstration in history." And a similar spirit became universally manifest with the international conference on the environment at Rio de Janeiro in 1992—despite the United States's resistance to treaties on the greenhouse effect and principles of biodiversity; and the general inattention to inequities between the nations of the northern and southern hemispheres. Such events nonetheless encourage the expansion of the ecological self in directions both protean and committed, both local and planetary. The ideal of a "biotic community" is extended to encompass the earth.

My emphasis on human species awareness in no way overlooks other species. I am convinced that any global identification must embrace all species both in their inherent value and in their importance to our own profound connections to nonhuman forms of life. Still, we need to maintain our focus on the human mind, on our ways of symbolizing our ecological connections, on relevant patterns of self and history; on human attitudes and actions that threaten the environment, and on our responses to that threat, which can include revitalization of both ourselves and our habitat. "Dead trees are what the forest grows on," we are told—a reminder that reaches back to Greek mythology and encompasses the vast cosmic pattern of death and renewal that frames, and vastly transcends, our human existence. Under profound threat, the biodiversity that helps sustain our planet reverberates with new intensity in the ecological self, a protean extension of the species self.

## TRAUMA AND THE REJECTION OF HISTORY

Ultimately, trauma and suffering become a basis for rejecting received versions of historical experience, including (as Nandy puts it) "the oppression which comes as 'history,'" and that state of being "victimized . . . by the idea of history itself." Trauma and suffering provided a worldwide basis for rejecting received history in the extraordinary events of 1989–90: the revolutions in Central and Eastern Europe, the assertion of Chinese democracy at Tiananmen Square, and the painful beginning emergence of South Africa from the official apartheid policy of white domination. The defiance of existing historical assumptions, on behalf of species principles, contributed greatly to the empathic excitement throughout the world. People everywhere sensed that what they were witnessing were not so much national revolutions as human milestones, that it was not just black South Africans or Chinese students and workers or Czech intellectuals asserting a measure of freedom: all of us, as human beings, were experiencing that freedom.

Species principles were also evident in the writings of European dissident leaders well before the changes in the regimes of their countries. Poland's Adam Michnik spoke of the broad principles of "defending hope" and of "people getting up from their knees" to resist spiritual or political oppression. Václav Havel advocated new forms of institutions and associations (see chapter 6, page 106) in a civic revolution aiming to redefine citizenship and human relationships so that they are rendered separate from, and in defiance of, the corrupt models of the oppressive state. Havel was later to speak of "a 'higher' responsibility, which grows out of a conscious or subconscious certainty that our death ends nothing, because everything is forever being recorded and evaluated somewhere else, somewhere 'above us.'" All this is "an integral aspect of the secret order of the cosmos, of nature, and of life, which believers call God, and to whose judgment everything is liable." Whether one wishes to interpret this last statement in Christian terms, or in my own secular model of symbolic immortality, it contains a transcendent principle of human beings reaching beyond themselves for the most encompassing connectedness, a principle consistent with the broadest expression of species consciousness.

And George Konrad extended a protean plea ("Creative intellectuals don't want to be bosses; they want to be able to tinker, to invent, to create what they have imagined") into a ringing declaration of resilient resistance to whatever can be imposed on human beings:

> That alleged and notorious reality which is there even when you are not, that reality before which you are very little (existing at all only by its leave)—try to look it in the eye. Whether its name is matter or communism or God, say to it with your jaw trembling: You are you, but I'm still me. I resist your power to possess. I don't want to acknowledge that you do with me whatever you like. You can't butter your bread with me. I don't belong to you.... I am trying to slow the onrush of schizophrenia into the charmed circle of a sound mind. Of course I am small before the great, weak before the powerful, cowardly before the violent, wavering before the aggressive, expendable before It, which is so vast and durable that I sometimes think it is immortal. I don't turn the other cheek to it, I don't shoot it with a slingshot; I look, and then I collect my words.

The words Konrad and others "collect" are applicable to everyone and can be disseminated almost instantly by the world's media and made available everywhere. Anyone's defiance of oppression can become everyone's experience, to the point of an emergence of a "global civil society": transnational efforts to stem depletion of the ozone layer; organizations such as Amnesty International for human rights and Greenpeace combatting nuclear and environmental dangers; and many other institutions and individuals with principles that transcend nationality and nations. This global society, Falk tells us, "becomes invisible . . . if we look at reality through a realist [traditional geopolitical] lens" but is nonetheless "being constituted before our eyes."

The civic revolutions in Europe, like many Third World movements for democracy, were part of a larger late-twentieth-century turning away from the lethal traditional politics associated with the cold war and, before that, with "statism" and the international war system. Havel connects these tendencies to the vain modern enterprise of "controlling everything that exists," and insists on the great lesson of the European revolutions: "Communism was not defeated by military force, but by life, by the human spirit, by conscience, by the resistance of Being and man to manipulation." In other words, whatever the political and military forces at play, closed totalism was overcome by a force inherent in our species, one that had to do with the mind's explorations and energies—a force I would call "protean vitality."

## The Struggle for the Soul of the Species Self

Unfortunately, civic politics and global civil society do not make the only claims on species consciousness and the species self. The lure of the global market, which has been intensified by the communications revolution, can be a powerful stimulus to self-serving transnational projections and identifications. Although multinational corporations can, to be sure, make some connection with principles of civic politics—including, for instance, those concerned with preserving the environment or promoting principles of individual freedom—that connection seems limited. What is likely—indeed, it is already occurring—is "a struggle for the soul of the species self" between the market orientation and the more humane global values of a civil society. Inevitably, any compromise will include aspects of the two contenders.

### ETHNICITY AND COMMONALITY

The worldwide plunge into ethnicity—particularly when totalized and fundamentalist in direction—is also a formidable antagonist to species awareness and the species self. But here, too, there are hopeful possibilities in the relationship of ethnicity to commonality. Until recently, most observers of the Third World have seen ethnicity as a remnant of tradition, one that would inevitably decline with "modernization," with cultural rationalization and national integration. In many parts of the Third World, however, there has been an "ethnic revival," which is by no means limited to a fanatical fringe but includes grass-roots efforts to reconstruct elements of kinship and community and to re-establish aspects of "the all-embracing emotional security offered by the family to the child." This ethnic resurgence occurs in varied political and moral contexts and is distinctly influenced by declining faith in the nation-state, which is perceived as no longer able to protect its citizens from technological danger (from advanced weaponry and pollution) or to provide purpose and meaning in the face of ever-accelerating change. With this diminishing psychological investment in the nation-state, ethnicity itself could become a focus for the experimentation and reshufflings of self I have been discussing throughout this book, bringing about new relationships between ethnicity and species consciousness. With the "weakening of former national identities," there could emerge "new identities . . . based on 'primordial loyalties,' ethnicity, 'race,' local community, language, and other culturally concrete forms"—their "proliferations and fluidities" in keeping with worldwide acceleration of cultural change.*

In Europe, Günter Grass was a voice in the wilderness in opposing the political merging of the two Germanies. He specifically objected to an all-powerful and unified German nation-state (see page 86), reminding the world "how much grief this unified state caused" in the past and insisting also that "the image of Auschwitz . . . weighs on [its] . . . conscience." Instead, he advocated forms of cultural innovation: "a confederation [that would] point . . . the way to a new, different, and desirable self-definition that would include joint responsibility for German history." This concept of "cultural nationhood," he explained, could result in "a modern, broader concept of culture, . . . a multiplicity of German culture without needing to assert unity in the sense of a nation-state." However politically unfeasible, Grass was advocating a form of species-oriented ethnic pro-teanism and warning of the dangers of ethnic purity and totalism.

But species consciousness is precarious, as demonstrated by the subse-quent political chaos in Germany, including bitter resentment toward East Germans and the economic burden they brought with them and, for more ethnic reasons, toward Turkish "guest workers" and the large num-bers of refugees from various European upheavals streaming into Ger-many. Although Grass's wisdom has been sadly confirmed by neo-Nazi violence, that violence was countered by millions of Germans, in peaceful demonstrations, reasserting a commitment not only to democracy but to larger human connectedness.

More generally, there is much evidence throughout Europe, during this last decade of the twentieth century, of national confusion and eth-nic antagonism and fragmentation, as well as of political and economic cooperation and tendencies toward regional enhancement and toward certain aspects of species consciousness. One European example of odd and creative combinations is the Hungarian political party FIDESZ (the acronym for Federation of Young Democrats) which, at first seen as the youth wing of the dissident movement, came to establish its own identity by means of its bold assertions at the time of the revolution overturning communism and its political style and content: an immersion in MTV and Western popular culture as well as Western democracy and law (a number of youth leaders having spent considerable time in Western Europe and America); a combination of liberalism and conservative eco-nomics, along with an interest in poll taking and political campaign plan-

---

*Writers such as Salman Rushdie and Ashis Nandy, different as they are in every way, explore in their works various aspects of these emerging "messier" Third World identities.

ning; and, above all, an embrace of the advantages of youth as the only portion of the population untainted by the country's Communist past.

It is sometimes suggested that the United States and Europe have reversed roles: the United States undergoing a decline in its longstanding capacity for collective forms of creative proteanism, while Europe shows signs of transmuting its traditional expressions of fragmentation into innovative institutional arrangements. But there are complex ebbs and flows in both places. Indeed, there are efforts everywhere to connect "personal dispositions"—that is, immediate individual protean struggles—with "globalising influences" that stem from shared world history.

## CULTURAL MULTIPLICITY

One striking globalizing influence, by no means clear in its effects, is the continued worldwide explosion of American popular culture. The sociologist Todd Gitlin speaks of American popular culture as "the closest approximation there is today to a global lingua franca, drawing urban classes in most nations into a federated culture zone." This "second culture" includes popular music (rock, country western, folk), films, television series, and Disney characters—the last often given an additional protean twist in being recast to connect with European or Japanese or Israeli cultural concerns. While American popular culture is often violent and vulgar, it can also touch species principles and carry liberating ideas.

For example, in 1991 a group of Serbian students were arrested and brutally tortured by Belgrade riot police after an opposition rally; in response to their request for defense lawyers for the phony trial being organized, they were told: "You have been watching too many American films!" More generally, American popular culture can help young people everywhere to articulate their protean yearnings and impulses. The Hungarian youth party FIDESZ is a case in point. Another (of a romanticized nature) is the experience I had when doing research on Japanese youth some years ago. When I asked a fiery young ultraradical student communist leader about what he did in his leisure time, he told me that he went to the movies, and then, sheepishly, that he especially liked American westerns. He explained that he was moved profoundly by the hero alone on his horse (or perhaps with a woman) riding out toward the horizon in complete individual freedom, no longer constrained by any social rules or requirements—and contrasted such images with the suffocating demands of Japanese society and family life. This overall model of "cultural bilingualism" need not be limited to American exports; it can take on increasing importance, and contribute much to species awareness, as people everywhere come to live simultaneously in both their own and an internationalized culture.

That cultural multiplicity is consistent with certain psychological and anthropological perspectives now being put forward by such observers as the psychoanalyst James Hillman and the anthropologist Richard Shweder. Hillman stresses the movement from a "monotheism" to a "polytheism" of consciousness (see chapter 1) as our only means of coping with the "fragmentary autonomous systems" of our minds. Shweder stresses the unlimited psychological sources of individuals and cultures as they "make each other up" and advocates a multiplicity of being or "ontological polytheism"—celebrating the reach of the anthropologist as "the student and beneficiary of all traditions, and the slave to none." And feminist anthropologists insist that gender variations be given a place among these "many voices clamoring for expression." In a parallel philosophical idiom, the philosopher Richard Rorty imagines an ideal culture so inclusive that no individual or group—"neither the priests nor the physicists nor the poets nor the Party"—would be considered more "rational" or "scientific" or "deeper" than any another; a culture in which heroes would be those people who excelled "doing the quite diverse things that they did, . . . simply people who were good at being human" (here revealing, perhaps unwittingly, his species commitment).

Implicit in Hillman, Shweder, and Rorty is an approach to knowledge in general, and to science in particular—an approach both simplified and opened out. The simplification lies in identifying science as one among a number of valid approaches to knowledge, thereby relieving it of any remaining burden of exclusivity or finality in its quest for truth. As the physicist and philosopher of science Gerald Holton has explained, science is no more and no less than a way of thinking systematically and developing and changing one's ideas according to evidence. From that standpoint, scientists require a certain capacity for proteanism. And the protean mind, with its skepticism and openness, can be receptive to the scientific mode, even as it explores more speculative and nonrational approaches to knowledge. But that same mind is also wary of the embrace of science or its falsification for purposes of mass murder and genocide. The protean self can carry forward important, unending dialogues on precisely these questions and ultimately on global ethical issues having to do with all practice and application of science. Those dialogues can be enhanced by reflections on science and nature and on the relationship of the former to the "biodiversity" of the latter.

Multiplicity on behalf of global enhancement, then, can become a protean way of perceiving both science and nature. In a similar spirit, the philosopher Richard Tarnas refers to "the plasticity and constant change of reality and knowledge," and says that our very involvement in reality

means "at once transforming it while being transformed." That principle
of continuous cultural transformation is embodied in Salman Rushdie's
perception of himself as "a bastard child of history": "Perhaps we all are,
black and brown and white, leaking into each other like flavours when
you cook. I say, let it continue."

## The Expanding Protean Field

*It was especially important to think what a human being really was.*

—Saul Bellow

Widespread expressions of proteanism create a psychological field that
expands toward species consciousness. As the forces responsible for proteanism (dislocation, mass media revolution, and the possibility of extinction) have provoked collective reappraisal, other protean characteristics
(shifts in ideas, work innovations, free-floating emotions and communities) enhance receptivity to broader human ties. With an ever greater
sharing of world history, communities in particular can become fluid
groups interconnecting with one another throughout the globe. The
links may be merely occupational (international gatherings of lawyers or
physicists) but, more important, can also be ethical and broadly political
(the international doctors' antinuclear movement and the Helsinki Citizens Assembly), environmental (international collaboration in theory
building and activism), gender-related (exchanges among feminist
groups), or pertaining to human rights (Amnesty International and
many other organizations). However temporary, intermittent, and fragile, such liaisons always have the potential for renewal and expansion.

The protean self can transcend time and space—to contain simultaneously elements from highly divergent historical periods and equally divergent geographical and cultural places. The protean self need not be just
here or there but can be here *and* there; it can take continuous leaps
from its immediate location, including the leap from the individual mind
to the shared aspirations and images of an entire historical era. Its "serial
equipoise" and "rolling configurations" can reach everywhere. Contributing to the process are energies derived from the modern self and its tendency to shift allegiances, to "dethrone the given, historic community as
a pole of identity" and seek another group it can associate with "adher-
ence to the good." The sequence does not sever our prior ties or "dependence on webs of interlocution," but merely "changes the webs, and the
nature of our dependence" on them. In this way, there is continuation of

the modern principle of "interpenetration of the local and global," now radically intensified by the mass media, as our television sets make it difficult for us to turn away from suffering—in Bosnia or Somalia or anywhere.*

In that way, one's *I* can be propelled by proteanism toward immortalizing species connections. The sustaining image becomes: "I am a human being," and, "However extensive or brief my own journey on the earth, I live on in humankind." That perception of larger connection can provide an experience of transcendence or a "high state," a contemporary more or less secular expression of a mystical sense of oneness. With that larger connectedness, one is freer to question categories of designated enemies, and the inevitable hostilities and rivalries can become much less absolute: for example, the principle expressed in the 1980s by the antinuclear movement that the enemy was not the Soviet Union or the United States, but rather any combination of weapons and people in either nation that pressed toward nuclear holocaust. Such principles help people become less inclined to die for a national cause and more inclined to live for an international one.

Dramatic changes also occur in leaders and in our perceptions of them. Consider Mikhail Gorbachev's life journey from communist functionary and leader, to architect of a stunning set of policies opening up an oppressive society and making possible the liberation of Eastern and Central European states from their communist regimes, to a man seen (in his advocacy of reform rather than replacement of Soviet Communist leadership) as "unable to keep up with the times," to wise commentator on America and the world. In his 7 May 1992 talk at Westminster College in Fulton, Missouri—where forty-six years earlier Winston Churchill (whose statue is permanently silhouetted against Gorbachev in a newspaper picture) had delivered the famous "Iron Curtain" speech that marked the official onset of the cold war—Gorbachev noted the "ending of the global confrontation of the nuclear superpowers," warned against "triumphalist claims of Cold War victory," and urged "global efforts to protect the ecology" and to right the balance between the rich and poor countries, while emphasizing the unpredictability of the future and history's refutation of Marx and other "know-it-alls and Messiahs." Historical acceleration can use up a leader quickly by rendering one's insights and commitments inadequate to radically new situations, but the very proteanness of such leaders can enable one, after being deposed, to reappear in a new functional incarnation and to pursue species goals.

---

*To be sure, repeated television images can also contribute to numbing and to a sense of unreality in relation to such events, but my observation has been that viewers maintain nonetheless some perception of others' pain and suffering which might ultimately be tapped.

The possibilities for improvisation are limitless. Since such improvisation may take the form of resistance to existing authorities and their claimed truths, the protean self can, in struggling for a species mentality, "dare to defy the given models of defiance."

A species mentality has been evident in a number of people we interviewed. Consider Carol C.'s sequence from her profound and fearful childhood response to the Crucifixion to her adult embrace of that searing image as a source of opposition to the torture of any human being. Or Arthur M.'s transformation of his own victimization by his father during childhood to vigorous and innovative world leadership in defending all human rights. Or Barbara M.'s identification with Harriet Tubman as a way of evolving a lifelong spirituality, a way both "Christocentric" and unlimited in its human outreach. Or Gordon Parks's befriending of a tubercular little boy from the slums of Rio de Janeiro as part of his conviction that "every life is valuable to our own existence." None of these people was born with species consciousness or automatically bequeathed it. Each had to make use of a protean self-process to explore combinations of local identification (personal, family, ethnic, religious, occupational, national) with principles of human commonality, to move back and forth between the two while at the same time blending them into an evolving species self.

The same is true of Francine C.'s relationship to the persecution of Jews: she is deeply concerned about anti-Semitism and the need for remembering the Holocaust, but says, "There are . . . other holocausts. I mean there is a holocaust in Nigeria. . . . I tend to think as much about the situation of the Palestinians, and the two wrongs, more than the Holocaust per se." And of people who, like Roslyn K., have been exposed early in life to ideas compatible with species consciousness. In a reverse sequence, she had to struggle to ground herself in immediate connections—with teaching, with specific community groups (especially involving youth and old people), with peace organizations (at both the grass-roots and decision-making levels), with prochoice advocates (in supporting the right to abortion), and with the homeless. She brought to them a spirit of species concern, whatever her moments of self-doubt and despair, just as she brought to her interests in painting and baseball passionate protean expression.

Strong species consciousness can occur unexpectedly, as in the case of George R., who rose from a sports-centered, lower-middle-class immigrant family to a corporate prominence that includes highly innovative methods and a policy of "always keep[ing] three balls in the air" as "the only way you can survive in the kind of crazy world we live in." He spoke of himself as "the eternal optimist" in connection with the larger world: "Obviously there are a lot of ills in the world that need to be addressed, but I generally believe . . . we're going to be . . . a healthy world. It'll be a world, I think, that people will be less tied to individual countries and be much more global in terms of people's ability to understand other societies. . . . And some of the kinds of changes that we see happening everyday around us suggest that, if they keep going the way they are, that we're . . . gonna have a much more significant movement of different peoples around the world. National boundaries will certainly break down in the sense of . . . ability of people from the United States to go to Eastern Europe, to go to China, to go to Russia . . . and on and on and on and on. Certainly more people are experiencing that now than probably . . . any of us ever imagined when we were young. I don't care what your economic status is, the opportunities are there." His worries about problems in our own country's "infrastructure," and even more about the validity of his own assertion that "corporate leaders or educational leaders or what have you" are bringing their wisdom to these problems, render his species vision even more impressive.

Aaron O., a New England rabbi, calls forth what is most universal in Judaism for his particular philosophical activism. From a religious family with strong social concerns, Aaron has been an activist since his high school days (he was in his late fifties when interviewed) and has long had the sense that "the Jewish community would have its own wisdom and its own ways." He illustrated the point by telling how some years ago he became active in holding, at the edge of the Nevada nuclear test site, a "pre-Passover seder" in which participants experienced their arrest as "an affirmation of what we talked about as opposing the ultimate pharaoh [here standing for oppressor of Jews]." He constantly invoked the Holocaust in terms of its species meanings: "Because people thought it was unthinkable, they didn't take the actions necessary to make sure it didn't happen. And . . . people say the same thing about the bomb. 'It's unthinkable.'" Hence, "Jewish experience has that special take on the world, that special experience of their own." Aaron invoked the Old Testament also in universalistic terms: "The flood story doesn't talk about . . . us versus them. . . . We have the whole human race and, indeed, all the species being [threatened]. . . . Noah was not against anybody or anybody against Noah. . . . Noah just has the good sense to respond when God says there's a danger."

Several mystical experiences have helped Aaron to integrate these various elements. At a time of intense antiwar and racial protest during the late 1960s, he remembers seeing National Guardsmen on the streets of Washington, D.C., and thinking, "That's Pharoah's army." And he felt, "Something about Jewish tradition . . . really spoke to . . . this piece of me that I cared about, and to the streets and to life, in a way it had never spoken to me before." Another time he had a vision of preparing "a liturgy that brought together mourning for the Holocaust and for

Hiroshima," and heard a "voiceless voice" tell him that if he could do that, "all of them will live again"—this experience coinciding with his recovery from a near-fatal illness. These mystical experiences were "like a volcano" for Aaron, giving him the courage (after experimenting with academic life and electoral politics) to "invent . . . my own direction" and work from a religiously and politically radical Jewish perspective. He prepared, among other things, readings for a Passover seder which wove the traditional story of Jewish liberation from bondage with sayings of Martin Luther King, descriptions of the Warsaw ghetto, and general pacifist struggles.

As they have traditionally done for religious and secular "seers," these mystical experiences enabled Aaron to break away from contraries and oppositions and move in directions consistent with species awareness. In that spirit, he has been working on a new prayer book "which includes some prayers in Arabic affirming the existence of one God, . . . intertwined with the Hebrew, deliberately, in order to face Jews with the question of whether they're willing to say in Arabic, as well as in Hebrew, there is one God." Through these spiritual explorations, Aaron's "ways of experiencing God . . . have gotten much richer than they used to be and much more varied." Like other people, Aaron is not without contradictions: on more than one occasion, when he felt Israel to be threatened, he strayed from his species principles in temporary advocacy of military force. But he would quickly retreat from that position and return to his "global" protean style and resume "talking about a world of conflict woven into cooperation" and of a "one earthness . . . so strong and so real that we simply can't afford to have the collisions [that could result in its destruction]."

## The Matter Remains Open

Freud once claimed that his most troubled patients revealed, in ways that were "larger and coarser," the kinds of psychological experience all of us undergo every day. In exploring proteanism and its antagonists, I have been discussing, perhaps in larger and coarser ways, the experience of ordinary human beings everywhere at this moment in history. It will come as no surprise that, in completing this book, I conclude that everything remains open. Indeed, the principle that the future is not predictable is inherent to virtually everything I have said. If nothing else, the last decades of the twentieth century have demonstrated the extreme fallacy of historical determinism, a fallacy that ignores the uncertainties of human behavior and the mystery of the symbolizing process, a mystery that takes on high relevance in our era. More than merely manifesting this unpredictability, proteanism provides us with a concept to help us grasp what it is about. The concept is also consistent with the idea that, in respect to culture, we are always caught up with "invention" rather than mere "representation"—that, as symbolizers, we always re-create what we observe or experience. In that way, we have no choice but to invent or reinvent our own evolving future—never with full clarity but never without possibility.

Calling forth one's proteanism on behalf of species consciousness becomes part of the social evolution of the self—part of seizing upon the evolutionary human capacity to connect with faraway places. Becoming human, that is, enabled an emerging self to locate itself outside of its immediate setting. That process took a quantum leap in the modern era; and the twentieth century, particularly its latter decades, still more radically expanded the self's access to distant locations, which now help form the self and contribute greatly to its definition and identity. Whatever the myriad confusions that result, the process is inexorable; we seek, almost automatically, some adaptation to it. We modify the self to include connections virtually anywhere while clinging to a measure of coherence. The individual self thus learns to develop a "place for many places," while the prevailing historical forces propel the process toward ever greater inclusiveness.

Much of this process consists of calling forth the innate plasticity of human development and behavior. At issue is an evolutionary principle in which the early forest environment favored "versatility in stance and locomotor pattern," so that "social relationships that led to brain evolution were then themselves altered when larger-brained—and more plastic—organisms were involved in them" in a broad "system of reciprocal influence." That "system of reciprocal influence" now contributes to, and is further enhanced by, proteanism reaching out toward the human species.

This multilocal self can draw images from far places and render them its own "memories." Whether painful and sad (images of Hiroshima or of starving African children) or joyous (the tearing down of the Berlin Wall or Nelson Mandela striding proudly out of prison), these image-memories can embed themselves powerfully within millions of individual selves. As this kind of multilocal proteanism moves toward species consciousness, it can enhance individual and collective commitment to nonviolence. Mutability and inclusiveness can replace, or at least undermine, the rigidity and exclusion inherent in the violent act.

I am speaking not of a sudden eureka moment, or even of a dramatic species mutation, but of a gradual shift in the function of self that may be discernible only at certain times and in certain places. As in all evolutionary developments, the shift involves innovation and adaptation. The varying levels of identification—from individual to family to social or ethnic group to nation and then species—continue to reverberate, their harmony imperfect but sufficient to permit a variety of loyalties and a capacity to resolve, if again imperfectly, conflicts among these loyalties. This evolution of the self toward its own species can help it overcome dissociative tendencies. One moves toward becoming what the early Karl Marx called a "species-being," a fully human being. Once established, the species identification itself contributes to centering and grounding. In no way eliminated, prior identifications are, rather, brought into new alignment within a more inclusive sense of self.

Inclusiveness is vital. Elements of the species self reach back to earliest recorded human history—from at least 1500 B.C. (in Hinduism) to subsequent developments in Taoism, Buddhism, Judaism, and Islam, as well as Christianity. Indeed Jesus' Sermon on the Mount was a powerful extension of already existing species principles rather than an initial expression of them. Drawing upon these early forms of consciousness, the species self is also influenced by every subsequent expression of commonality extending to contemporary global visions. In style, the species self incorporates premodern holism and spirituality, the modern quest for the universal, and the pluralism that has come to stamp the postmodern. In gender, the species self tends to include both "male" and "female" elements—that is, to move beyond narrow definitions of what it is to be either male or female and explore combinations of those elements. The self in social evolution helps us redefine that elusive entity we call "human nature"—not as a fixed set of structures or behaviors but as a mutable array of potentialities one can always draw upon.

Proteanism is a means of coordinating one's energies toward at least minimal integration and maximal reach. That tendency has been validated by twentieth-century thinkers who focus on form and configuration, on experience and meaning, as inseparable from reason and necessary to survival. The tradition provides a certain centering to balance the risky decentering inherent in contemporary forays, an element of cultural grounding necessary for the stretch toward the species. It is a tradition that provides a context for transcendence of context. The protean self, then, becomes a bridge between the modern and the postmodern, a source of continuity that takes in radical discontinuity. The ongoing process is primarily cultural and psychological, though never free of the political. Whatever the impediments—and there are bound to be many—only the increasingly unbound human imagination can press toward a species mentality.

In writing about human resilience at a time of considerable fragmentation, I advocate the life-enhancing expressions of that resilience, even as I seek sufficient detachment to probe both its possibilities and its impediments. However I may imagine the future of proteanism, I speak from the vantage point of the present. Any future species direction I or others imagine must have roots in contemporary commonality. As the self-reflecting species, we are bound to each other and to every other species. And the protean self, rendered collective, has a certain power to alter and strengthen those larger human bonds. That power inevitably relates to our symbolization of life and death. Just as, in primitive cultures, the soul of the individual who dies was thought to blend with its "ancestor souls" in maintaining human continuity, so may we understand the capacity, in life, for an individual *I* to connect with every other *I* that exists, has existed, or will exist. Now the human community has been radically broadened: our "ancestor souls" populate the globe. At stake for all is what I speak of as "the future of immortality."

I have suggested several models for a proteanism that is, in its very fluidity, tough-minded and morally committed. Václav Havel discovered in himself, in his struggle to break out of a context of falsity, a "hidden openness to truth": "Individuals can be alienated from themselves only because there is *something* in them to alienate." That "something" has to do with authenticity, with meanings and human associations that, over the course of a life, one experiences as genuine. The protean quest, however flawed, enhances that authenticity.

By enabling one to transform discontinuity and pain, proteanism "allows the traumatized to speak, and to be heard." It can give new voice and vitality to many who would otherwise be silent and deadened, and provide new byways to human connection. The protean path I describe, of individual people reaching toward global belonging, is a path of hope. One may experience that hope, and even a modest personal liberation, in consciously embracing that direction. The embrace is an act of imagination and, as such, a profound beginning.

# NOTES

## Chapter 1: The Changing Psychological Landscape

2     For the interviews of Chinese in Hongkong, of Japanese youth, of innovative young American professionals, and of Vietnam veterans, see my *Thought Reform and the Psychology of Totalism: The Study of "Brainwashing" in China* (Chapel Hill: University of North Carolina Press, 1989 [1961]); *History and Human Survival: Essays on the Young and Old, Survivors and the Dead, Peace and War, and on Contemporary Psychohistory* (New York: Random House, 1970); *The Life of the Self: Toward a New Psychology* (New York: Basic Books, 1984 [1976]); and *Home from the War: Learning from Vietnam Veterans* (Boston: Beacon Press, 1992 [1973]), which is the source (284–85) of the phrase on freedom, "to just move anywhere and feel anything."

4     "Surprising quickness of the collapse" and "define and redefine the identity of the state" from Jiri Musil, "Czechoslovakia in the Middle of Transition," *Daedalus* (Spring 1992): 175–95.

5     Homer, *The Odyssey*, trans. Robert Fitzgerald (Garden City, NY: Doubleday, 1963), Book 4, 66.

5     "Who of those" . . . "chastity inviolate" from W. H. Roscher, "Proteus," *Ausführliches Lexikon der griechischen und römischen Mythologie*, vol. 5 (Leipzig: 1884), 3172, 3174, 3175–76, 3177.

6     The study of "Nuclear Threat and the American Self" was conducted over a three-year period (1987–90), funded by a grant from the John D. and Catherine T. MacArthur Foundation, whose support is gratefully acknowledged.

8     "Swims, even wallows, in the . . . " from David Harvey, *The Condition of Postmodernity* (Cambridge, MA: Blackwell, 1989), 44.

8     "Contingency, multiplicity, and polyvocality" from Henry M. Sayre, *The Object of Performance: The American Avant-Garde since 1970* (Chicago: University of Chicago Press, 1989), xii–xiii.

8     "Playful, self-ironizing" from Harvey, *Condition of Postmodernity*, 7–8.

9     "Deep/in the green sea/I saw . . . " from W. S. Merwin, "Sight," *The Rain in the Trees* (New York: Knopf, 1988), 35.

234                                                                     *Notes*

10    "My whole life . . . " from Malcolm X, *The Autobiography of Malcolm X,* as
      told to Alex Hailey (New York: Ballantine, 1964), 390.

10    "Like many people who invent . . . " quoted in *Business Week,* 19
      November 1990, 28.

10    Quotes from Václav Havel are from *Disturbing the Peace* (New York:
      Knopf, 1990), 202—4.

10–11 On totalism, absolute dogma, and a monolithic self, see my *Thought
      Reform.*


## Chapter 2: History and the Self

13    *"Open-ended behavioral repertoire"* . . . "better brains" from Dean Falk,
      "Brain and Evolution in Homo: The 'Radiator' Theory," *Behavioral and
      Brain Sciences* 13 (1990): 344.

13–14 Enlargement of brain depends upon culture, and culture "ingredient
      to human thought," Clifford Geertz, *The Interpretation of Cultures* (New
      York: Basic Books, 1973), 89.

14    "Homo . . . [the] generalist . . . " from Pat Shipman, quoted in
      William K. Stevens, "Global Climate Changes Seen as Force in Human
      Evolution," *New York Times,* 16 October 1990, C1 and C6. See also Ship-
      man, "The Ancestor That Wasn't," *The Sciences* (March–April 1985):
      43–48.

15    "The bond between the sacred" . . . "thou shalt prefer." This series of
      quotes is from Stephen A. McKnight, *Sacralizing the Secular: The Renais-
      sance Origins of Modernity* (Baton Rouge: Louisiana State University
      Press, 1989), 65–66.

15    The phrase "sacralization of the secular" is from McKnight, ibid.

16    "Activist, engineering attitude toward nature . . . " from Zygmunt Bau-
      man, *Modernity and the Holocaust* (Ithaca, NY: Cornell University Press,
      1989), 70.

16    "Self-emancipation" see McKnight, *Sacralizing the Secular,* 2.

16    Diverse cultural elements of Meiji Japanese innovators, as two co-
      authors and I discovered in our investigation of a few of them. See
      Lifton, Shuichi Kato, and Michael Reich, *Six Lives/Six Deaths: Portraits
      from Modern Japan* (New Haven, CT: Yale University Press, 1979).

17    "Peculiar phenomenon" . . . "sub-systems" from Henri Lefebvre, *Every-
      day Life in the Modern World* (New York: Harper Torchbooks, 1971
      [1968]), 183.

18    "The sensuous and the intellectual . . . " from Philip Marchand, *Mar-
      shall McLuhan: The Medium and the Messenger* (New York: Ticknor and
      Fields, 1989), 69

18    "Galaxy" . . . "print culture" from McLuhan, *Gutenberg Galaxy*
      (Toronto: University of Toronto Press, 1988 [1962]), 47, 124, 125.

18    "Split between" . . . "rejected awareness," ibid., 170, 199, 222, 235–36,
      245.

18    "Curved space" . . . "Gutenberg man," ibid., 133.

19    "Discarnate man" . . . "patterns of information" from Marchand, *Marshall McLuhan*, 238.

19    "The medium is the *massage*" . . . "unaltered," ibid., 26.

19    "What if he is right?" from Tom Wolfe, *The Pump House Gang* (New York: Farrar Straus and Giroux, 1968), 133–73.

20    Elements of McLuhan's proteanism, from Marchand, *Marshall McLuhan*.

20–21 Long quote from Penelope Lively, *City of the Mind* (New York: Harper-Collins, 1991), 2–3.

21–22 "Cultures without terminal visions" from W. Warren Wagar, *Terminal Visions: The Literature of Last Things* (Bloomington: Indiana University Press, 1982), 36.

22    "Age of darkness" from Mircea Eliade, *Cosmos and History: The Myth of the Eternal Return* (New York: Harper Torchbooks, 1959 [1954]), 118.

22    "The myth of universal conflagration" . . . "come to the living" from Eliade, *Cosmos and History*, 124.

22    "I am thy creature" from Langdon Winner, *Autonomous Technology* (Cambridge, MA: MIT Press, 1978), 310.

23    "Literary ghetto" . . . "world-historical signals" from Wagar, *Terminal Visions*, 9–10, 200.

23    "So in his own way . . . " from Martin Amis, *London Fields* (New York: Harmony Books, 1989), 254.

23    "A predicament for the individual," Frank Kermode, from Wagar, *Terminal Visions*, 10.

24    "To strengthen the ego" . . . "its organization" from *New Introductory Lectures on Psychoanalysis*, Volume 22 of *The Standard Edition of the Complete Psychological Works of Sigmund Freud* (London: Hogarth Press, 1964), 80.

25    "A rider" . . . "the id," ibid., 77.

25    "Systematic self-restriction" . . . "self-ideal" from Ernest Becker, *The Denial of Death* (New York: Free Press, 1973), 210.

25    "Transcendent function" . . . "conjoined opposites" from Carl Jung, "The Transcendent Function," in *The Structure and Dynamics of the Psyche, Collected Works*, vol. 8, trans. R. F. C. Hull (Princeton, NJ: Princeton University Press, 1969), 90.

25    "Will" . . . "instinctual drives," Otto Rank, quoted from E. James Lieberman, *Acts of Will: The Life and Work of Otto Rank* (New York: Free Press, 1985), 357–58.

25    "Cultural development " . . . "life itself" from Otto Rank, *Beyond Psychology* (New York: Dover, 1958 [1939]), 48, 161, 278.

26    "Self-system" . . . "is forward" from Harry Stack Sullivan, *Conceptions of Modern Psychiatry* (New York: Norton, 1953), 19–21, 97.

26    For Erikson on identity, see his *Identity: Youth and Crisis* (New York: Norton, 1968).

26    For Laing's work, see his *The Divided Self* (Harmondsworth: Penguin, 1965 [1960]), and *Self and Others* (Harmondsworth: Penguin, 1969 [1961]).

26     "An extinction" . . . "the no-self" from C. Fred Alford, *The Psychoanalytic Theory of Greek Tragedy* (New Haven, CT: Yale University Press, 1992), 135, 119. See also Jacques Lacan, *Ecrits,* trans. Alan Sheridan (New York: Norton, 1977).

27     For Kohut's work, see his *The Restoration of the Self* (New York: International Universities Press, 1977).

27     "Polytheistic psychology" . . . "and centers" from James Hillman, *Revisioning Psychology* (New York: Harper and Row, 1975), 26–27.

27     "Human plasticity" from Richard E. Lerner, *On the Nature of Human Plasticity* (Cambridge: Cambridge University Press, 1984).

27     "The saturated self" from Kenneth J. Gergen, *The Saturated Self* (New York: Basic Books, 1991).

27     "The empty self" from Philip Cushman, "Why the Self Is Empty," *American Psychologist* 45 (May 1990): 599–611.

27     "Possible selves" from Hazel Markus and Paula Nurius, "Possible Selves," *American Psychologist* 41 (September 1986): 954–69.

27     "The dialogical self" from Herbert J. M. Hermans et al, "The Dialogical Self," *American Psychologist* 47 (January 1992): 23–33.

27     "The decentralized identity" from Edward E. Sampson, "The Decentralization of Identity," *American Psychologist* 40 (November 1985): 1203–11.

27     "Many dimensional man" from James Ogilvy, *Many Dimensional Man* (New York: Oxford University Press, 1977).

27     "The quantum self" from Danah Zohar, *The Quantum Self* (New York: Quill/William Morrow, 1990).

27     "Multimind" from Robert Ornstein, *Multimind* (Boston: Houghton Mifflin, 1986).

27     "The society of mind" from Marvin Minsky, *The Society of Mind* (New York: Simon and Schuster, 1985).

27     Mumford's review of Jung's autobiography from *New Yorker,* 23 May 1964.

28     "Is no mere receiving" . . . "formation" from Ernst Cassirer, *The Philosophy of Symbolic Forms,* Volume 3: *The Phenomenology of Knowledge* (New Haven, CT: Yale University Press, 1973 [1957]), 13.

28     "*Transformational* nature" . . . "of experiences" from Susanne K. Langer, *Philosophy in a New Key: A Study in the Symbolism of Reason, Rite, and Art* (New York: New American Library, 1951 [1942]), viii, 32, 45, 48.

28     "Tremendous complexity" . . . "the world" from Langer's three-volume study, *Mind: An Essay in Human Feeling* (Baltimore, MD: Johns Hopkins Press, 1967–1982), vol. 1, 67.

28     "The great dreams of mankind . . . " from Langer, *Philosophy in a New Key,* 168.

29     [Footnote] Quoted in Lerner, *On the Nature of Human Plasticity,* 2.

29     For the principle of the symbolizing self and the paradigm of life-continuity, see Robert Jay Lifton, *The Broken Connection: On Death and the Continuity of Life,* (New York: Basic Books, 1983 [1979]).

29    "The constant reformulation of . . . " from Langer, *Mind,* vol. 1, 80.

30    "In moral " . . . "the good" from Charles Taylor, *Sources of the Self: The Making of the Modern Identity* (Cambridge, MA: Harvard University Press, 1989), 27, 34.

30    "Specific difference" . . . "but interdependent" from Ernst Cassirer, *An Essay on Man* (New Haven, CT: Yale University Press, 1944), 26, 228.

30    "That newest of natural phenomena—Mind—still . . . " from Langer, *Mind,* vol. 3, 219.

30    "Grand narratives" . . . "metanarratives," see Pauline Marie Rosenau, *Post-Modernism and the Social Sciences* (Princeton, NJ: Princeton University Press, 1992), 85, and David Harvey, *The Condition of Postmodernity* (Oxford: Basil Blackwell, 1989 [1980]), 9.

30    "Postindustrialized, postmodernized, postsemioticized, post-toastied . . . " from John Leonard, "Exgrasspororating German," *Nation,* 24 December 1990, 817.

30    "Amazing what the mind . . . " from Robert Creeley, "Thinking," in Jorie Graham and David Lehman, eds., *Best American Poetry 1990* (New York: Collier Books, 1990), 41.

30    "A so-called steady state . . . " from Langer, *Mind,* vol. 2, 266.

30    "Rolling configurations" . . . "serial equipoise" from Ronnie Dugger, Wellfleet psychohistory meetings, October 1991.

31    "Even conceivable . . . " from Langer, *Mind,* vol. 1, 53.

31    "Idols of " . . . "of mathematization," ibid., 50.

## Chapter 3: America, The Protean Nation

32    Both epigraphs from Lewis Lapham, "Who and What Is American?" *Harper's,* January 1992, 45–46, 48.

32    "An endless inpouring of strangers . . . " from Tony Tanner's introduction to Herman Melville, *The Confidence Man* (New York: Oxford University Press, 1989 [1856]), xvi.

32    "No prudent man" . . . "or a jail" quoted from Boorstin in Lapham, "Who and What Is American?" 43, 46.

33    "The 90's, which began in the 80's . . . " from Daphne Merkin, "Name That Decade," *New York Times,* 24 May 1992.

33    "We are a nomad people . . . " from Richard Reeves, "Must We Live and Die Alone?" *Honolulu Advertiser,* 27 January 1992.

33    "Profusion of individual" . . . "and so on" from Henry M. Sayre, *The Object of Performance,* xii.

33    "Rich diversity " . . . "of change" from Ellison, *Shadow and Act* (New York: Random House, 1964), 105–6.

34    De Tocqueville epigraph quoted in Tanner's introduction to Melville, *Confidence Man,* xv.

34    "Great historic" . . . "real sense" from Frederick Jackson Turner, "The Significance of the Frontier in American History," in Turner, *Frontier and Section* (Englewood Cliffs, NJ: Prentice-Hall, 1961), 39; essay origi-

nally published in the *American Historical Association, Annual Report for 1893* (Washington, DC: American Historical Association, 1893), 199–227.

34 "Civilization" . . . "move about" from Gary Lindberg, *The Confidence Man in American Literature* (New York: Oxford University Press, 1982), 5.

34 "A tanned" . . . "his land" from Tanner's introduction to Melville, *Confidence Man,* viii.

34 "Tries out " . . . "in performance" from Lindberg, *Confidence Man in American Literature,* 88, 91–2.

34–35 "The bonds" . . . "after West" from Turner, "The Problem of the West," in *Frontier and Section,* 63.

35 "Regeneration through violence" from Richard Slotkin, *Regeneration through Violence: The Mythology of the American Frontier, 1600–1860* (Middletown, CT: Wesleyan University Press, 1973), 83–84.

35 "Indian removal" . . . "of villages" from Howard Zinn, *A People's History of the United States* (New York: Harper Perennial Library, 1990 [1980]), 124.

35 "The rogues, adventurers" . . . "higher reality" from Slotkin, *Regeneration,* 4, 18, 27.

36 "Powers as" . . . "southern virtues," ibid., 398.

36 "This perennial rebirth . . . " from Turner, "The Significance of the Frontier," in *Frontier and Section,* 38.

36 "Not one free from the . . . " from Zinn, *A People's History of the United States* (New York: Harper Colophon, 1980), 221.

36 "Wiles that have hitherto been . . . " from John Higham, *Strangers in the Land: Patterns of American Nativism 1860–1925* (New York: Atheneum, 1963 [1955]), 93.

36 "No variety of anti-European sentiment . . . ," ibid., 25.

36 "Swarms of hybrids" from Madison Grant, *The Passing of the Great Race; or, The Racial Basis of European History* (New York: Charles Scribner's Sons, 1916).

37 "A stranger am I to" . . . "am free" quoted in Zinn, 261.

37 Long quote from Saul Bellow, *The Adventures of Augie March* (New York: Viking Press, 1953), 125.

37–38 "Melted into" . . . "yet unknown" from Nathan Glazer and Daniel P. Moynihan, *Beyond the Melting Pot: The Negroes, Puerto Ricans, Jews, Italians, and Irish of New York City* (Cambridge, MA: MIT Press, 1989 [1963]), 288, 290–91, 13, 17, 315.

39 "A regular institution" . . . "a slaughterhouse" from Zinn, 23.

39 "If you" . . . "the ell" from *Narrative of the Life of Frederick Douglass, an American Slave, Written by Himself,* edited by Benjamin Quarles (Cambridge, MA: Harvard University Press, 1960), 58, 59, 64–65.

39–40 "Double meanings" from Henry Louis Gates, Jr., *The Signifying Monkey: A Theory of African-American Literary Criticism* (New York: Oxford University Press, 1988). See also Lawrence W. Levine, *Black Culture and Black Consciousness* (New York: Oxford University Press, 1977); Ralph Ellison,

*Shadow and Act* (London: Secker & Warburg, 1967) and *Going to the Territory* (New York: Vintage Books, 1987); Stanley M. Elkins, *Slavery* (Chicago: University of Chicago Press, 1976 [1959]); Ann J. Lane, ed., *The Debate over Slavery: Stanley Elkins and His Critics* (Champaign-Urbana: University of Illinois Press, 1971); Winthrop D. Jordan, *White over Black* (Baltimore: Penguin Books, 1969 [1968]); Eugene D. Genovese, *Roll, Jordan, Roll: The World the Slaves Made)* (New York: Vintage Books, 1976 [1972]); and Toni Morrison, *Beloved* (New York: New American Library, 1988 [1987]).

40    "Now trickster, ladies' man, and . . . " from Sterling Stuckey, "Through the Prism of Folklore: The Black Ethos in Slavery," in Lane, *Debate over Slavery*, 264.

40    "Virtuoso of the system" from George M. Frederickson and Christopher Lash, "Resistance to Slavery," in Lane, *Debate over Slavery*, 241.

40    "I want you to overcome . . . " from Ralph Ellison, *Invisible Man* (New York: Vintage Books, 1989 [1952]), 16.

40    On the "great migration" to the North, see Nicholas Lemann, *The Promised Land: The Great Black Migration and How It Changed America* (New York: Knopf, 1991).

40    On black family breakdown during sharecropping era, see Herbert G. Gutman, *The Black Family in Slavery and Freedom 1750–1925* (New York: Vintage Books, 1976).

40    "He composed" . . . "to lie?" from Ellison, *Invisible Man*, 102, 139.

40    "World . . . without boundaries " . . . "perhaps all at the same time," ibid., 498–99, 510.

41    "The murky" . . . "flood the marketplace" from Cornel West, "Nihilism in Black America," *Dissent* (Spring 1991): 221–26.

41    Ellison on the "beautiful absurdity of their American identity and mind" from *Shadow and Act*; see also his *Going to the Territory* (New York: Vintage Books, 1987).

41    Epigraph quoted in Lindberg, *Confidence Man in American Literature*, 143. Subsequent quotes, "linking land boomers" . . . "con man in the clearing," ibid., 6, 148.

42    A "shell game of identity" from Tanner's introduction to Melville, *Confidence Man*, xxxiii.

42    "I try" . . . "rapid petrifaction" from Lindberg, *Confidence Man in American Literature*, 154, 140, 5, 129, 125, 161.

42    "Metamorphosis is" . . . "to freeze" ibid., 171, and Tanner's introduction to Melville, *Confidence Man*, ix.

42    "I have" . . . "that one" from Lindberg, *Confidence Man in American Literature*, 172–73.

42    For Ernest Hemingway on the "shapelessness" of the world, Alfred Kazin, *Bright Book of Life: American Novelists and Storytellers from Hemingway to Mailer* (South Bend, IN: University of Notre Dame Press, 1980 [1974]) 7.

42    For quotes on Neal Cassady, see Lindberg, *Confidence Man in American Literature*, 261–63.

43      "In a spirit"... "the mind" from Kazin, *Bright Book of Life*, 263, 268–69.

43      "Fury of"... "happening to them," ibid., 150, 154, 192, 199.

43      "The more a man trades ... " from Russell Banks, *Continental Drift* (New York: Harper and Row, 1985), 283.

43      "Smell of too much freedom ... " from Frederick Barthelme's novel *Natural Selection* (New York: Penguin, 1991), 191.

43      "A crook"... "and self" from Lindberg, *Confidence Man in American Literature*, 138.

43      "I touched all sides... " from Bellow, *Augie March*.

43      "Rogue-survivor"... "be regenerated" from Lindberg, *Confidence Man in American Literature*, 251, 454–55.

43      "A representative modern intelligence, swamped... " from Tony Tanner, *City of Words: American Fiction, 1950–1970* (New York: Harper and Row, 1971).

43      "The personification"... "the other" from Ellison, *Shadow and Act*, 181––82.

43–44   On Ellison probing of deep disorder, see Lindberg, *Confidence Man in American Literature*, 250.

44      "A prose which is... " from Ellison, *Shadow and Act*, 104–5.

44      Epigraph from Graham and Lehman, *Best American Poetry 1990*, xix.

44–45   Series beginning "American environments" and ending with long quote "I've come to understand" from Don DeLillo, *White Noise* (New York: Viking Press, 1985), 66, 51.

45      "A person sits in a ... " through the end of the long quotation ("how to assimilate him"), from Don DeLillo, *Mao II* (New York: Viking Press, 1991), 132.

46      For war's having little unpleasantness, see my article, "Techno-bloodshed," *Guardian* (London), 14 February 1991.

46      On the four-year-old child during the Gulf War, see my article, "Parents: To Children Danger Isn't Distant—It's in the Television," *Los Angeles Times*, 3 February 1991.

47      Epigraph from Paul S. Boyer, *By the Bomb's Early Light* (New York: Pantheon, 1985), 15.

47      First *New York Times* quote, 8 August 1945; second from Spencer Weart, "The Atomic Age: The Heyday of Myth and Cliché," *Bulletin of the Atomic Scientists* 41 (August 1985), 43.

47      For discussion of nuclear fear, its relationship to environmental threat, and psychological shifts at the end of the cold war, see Charles B. Strozier's, Michael Perlman's, and my, *Nuclear Threat and the American Self*, forthcoming. See also Strozier's and my, "The Threat Is Going, but Not the Terror," *New York Newsday*, 22 December 1991.


## Chapter 4: Odd Combinations

50      First epigraph from Ann Beattie, *What Was Mine* (New York: Random House, 1991).

50      Second epigraph quoted in Herta Wescher, *Collage,* trans. Robert E. Wolf, (New York: Abrams, 1968), 163.

50      "A world dominated by metamorphoses . . . " from Umberto Eco, *The Middle Ages of James Joyce* (London: Hutchinson Radius, 1989 [1962]), 36.

50–51   "One-way motion" . . . "individual fate" from Brian Boyd, *Vladimir Nabakov: The American Years* (Princeton, NJ: Princeton University Press, 1991), quoted in *New York Times Book Review,* 22 September 1991.

51      "Like particles in modernity's accelerator" from Michael J. Shapiro, *Reading the Postmodern Polity: Political Theory as Textual Practice* (Minneapolis: University of Minnesota Press, 1992), 78.

51      "Time . . . is up for grabs" from Janette Turner Hospital, *Charades* (New York: Bantam Books, 1989), 29.

51      "Tak[e] . . . the time to drift and think" from Mary Ann Caws, "Presidential Talk: [American Comparative Literature Association] A Floating Text" (typescript, 1991).

51      "*How Many More Shapes* . . . " from Bharati Mukherjee, *Jasmine* (New York: Grove Widenfeld, 1989), 215.

55      "I saw another cross with . . . " from Carruth's poem "Crucifixion" in Graham and Lehman, *Best American Poetry 1990,* 16–17.

67      "We live because there are a number of encounters . . . " from Ivan Klima *Love and Garbage* (London: Chatto & Windus, 1990 [1986]), 51.

67      "A stable" . . . "dynamic inconsistency" from Karl Miller, *Doubles: Studies in Literary History* (Oxford: Oxford University Press, 1985), 24.

67      "Post-quixotic, post-Copernican U.S.A. where a . . . " from Saul Bellow, *Herzog* (New York: Viking Press, 1961), 286.

67      "Disencumber . . . himself . . . " from H. Porter Abbott, "Saul Bellow and the 'Lost Cause' of Character," in Gloria L. Cronin and L. H. Goldman, eds., *Saul Bellow in the 1980s: A Collection of Critical Essays* (East Lansing: Michigan State University Press, 1989), 134.

67      "The back-and-forthness" . . . "nothing is out of place" from Don DeLillo, *Mao II* (New York: Viking Press, 1991), 51, 22.

67–68   "Out of God's sight" . . . "the ride I'm on" from Mukherjee, *Jasmine,* 85, 215.

68      "Nymphet" . . . "of being" from Kazin, *Bright Book of Life,* 306–7.

68      Quoted comments by Leonard about Grass—"a career" to "Nobel Prize"—from "Exgrassperorating German," *Nation,* 811, 812, and 816.

68      Frost's "ideals of" . . . "genuinely rescued" quoted in Graham and Lehman, *Best American Poetry 1990,* xxvii.

68      For discussion of breakdown of fixed poetic criteria and experimentation with nonpoetic forms see Jonathan Holden, *Style and Authenticity in Postmodern Poetry* (Columbia: University of Missouri Press, 1986), 11.

68–69   "From Manhattan, a glittering shambles/of . . . " from Amy Clampitt, "My Cousin Muriel," in Graham and Lehman, *Best American Poetry 1990,* 34. Carson, "Towns are the illusion" . . . "Judas Town," 18–31.

69      "A conception" . . . "many dimensions" in Robert L. Herbert, ed., *Modern Artists on Art* (Englewood Cliffs, NJ: Prentice-Hall, 1964), 77–78.

69      "Meanings [that]" . . . "and final" from Sayre, *The Object of Performance,*
        7.

69      "Replacement of" . . . "of possibility" from Harold Rosenberg, *The Anx-
        ious Object: Art Today and Its Audience* (New York: Horizon Press, 1964),
        32–33.

69      "To dispense" . . . "action painting" from Harold Rosenberg, *The Tra-
        dition of the New* (New York: Grove Press, 1961), 27. Italics added.

69      "The process of painting *is* . . . " quoted in the *New York Times,* 28 July
        1991.

69      About "'bad' painting . . . " see Sayre, *Object of Performance,* xii.

69      "Great plethora" . . . "willful eclecticism" from Rosalind Krauss,
        quoted in Sayre, *Object of Performance,* xi.

69–70   "Small scratches" . . . "World exoticism" from Sayre, *Object of Perfor-
        mance,* 11–12.

70      "A revolution" . . . "component parts" from Naum Gabo, "The Con-
        structive Idea in Art," in Herbert, *Modern Artists on Art,* 107.

70      "Moment of Cubism" from John Berger, *The Look of Things* (New York:
        Viking Press, 1971), 133–62. All subsequent quotations in this para-
        graph are from the Berger essay.

70      Picasso and Braque inserting objects into their paintings, Herta
        Wescher, *Collage,* trans. by Robert E. Wolf, (New York: Abrams, 1968),
        20. While working with me on proteanism, Eric Olson developed an
        imaginative collage method for use in evaluation and therapy. I am
        indebted to him for our close collaboration and continuous dialogue
        during the 1970s. See Eric Wicks Olson, "The Mind's Collage: Psychic
        Composition in Adult Life," thesis for program in clinical psychology
        and public practice, Harvard University, May 1976.

70      "It is not the paste . . . " and quotations from footnote from Wescher,
        *Collage,* 163.

71      "Beat Zen . . . " from Sayre, *Object of Performance,* 9.

71      "Transformation of . . . dog into artist," ibid., 56–57.

71      "Pasadena Lifesavers" . . . "psychic level," ibid., 95.

71      "Chance collisions" . . . "perpetual nomadism," ibid., 154; and Janet
        Kardon, *Laurie Anderson: Works from 1969 to 1983* (Philadelphia: Insti-
        tute of Contemporary Art, University of Pennsylvania, 1983).

71      On architectural postmodern pluralism, see Charles Jencks, "Death for
        Rebirth," *Architectural Design,* 60 (September–October/1990), 7. See
        also Jencks, *The Language of Post-Modern Architecture* (New York, Rizzoli,
        1987 [1977]); and David Kolb, "Postmodern Sophistications," in *Archi-
        tectural Design,* op. cit., 13.

72      "We look at architecture now . . . " from Paul Goldberger, "After Opu-
        lence, a New 'Lite' Architecture," *New York Times,* 20 May 1990, Section
        2, 1, 18.

72      "Locus of meanings" from Steven Connor, *Postmodernist Culture* (New
        York: Basil Blackwell, 1989), 74, 75, 78.

72      For Jencks on Kurokawa museum in Hiroshima, see his "Death for
        Rebirth."

72     "Vast and uninterrupted dialogue" from Sayre, *Object of Performance*, 31.

72     "How is it possible" . . . "messages and meanings" from DeLillo, *Mao II*, 134, 157.

72     "Criss-cross" fashion to "music of ideas" from Eco, *Middle Ages*, 45, 43, 50.

72     "The history of the world . . . " from Lefebvre, 3–5.

72     "The world with which contemporary . . . " from Eco, *Middle Ages*, 85.

73     "Equally fragmented" . . . "dangerous as it is" from Salman Rushdie *The Satanic Verses* (New York: Viking Press, 1988), 4, 8.

73     "Celebrates hybridity, impurity, intermingling . . . " from W. J. Weatherby, *Salman Rushdie: Sentenced to Death* (New York: Carroll & Graf, 1990), 233.

73     "Postmodern prophet of the confluence . . . " from Mark Edmundson, in Weatherby, *Salman Rushdie*, 148.

## Chapter 5: Sources of Flux and Form

74     Janette Turner Hospital epigraph from her *Charades*, 223.

74     James Joyce epigraph from his *A Portrait of the Artist as a Young Man* (New York: Viking-Compass, 1956 [1916]), 248–49.

75     "There is" . . . "no superego" from Jean-Paul Sartre, *The Words* (New York: Braziller, 1964), 19.

75     "Soul free and fancy free . . . " from Joyce, *A Portrait of the Artist*, 248–49.

75     "His mind seemed older . . . ," ibid., 95.

75     Daniel Day-Lewis quote is from Joan Juliet Buck, "Actor from the Shadows," *New Yorker*, 12 October 1992, 53.

76     "Home is a failed idea" from DeLillo, *Mao II*, 92.

79–80  Jamaica Kincaid quote, from her story, "Mariah," in *The Graywolf Annual Seven: Stories from the American Mosiac* (St. Paul, MN: Graywolf Press, 1990), 92.

80     "To nullify its promissory notes" . . . "of the living" from Rosenberg's *The Tradition of the New*, 30, 75, 155.

80     "A strange 'thing,' an object . . . " from Budd Hopkins, *Sculpture*, privately published pamphlet, 1988.

80     "[W]ith *my* memory—all the . . . " from Bellow, *Herzog*, 134.

80     Faulkner's ambition "to put everything in one sentence . . . " quoted in Kazin, *Bright Book of Life*, 31.

81     Epigraph, ibid., 75.

81     "Shock" . . . "learned something," ibid., 75.

81–82  A lasting *death imprint* . . . "failed enactment" from my *Broken Connection*, 170–72; see also the essay, "The Concept of the Survivor," in my collection, *The Future of Immortality and Other Essays for a Nuclear Age* (New York: Basic Books, 1987), 231–43.

85     On Kurt Vonnegut novels, see his *Slaughterhouse 5* (New York: Delacourt, 1969); *Mother Night* (New York: Delacourt, 1971); and *Cat's Cradle* (New York: Delacourt, 1971).

86      "So many possibilities" from Gunter Grass, *The Tin Drum* (New York: Pantheon, 1961 [1959]), 585.

86      Gunter Grass quotations are from his *Two States, One Nation?* (New York: Harcourt Brace Jovanovitch, 1990), 6, 7, 123, 112–13, 118.

86–87   "Destructive character" . . . "will bring" in David Frisby, *Fragments of Modernity* (Cambridge, MA: MIT Press, 1986), 1.

87      "Where is that human life . . . " from Bellow, *Herzog,* 220.

87      Bellow epigraph, ibid., 303.

87      For Clifford Geertz on "The Western conception of the person," see his "'From the Native's Point of View': On the Nature of Anthropological Understanding," in Richard A. Shweder and Robert A. LeVine, eds. *Culture Theory: Essays on Mind, Self, and Emotion* (New York: Cambridge University Press, 1984), 126.

88      "Multiple, unintegrated or partially integrated" . . . "experience a sense of continuity" from Katherine P. Ewing, "The Illusion of Wholeness: Culture, Self, and the Experience of Inconsistency," *Ethos* 18 (1990): 273.

88      "How my mind has struggled to make coherent sense" from Bellow, *Herzog,* 325.

88      "A shaky edifice" . . . "the world's community of displaced writers" from Salman Rushdie's collection, *Imaginary Homelands* (London: Granta Books, 1991), 12, 15.

88      "The experience of my own . . . " from DeLillo, *Mao II,* 159.

88      "I changed because I wanted to" . . . "into adventurous Jase" from Mukherjee, *Jasmine,* 186, 174.

88      "Simultaneous existence" . . . "the planet" from Kazin, *Bright Book of Life,* 316, 317.

91      "[T]urns to its own figurations . . . " quoted in Mary Ann Caws, "Singing in Another Key: Surrealism through a Feminist Eye," *Diacritics* (Summer 1984): 63.

91      "Law-abiding" from Allan Wheelis, *The Path Not Taken* (New York: Norton, 1990), 96. Wheelis was discussing the morality that constrains individuals to serve the collective: "The man may be a killer, but he expects the parts of his body to be law-abiding."

91      "Narrative configuration" . . . "will be" from Donald Polkinghorne, *Narrative Knowing and the Human Sciences* (Albany: State University of New York Press, 1988), 150.

91      "Significant form" from Langer, *Mind,* Vol. 1, 67.

91–92   Charles Taylor's discussion of "escape from self" and "common space" from his *Sources of the Self,* 526–27.

92      Geertz on *nisba* and selfhood, from " . . . Native's Point of View," 130–34.

92      "A particular" . . . "moral space" from Taylor, *Sources of the Self,* 25–52.

## Chapter 6: Poise and Equipoise

93     Rushdie chapter epigraph, from Weatherby, *Salman Rushdie*, 127.

94     Havel section epigraph, from *Disturbing the Peace*, 57.

96     "Hitler Studies" . . . "less marked than you think" from Don DeLillo, *White Noise* (New York: Viking Penguin, 1985 [1984]), 150, 38.

96     "Naturalized Americans" . . . "Peter Sellers" from Bharati Mukherjee, *The Middleman and Other Stories* (New York: Fawcett Crest, 1988), 101.

96     "Rattling cab" . . . who knows what the mixture is!" from Bellow, *Herzog* 206–7.

97     "Thanatoids" . . . "of death" from Thomas Pynchon, *Vineland* (Boston, MA: Little, Brown and Co., 1990), 171.

97     "Knew perceived reality . . . " and all subsequent quotations in the paragraph are from Mary Anne Caws, *The Art of Interference* (Princeton, NJ: Princeton University Press, 1989), 73, 75–76, 77.

97     "Theatrical images . . . " and the remaining quotes in the paragraph are from Václav Havel, *Disturbing the Peace*, 53, 44, 113, 114.

98     "Disturbing magic" . . . "must understand," ibid., 126–27.

98     For anti–Vietnam War impact of "I-Feel-Like-I'm-Fixin'-to-Die Rag," see my *Home from the War*, 217–21.

98     "A somewhat" . . . "burlesque treatment" from Roscher, "Proteus."

99     Section epigraph from DeLillo, *Mao II*, 4.

99     "I felt it was stupid . . . " from Barthelme, *Natural Selection*, 93.

99     "Someone is living my life"; see epigraph for chapter 10, page 190, and note on the epigraph.

101     "A quality" . . . "free-floating condition" from *Standard Edition*, vol. 20, 165; and Hensie and Campbell, *Psychiatric Dictionary* (New York: Oxford University Press, 1960), 53.

102     "Herzog experienced nothing but his" . . . "but what is it?" from Bellow, *Herzog*, 240, 129.

102     Motherwell, "The need" . . . "men feel," in Stephen Polcari, *Abstract Expressionism and the Modern Experience* (New York: Cambridge University Press, 1991), 302.

102     "It's hate I long for . . . " from Mukherjee, *The Middleman and Other Stories*, 26.

102     Graham quote, from Graham and Lehman, *The Best American Poetry 1990*, xxix.

102     "Struggle between" . . . "reassuring uncertainty" from Hopkins, *Sculpture*.

103     "Lifestyle enclaves" and remaining quotations in the paragraph, from Bellah et al., *Habits of the Heart* (Berkeley: University of California Press, 1985), 72.

105     Anne Carson, "Towns are" . . . "a town" from *Best American Poetry 1990*, 18.

105     "His old bass player and . . . " from Pynchon, *Vineland*, 9.

106     "There should be forms of . . . " from Timothy Garton Ash, *The Magic Lantern: The Revolution of '89 Witnessed in Warsaw, Budapest, Berlin, and Prague* (New York: Random House, 1990), 147. Ash understood that

principle to apply throughout most of the European revolutions against Communist governments.

106    "Spiritual authority" . . . "its head" from George Konrad, *Antipolitics* (New York: Harcourt Brace Jovanovich, 1984), 118–19.

106    "Civic Catechism" . . . "the state" from Adam Michnik, *Letters from Prison and Other Essays* (Berkeley: University of California Press, 1985), 58, 124.

106    Klima quotation from his *Love and Garbage*.

107    Barthelme epigraph from Joseph David Bellamy, ed., *In the New Fiction* (Champaign-Urbana: University of Illinois Press).

107    "I am not worried about . . . " from "Symposium on Transcending Ideological Conformity," *New Oxford Review* (October 1991): 18.

107    "I do not wish to . . . " from Joyce, *Portrait of the Artist*, 239.

107    "Uncontrollable spontaneity" . . . "self-organization" quoted and discussed in my *History and Human Survival* (New York: Random House, 1970), 343.

108    "Do you believe" . . . "disbelieve in it," Joyce, *Portrait*, p. 239.

110    For discussion of Berrigans, Hoffman, and 1960s modes of protest, see Todd Gitlin, *The Sixties: Years of Hope, Days of Rage* (New York: Bantam, 1987).

110    "The central" . . . "off limits" from Weatherby, *Salman Rushdie*, 127.

110    "[H]umankind lives mainly" . . . total *explanations*" from Bellow, *Herzog*, 319, 166.

110    "Dangerous and destructive" from H. Porter Abbott, "Saul Bellow and the 'Lost Cause' of Character," in Gloria L. Cronin and L. H. Goldman, eds., *Saul Bellow in the 1980s: A Collection of Critical Essays* (East Lansing: Michigan State University Press, 1989), 121.

110    "The comic-book" . . . "of speech" from "The author to his body on their 15th birthday 29 ii 80 [actually 60th birthday]," in Richard Ellmann and Robert O'Clair, eds., *The Norton Anthology of Modern Poetry*, 2nd ed., (New York, 1988), 1023.

110    "Every thought is permitted. And . . . " from DeLillo, *Mao II*, 132.

110    "Hermeneutic of suspicion" of Nietzsche, from David Miller, "Chiliasm: Apocalyptic with a Thousand Faces," in Valerie Andrews, Robert Bosnak and Karen Walter Goodwin, eds., *Facing Apocalypse* (Dallas: Spring Publications, 1987), 8.

111    "Antipolitics strives to put politics . . . " from Konrad, *Antipolitics*, 92.

111    "Someone who subscribes to an . . . " from Havel, *Disturbing the Peace*, 80.

111    "Fighting with clients . . . " from Barthelme, *Natural Selection*.

111–12  "An English architect stuck in . . . " and remaining quotations in this and the next paragraph, from Lively, *City of the Mind*, 2, 7, 13, 3, 91, 214.

114    "An ape" . . . "those apes" and subsequent long quotation about bills, from Barthelme, *Natural Selection*, 103, 13.

115    "But somehow" . . . "into science" from Bellow, *Herzog*, 311.

118    Long Havel quote from *Disturbing the Peace*, 167.

119     "It was" . . . "established opposition," ibid., 128–30.

119     "Something new" and subsequent quotations in the paragraph from Greil Marcus, *Lipstick Traces: A Secret History of the 20th Century* (Cambridge, MA: Harvard University Press, 1989), 2, 14–15, 24.

## Chapter 7: Enduring Connections

120     "When the Old God" . . . "flies and bottletops" from DeLillo, *Mao II,* 7.

120     "You get one last chance . . . " from Bellow, *Herzog,* 303.

120     "Life and death are fascinatingly . . . " from Kazin, *Bright Book of Life,* 302.

121     Section epigraph quoted in Gwyneth Cravens, "Past Present," *Nation,* 24 June 1991, 862.

121     "Potato love" from Bellow, *Herzog,* 66.

123     "That's O.K., Dad" through "men are always after them" from Barthelme, *Natural Selection,* 92, 11.

124     "He knew when he kissed . . . " from F. Scott Fitzgerald, *The Great Gatsby,* quoted in Lindberg, *Confidence Man in American Literature,* 137.

124     "At least until such time" and subsequent quotations from *Herzog* in the remainder of the paragraph can be found in Jonathan Wilson, *Herzog: The Limits of Ideas* (Boston, MA: Twayne Publishers, 1990), 23–26, 28–30.

124     Section epigraph from Arville G. Brim and Jerome Kagan, "Constancy and Change: A View of the Issues," in Brim and Kagan, eds., *Constancy and Change in Human Development* (Cambridge, MA: Harvard University Press, 1980), 1.

125     Brim and Kagan's rejection of early childhood determinism, ibid., 1.

126     "Decentering of the self" is discussed in my *Life of the Self,* 72.

126     "Revenants" . . . "imaginative reach" from review of *Love in a Life* by Andrew Motion, *Times Literary Supplement* (March 1988).

127     "I shall die . . . " from "Conscientious Objector," in Edna St. Vincent Millay, *Collected Lyrics* (New York: Harper Colophon, 1981), 216.

128     Spaceship *Voyager.* Allusion to the search for extraterrestrial intelligent life. See "Voyager points camera at the planets tonight," *New York Times,* 13 February 1990, C2.

131     Section epigraph from Rushdie, *Satanic Verses,* 295.

131     "Moments that seem to leave" . . . "back into play" from Markus, *Lipstick Traces,* 4, 24.

131–32  "The world is incompatible" . . . "only to suffer the effects" from Rushdie, *Satanic Verses,* 295, 432.

132     "A net, the kind . . . " from "The Tenant," in Mukherjee, *The Middleman and Other Stories,* 96.

133     "No reason to see history" from Isaiah Berlin interview in *New York Review of Books,* 28 May 1992.

## Chapter 8: Life Stories

148        *The Day After.* Television movie on the aftermath of nuclear war, first
           aired in November, 1983.

151–59     All quotations in this section (pages 26–38) are from Gordon Parks,
           *Voices in the Mirror: An Autobiography* (New York: Anchor Books, 1990).
           The page numbers of quoted passages, in sequence, are as follows:
           340–341, ix, 273, 13, 7, 17, 5, 20, 64, 65, 66, 95–6, 102, 161, 117, 133,
           111, 147, 216, 219–20, 221, 254, 257, 287, 332, 179–80, 21, 22, 208, 210,
           275, 281, 321, 327–28, 323, 24, 222, 341, 342.

## Chapter 9: The Fundamentalist Self

160        Section epigraph from Rushdie, *Satanic Verses,* 210–11.

161        "Modernism in theology" . . . "gently" from George M. Marsden, *Fun-*
           *damentalism and American Culture* (New York: Oxford University Press,
           1980), 159, 263.

161        For discussion of American Bible-centeredness and revivalism, see
           Ernest R. Sandeen, *The Roots of Fundamentalism: British and American*
           *Millenarianism 1800–1930* (Chicago: University of Chicago Press, 1970),
           107.

161        For use of the term *fundamentalist,* see Martin Marty, "Fundamentalism
           as a Social Phenomenon," *Bulletin of the American Academy of Arts and Sci-*
           *ences* 42 (1988): 15–29. Marty uses the term *fundamentalist-like* to convey
           broader applicability.

161–62     For discussions of ideological totalism and fundamentalism, see my
           *Thought Reform,* 419–37; and (with Richard Falk), *Indefensible Weapons:*
           *The Political and Psychological Case against Nuclearism* (New York: Basic
           Books, 1982), 100–110.

161–62     "Terrifying singularity" . . . "unregulated, free" from Rushdie, *Satanic*
           *Verses,* 102–3, 363–64.

162        "To weight the balance" . . . "standards of rationality" from Sandeen,
           *Roots,* 108, 131.

162        "Through the lens of Scripture" . . . "find and assert symbols" from
           Marty, "Fundamentalism as a Social Phenomenon," in George Mars-
           den, ed., *Evangelicalism and Modern America* (Grand Rapids, MI: Erd-
           mans, 1984), 57, 66. (This is an earlier, and somewhat different, ver-
           sion of the paper quoted earlier.)

162        "Subsumed within a religious framework" from Michael Barkun,
           "Imagining Apocalypse: The Religious Bases of the Extreme Right"
           (Paper delivered at the Conference on Historical Trauma, Center on
           Violence and Human Survival, City University of New York, John Jay
           College, 19 April 1990).

162        On "Christian identity," see Michael Barkun, "Millenarian Aspects of
           'White Supremacist Movements," *Terrorism and Political Violence,* vol. 1
           (January 1989), 409–34.

163        "Messianic sanctions for terror" and "holy terror" from David C.

Rapoport, "Messianic Sanctions for Terror" (typescript).

163 On Nazi millenarianism, see James M. Rhodes, *The Hitler Movement: A Modern Millenarian Revolution* (Stanford, CA: Hoover Institution Press, 1980); and Charles B. Strozier, "Christian Fundamentalism, Nazism, and the Millennium, *Psychohistory Review,* 18 (1990): 207–17.

163 "Time presses,/Ten" . . . "enemy remains" from Stuart Schramm, *Mao Tse-tung* (London: Penguin, 1966).

164 "The general fear of Mahound" . . . "unsullied, unaltered, pure" from Rushdie, *Satanic Verses,* 362, 207.

164 "Total politics, total authority, total being" from DeLillo, *Mao II,* 185.

164 "More compromising, more assimilable" from Marty, in Marsden, *Evangelicanism and Modern America,* 67.

164–65 "Hard-pressed to" . . . "of promoter" from Timothy P. Weber, *Living in the Shadow of the Second Coming: American Premillennialism, 1875–1982* (Chicago: University of Chicago Press, 1987 [1979]), xi.

165 Sentence beginning with "Jim Bakker, with his wife, Tammy," is my own description, drawn from various sources. "Praise the Lord" . . . "make him cry" from Martin Gardner, "Giving God a Hand," *New York Review of Books* 13 August 1987, 22.

165 "Cancer that needed to be excised" . . . "Devil has to have a hand in it" from "Sex, Demons and TV Ratings Fight Enliven Court Battle of Two Evangelists," *New York Times,* 21 July 1991, 14.

166 Long quote beginning, "the greatest show on earth" from Gerard Straub, *Salvation for Sale,* quoted in Gardner, "Giving God a Hand," 22–23.

166 "Divorce is never legitimate" and other quotations in this and the next paragraph are from Nancy Tatum Ammerman, *Bible Believers: Fundamentalists in the Modern World* (New Brunswick, NJ: Rutgers University Press, 1987), 143, 144, 156, 57, 211.

166 Section epigraph from Albert Camus, *The Fall* (New York: Knopf, 1957), 138.

166–67 Characteristics of fundamentalists interviewed at our Center described in Charles B. Strozier and Laura Simich, "Christian Fundamentalism and Nuclear Threat," *Political Psychology* 12 (March 1991): 81.

167 "Endist" focus. Strozier defines "endism" as "the location of the self in some future narrative," in his forthcoming book, *The Apocalyptic Imagination* (Boston: Beacon Press, 1994). Strozier's work has contributed greatly to this chapter.

167 "The 'nuclearization' of the Bible" from Andrew G. Lang, "The Political Eschatology of the Religious Right" (typescript), 2.

167 For influence of nuclear threat on spread of fundamentalism, see my discussion in *Indefensible Weapons,* 80–99, and Strozier's "Christian Fundamentalism, Nuclear Threat and the Middle East War," working paper, Center on Violence and Human Survival.

167 "The most widely-read writer on . . . " from Weber, *Living in the Shadow,* 211.

167 "Their world is a mission field" from Ammerman, *Bible Believers,* 91.

168        "Simple antitheses" . . . "of Satan" from Marsden, *Fundamentalism and American Culture,* 224.

168        "What is good and evil . . . " from Strozier and Simich, "Christian Fundamentalism," 92.

168        "Well-marked road map . . . " from Ammerman, *Bible Believers,* 41, 46.

168        "How to have a Christian marriage . . . " from Strozier and Simich, *Christian Fundamentalism,* 85.

168        "A sheltering canopy" . . . "for his worst attacks" from Ammerman, *Bible Believers,* 51, 136, 70, 156, 64.

169        "Where the believer, in a . . . " from Randall Balmer, *Mine Eyes Have Seen the Glory: A Journey into the Evangelical Subculture in America* (New York: Oxford University Press, 1989), 25.

169–70     Narrative that "fits," Strozier and Simich, "Christian Fundamentalism," 91–94.

170        "A hostile rejection of God's . . . " from Weber, *Living in the Shadow,* x.

171        "Concerted supernatural intervention" from William Martin, quoted in Weber, *Living in the Shadow,* 233.

171        "High measure of control" from Marty, "Fundamentalism as a Social Phenomenon," *Bulletin of the American Academy of Arts and Sciences,* 22.

174        "I am the way, the truth . . . " from John, chapter 14, verse 6.

174–75     On divergent approach to end-time ideology, see Strozier and Simich, "Christian Fundamentalism," 85–86.

175        Darlene's nuclear verb, "if God doesn't escalate the time," quoted in ibid., 87.

176        "Violence washes over everything" from Strozier, *The Apocalyptic Imagination.*

188        "War all day long" from Ammerman, *Bible Believers,* 97.

## Chapter 10: The Dark Side

190        Pirandello epigraph quoted in Gwyneth Cravens, "Past Present," *Nation,* 24 June 1991, 861.

190        John Edgar Wideman epigraph from his *Philadelphia Fire* (New York: Vintage Books, 1991 [1990]), 22, 34.

190        "Chaos of possibilities" from Barthelme, *Natural Selection,* 198.

190        "The Post-Impulsives Are Here . . . " from Bruce McCall, "The New Rabelaisians," *New Yorker,* 18 June 1990, 30.

191        "Don't trust anyone" . . . "horsefeathers" from Daniel Akst, "California & Co.," *Los Angeles Times,* 21 February 1992.

191        "Shamelessly and unequivocally laughing . . . " from Václav Havel, "Paradise Lost," *New York Review of Books,* 9 April 1992, 6.

191        "Drifter" . . . "signatures, pseudonyms" from Don DeLillo, "American Blood: A Journey through the Labrinth of Dallas and JFK," quoted in Shapiro, *Reading the Postmodern Polity,* 69. Subsequent quote from Shapiro, 74.

191        "Astonishing new offer" . . . "didn't matter already?" from Amis, *Lon-*

*don Fields,* 297, 254.

192    "Battered identities" from West, "Nihilism," 222.

192    "Turn . . . their ordinary lives . . . " from Banks, *Continental Drift,* 339.

192    Russell Banks's depiction of transmission of violence, in *Affliction* (New York: Harper and Row, 1989).

192    "Cursed" . . . "doomed" from Maxwell Geismar, *American Moderns: From Rebellion to Conformity* (New York: Hill and Wang, 1958), 99.

192    "Neutralization" . . . "Zero point" (Roland Barthes's term) from LeFebvre, *Everyday Life,* 59, 260.

193    Recent study revealing depression in American settlers discussed in Howard I. Kushner, *American Suicide: A Psychocultural Exploration* (New Brunswick, NJ: Rutgers University Press, 1991 [1989]). See especially the epilogue, 179–201.

193    "True self-consciousness" . . . "eyes of others" from W. E. B. DuBois, "Of Our Spiritual Strivings," in *The Souls of Black Folk: Essays and Sketches* (Greenwich, CT: Fawcett, 1961 [1903]), 16–17.

193    "Double voice" from Gates, *Signifying Monkey,* xxiv, xxv.

193    Brutal absurdity and "collapse in meaning" from West, "Nihilism," 223, 221.

193    "Put a handful" . . . "goddamned selves" from Wideman, *Philadelphia Fire,* 76–77.

195    *Roots.* The television series on black heritage first aired in 1977.

197    For discussion of violence as a form of personal transcendence, see Jack Katz, *Seductions of Crime* (New York: Basic Books, 1988).

202    Beckett epigraph from Lawrence Shainberg, "Exorcising Beckett," *Paris Review,* no. 4 (1987), 104, 108.

202    "Terrorist society" . . . "chastises himself" from LeFebvre, *Everyday Life,* 147.

203    "All things go together . . . " from summary by Michael Perlman, for Strozier, Perlman, and Lifton, *Nuclear Threat and the American Self,* forthcoming.

204    For discussion of nuclearism and nuclear fundamentalism, see my *Broken Connection* and *Indefensible Weapons.*

204    "A call to arms" . . . "Nukes Forever!" from Robert L. Park, "Star Warriors on Sky Patrol," *New York Times,* 25 March 1992, A23.

204–5  "The Butcher of Tompkins Square" from *New York Newsday,* 18 February 1992.

205    William Barret reference is from his book *The Illusion of Technique* (New York: Doubleday Anchor, 1978)

206    "Being a sensory" . . . "fragmented and obscured" from Erik Erikson, *The Life Cycle Completed* (New York: Norton, 1985), 85–86.

206    "A righteous" . . . "enraged slaughter" from Katz, *Seductions of Crime,* 18–19.

206    Michael Basch on empathy, from personal communication, 1991.

206–8  I discuss these aspects of centering and decentering in the *The Life of the Self,* the application of a life-continuity paradigm to psychiatric syndromes in the *The Broken Connection,* and doubling and other forms of dissociation in *The Nazi Doctors* (New York: Basic Books, 1986) and *The Genocidal Mentality* (New York: Basic Books, 1990).

207        "Psychological depression . . . despair," from West, "Nihilism," 222.

208–9    "[S]ome means of denial to . . . " from W. Confer and B. Ables, *Multiple Personality: Etiology, Diagnoses, and Treatment* (New York: Human Sciences Press, 1983).

209        "Division of" . . . "self-replacement therapy" from Nicholas Humphrey and Daniel C. Dennett, "Speaking for Our Selves: An Assessment of Multiple Personality Disorder," Center for Cognitive Studies, Tufts University, 11. In another version, Occasional Paper No. 8 of the Center on Violence and Human Survival, John Jay College, City University of New York.

209        "Double bind" . . . "and take charge" from David Spiegel, "Dissociation, Double Binds, and Posttraumatic Stress in Multiple Personality Disorder," in Bennett G. Braun, ed., *Treatment of Multiple Personality Disorder* (Washington, DC: American Psychiatric Press, 1986), 69–71.

209–10   On historical record and increase in cases of multiple personality, see Braun introduction, ibid.

210        On overlap between borderline states and multiple personality disorder, see Richard P. Horevitz and Bennett G. Braun, "Are Multiple Personalities Borderline?" in *Psychiatric Clinics of North America*, vol. 7, no. 1 (March 1984): 69–87.

211        "Mythic version" from Humphrey and Dennett, "Speaking for Our Selves."

211        On the "false memory syndrome," see Richard Ofshe and Ethan Watters, "Making Monsters," *Society* (March–April 1993): 4–16.

211        "I could see the centre of you . . . " from Rushdie, *Satanic Verses*, 183.

211        "Splendidly safe and happy" . . . "place I could stay forever" from Barthelme, *Natural Selection*, 201.

211        "It is innocent to hope . . . " from Naum Gabo, quoted in Herbert, *Modern Artists on Art*, 104.

212        "Mappings" . . . "free individual" from Gerald M. Edelman, *Bright Air, Brilliant Fire* (New York: Basic Books, 1992), 167.

212        "There need be no psychic self . . . " from Stephen Priest, *Theories of the Mind* (Boston: Houghton Mifflin, 1991), 221.

212        "Finished, it's finished . . . " from Samuel Beckett, *Endgame* (New York: Grove Press), p. 1.


## Chapter 11: The Protean Path

213        First epigraph from Václav Havel's essay, "The Power of the Powerless," in his *Living in Truth* (London: Faber and Faber, 1987), 122.

213        Second epigraph from Ashis Nandy, "Oppression and Human Liberation: Toward a Third World Utopia," in his *Traditions, Tyranny, and Utopias* (Delhi: Oxford University Press, 1987), 150.

213        "We are multiple from the start" from Richard Shweder, *Thinking*

*Through Cultures: Expeditions in Cultural Psychology* (Cambridge, MA: Harvard University Press, 1991), 5.

214 Dahrendorff section epigraph, from his *Reflections on the Revolution in Europe* (New York: Random House, 1990).

214 "Long-lost hunter's" ... "home to" from Stephen Harrigan, "The Long-Lost Hunter," *Audubon* (September–October 1992): 95.

214 "Experiencing their experience" from Michael Basch, "Empathic Understanding: A Review of the Concept and Some Theoretical Considerations," *Journal of the American Psychoanalytic Association,* 31 (1983): 101–26; and personal communication.

214 "Natural psychology" ... "*another person*" from Nicholas Humphrey, *Consciousness Regained* (Oxford: Oxford University Press, 1983), 6.

214–15 Infants' imitation of facial expressions, in Basch, "Empathic Understanding."

215 "In some precursor form" ... "social milieu" from Leslie Brothers, "A Biological Perspective on Empathy" (typescript), 17.

215 "Female connectivity" ... "the world" from Catherine Keller, *A Broken Web: Separation, Sexism, and Self* (Boston: Beacon Press, 1986), 132–33.

216–17 "Putting the unimaginable to imaginative use" and subsequent description of new artistic approaches to the Holocaust, from *New York Times,* 1 March 1992, Arts and Leisure section, 1.

217 "A great teacher" ... "or a counter-player" from Nandy's "Towards a Third World Utopia," 31; another version of this essay was called, "Oppression and Human Liberation."

217 "An injunction ... " and remaining quotations in the paragraph from Michael F. Jimenez, "'Citizens of the Kingdom': Toward a Social History of Radical Christianity in Latin America," *Religion and the Working Class* (Fall 1988), 11, 13, 18.

217–18 "Technical in character ... " and remaining quotations in the paragraph from Richard Falk, "New Dimensions in International Relations and the Infancy of Global Civil Society" (typescript, 1992), 11–13, 18.

218 For Hiroshima rumor suggesting ultimate desolation, see my *Death in Life: Survivors of Hiroshima* (Chapel Hill: University of North Carolina Press, 1991 [1968]), 68–69.

218 "The movement's 'basic themes—dismay ... " from Spencer T. Weart, *Nuclear Fear: A History of Images* (Cambridge, MA: Harvard University Press, 1988), 325.

218 "Ecological self" ... "intimately related" from Sarah Conn, as quoted in *Center Review* (a publication of the Harvard University Center for Psychological Studies in the Nuclear Age) (Fall 1990), 16.

218 On the "biotic community" see Aldo Leopold, *A Sand Country Almanac: With Essays from Round River* (New York: Ballantine, 1990 [1966]).

219 "Dead trees are what the ... " from Ted Williams, "Big Timber, the U.S. Forest Service and the Rape of the Northwest," *Forest Voice,* 2 (March 1990): 7. See discussion of this theme of revitalization in Michael Perlman *The Power of Trees: The Reforesting of the Soul* (Dallas, TX: Spring Publications, in press).

219        "The oppression" . . . "history itself" from Nandy, "Towards a Third
           World Utopia," 46.

219        Adam Michnik quotes from his *Letters from Prison and Other Essays*
           (Berkeley: University of California Press, 1985), 10.

219–20     "A 'higher' " . . . "is liable" quoted in Elshtain, "A Man for This Season:
           Václav Havel on Freedom and Responsibility," (typescript), 19–20.

220        Quotes in this paragraph from Konrad, *Antipolitics,* 242–43.

220        "Becomes invisible" . . . "our eyes" from Falk, "New Dimensions in
           International Relations . . . "

220        "Controlling everything" . . . "to manipulation" from Havel, "The End
           of the Modern Era," *New York Times,* 1 March 1992.

221        Richard Falk used the term, "A struggle for the soul of the species self,"
           at an informal discussion meeting at Princeton University in May, 1991.

221        "Ethnic revival" . . . "the child" from David Brown, "Ethnic Revival:
           Prospectives on State and Society," *Third World Quarterly* (October
           1989), 6.

221–22     The declining faith in the nation-state was discussed by A. S. Singham,
           in a presentation on the "Garrison State," to the Wellfleet psychohis-
           tory group in October, 1989. This talented thinker and extraordinary
           human being would have said much more on the subject had his life
           not been sadly cut short.

221–22     "Weakening of" . . . "concrete forms" from Jonathan Friedman, "Cul-
           ture, Identity, and World Process," *Review* 12 (1989): 52, 62.

222        "Proliferations and fluidities" . . . "messier" identities (footnote), from
           Rob Walker, "The Coming Global Civilization Project: What About
           'Culture?'" (typescript, January 1990).

222        "How much grief" . . . "sense of a nation-state" from Gunter Grass, *Two
           States—One Nation?* 6, 5.

223        "Personal dispositions" . . . "globalising influences" from Anthony Gid-
           dens, *Modernity and Self-Identity: Self and Society in the Late Modern Age*
           (Stanford, CA: Stanford University Press, 1991), 1.

223        "The closest approximation" . . . "too many American films" from
           Todd Gitlin, "World Leaders: Mickey, et al.," *New York Times,* 3 May
           1992, Arts and Leisure section.

224        "Monotheism" . . . "fragmentary autonomous systems" from Hillman,
           *Re-visioning Psychology,* 26–27.

224        "Make each other up" . . . "slave to none" from Shweder, *Thinking
           through Cultures,* 29.

224        "Many voices clamoring for expression" from Frances E. Mascia-Lees,
           Patricia Sharpe, and Colleen Ballerino Cohen, "The Postmodernists
           Turn in Anthropology: Cautions from a Feminist Perspective," *Signs:
           Journal of Women in Culture and Society* 15 (1989): 7–33.

224        "Neither the priests" . . . "good at being human" from Richard Rorty,
           *Consequences of Pragmatism* (Minneapolis: University of Minnesota Press,
           1986 [1982]), xxxviii–xxxix.

224        Holton on science, personal communication, 1990.

224–25     "The plasticity" . . . "being transformed" from Richard Tarnas, *The Pas-

*sion of the Western Mind* (New York: Harmony Books, 1991), 395–96.

225     "A bastard child" ... "let it continue" from Salman Rushdie in *Newsweek,* 12 February 1990, 53.

225     Section epigraph from Saul Bellow, *The Dean's December* (New York: Harper & Row, 1982).

225     "Dethrone the given" ... "nature of our dependence" from Charles Taylor, *Sources of the Self: The Making of the Modern Identity* (Cambridge, MA: Harvard University Press, 1989), 29, 39, 34.

226     "Interpenetration of the local and ... " from Giddens, *Modernity and Self-Identity,* 210–17.

226     Concerning mass media and Bosnia, see my article, "Can Images of Bosnia's Victims Change the World?" *New York Times,* 26 August 1992.

226     Description of and quotations from Mikhail Gorbachev speech in *New York Times,* 8 May 1992, A14.

227     "Dare to defy the given ... " from Nandy, dedication to *Traditions, Tyranny, and Utopias.*

230     Concerning our being caught up with the invention of culture, rather than its representation, see Shweder, *Thinking through Culture;* and James Clifford, *The Predicament of Culture: Twentieth-Century Ethnography Literature, and Art* (Cambridge, MA: Harvard University Press, 1988).

230     "Place for many places" from Michael Perlman, personal communication, 1991.

230     "Versatility in stance and locomotor ... " from F. A. Jenkins, Jr., "Tree Shrew Locomotion and the Origins of Primate Arborealism," in Russell L. Ciochon and John G. Fleagle, eds. in *Primate Evolution and Human Origins* (New York: Aldine de Gruyter, 1987), 12–13.

230     "Social relationships" ... "reciprocal influence" from Lerner, *Human Plasticity,* 94.

231     "Species-being" quoted in David McLellan, ed., *Karl Marx: Selected Writings* (New York: Oxford University Press, 1977), 81–82.

231     On exploratory combinations of maleness and femaleness, see David J. Krieger, "Conversion: On the Possibility of Global Thinking in an age of Particularism," *Journal of the American Academy of Religion* 58 (Summer 1990): 223–43.

231     Among these twentieth-century thinkers who focus on form, configuration, experience, and meaning, I would include psychoanalytic theorists Harry Stack Sullivan, Erik Erikson, and Heinz Kohut; as well as philosophical writers John Dewey, Alfred North Whitehead, Albert Camus, Jorgen Habermas, Ernst Cassirer, and Susanne Langer.

232     "Hidden openness" ... "to alienate" from Havel, *Living in Truth,* 57.

232     "Allows the traumatized to speak ... " from Cathy Caruth, comments at Wellfleet psychohistory meetings, October, 1991.

# INDEX